M000078327

Beating the Odds

Beating the Odds

The Story of One Black Man's Life in Twentieth Century America

Rufus W. McKinney

To Wilbur Williams, with my best wishes!

Rufus W. McKinney

VANTAGE PRESS
New York

Cover design by Susan Thomas

FIRST EDITION

Published by Vantage Press, Inc.
419 Park Ave. South, New York, NY 10016

Manufactured in the United States of America
ISBN: 0-533-14905-3

Library of Congress Catalog Card No.: 2004092482

0 9 8 7 6 5 4 3 2 1

To my wife, Donie, who, with my son, Fred, inspired me to write this book, which I dedicate also to Rudy, Anne, Paula, and all ten of my grandchildren

Contents

Beating the Odds

1

In the Beginning

My name is Rufus William McKinney. I live in the Washington, D. C., suburb of Bethesda, Maryland, but I was born in Jonesboro, Arkansas 74 years ago, August 6, 1930. Whenever I am asked, "Where are you from?" I always answer "Arkansas," even though I have not lived there for more than fifty years. Arkansas is my home, the place where I grew up, where my basic values were formed.

Jonesboro is a very small town in the northeast corner of Arkansas. To the south and east of town the land is flat and fertile, part of the Mississippi River Delta. North and west of town are the foothills of the Ozarks. The cotton and rice farmers south and east of town came to Jonesboro, the county seat of Craighead County, to conduct business. The cotton brokers and traders in other farm commodities were there; so were the government offices important to land ownership. The cotton gin was there. Farmers would bring their cotton first to the gin where the seeds were separated mechanically from the raw cotton. Next to the gin was a plant where cotton would be compressed into 500-pound bales for ease of shipment to textile mills in the eastern part of the United States and overseas.

Two busy railroad lines came through Jonesboro—the "Cotton Belt Railroad" and the "Frisco" line. The cotton belt maintained a "roundhouse" in Jonesboro where its steam and diesel locomotives, railroad cars and other equipment were brought for repairs. Jonesboro was the center of commerce for all of Craighead County.

Jonesboro and Craighead County were different from most other farming communities in eastern Arkansas. Blacks comprised only eight to ten percent of the population; the black percentage in the county was even less. Farms around Jonesboro tended to be smaller, in contrast with the cotton, rice and soybean plantations that stretched for miles around Blytheville, Marked Tree, West Memphis, Stuttgart and Helena. Jonesboro public schools operated on the traditional schedule from September to May. In other farm communities public schools ran split sessions, suspending operations during the spring planting and fall harvesting seasons. Split sessions made it possible for farm boys and girls to help plant and harvest the crops without losing time from school. When the cotton was laid by, i.e., left alone to mature, around mid-July, the schools would reopen to make up for the suspended periods. They remained in session until cotton picking time in mid-September when they closed again until the harvest was over a month or so later.

Many of the smaller communities around Jonesboro provided public schools for blacks only up to the eighth grade. Jonesboro's school system offered blacks the opportunity of attending Booker T. Washington School, which included first through the twelfth grades. Because the Jonesboro schools were not on split sessions, school children whose services were required on nearby farms during planting and harvest time attended school during those periods only when it rained or the weather was otherwise too bad for outdoor work.

My father, George Dallas McKinney, moved to Jonesboro with his wife Roseanna and two young daughters in 1918. George McKinney was born in west Tennessee in 1894, but grew up in Hughes, Arkansas. My mother was born in Marvel, Arkansas. Both were very small farming communities in the Mississippi River Delta 20 miles or so apart on Highway 79 southwest of Memphis, Tennessee. Their parents were farmers working 40 or so acres of land, which they owned themselves. George's father, Rufus McKinney, also was a skilled shoemaker, a trade he learned from his father, which he also taught his son George.

This is the story of Rufus William McKinney, the eighth of thirteen children born to George and Roseanna McKinney. I write this story some ten years after retiring from a career, first as a lawyer and later as an executive with one of the largest natural gas utility companies in America. That career occurred during a most turbulent time in American history; when the status of blacks in the society was transformed from near servitude to citizenship.

2

This real life tale takes us through a black boy's world growing up in the Deep South during the depths of the Depression. It demonstrates how that world changed for him as a consequence of his gaining access to education, the nurture and support of family, and his unwavering belief that he could succeed despite the circumstances of his birth and the limitations American society prescribed for black people.

The story of my life may be similar to that of other black men of my generation who lived to see the dawn of the twenty-first century. However, in many respects my experiences have been rather unique. I was in the first wave of black men to enter the higher level managerial and professional ranks of Fortune 500 companies. I believe the distance I traveled from where I began to where I ended up probably was greater than that covered by many more notable black men. None of my ancestors had the benefit of a college education. Neither were any of them successful in business or the professions. They were not well traveled, nor were any of them active in the political life of their community. While my parents like many others worked hard, they did not have "good" jobs that paid steady, reliable wages. What I am saying is there are degrees of privation and that which I experienced in childhood would rank toward the very bottom of that list.

When I tell people, even friends, I am writing my life story a common reaction I get is, "Why are you doing that? What have you done that anyone would be interested in knowing about?" My response usually is, I'm doing it for myself, for my children and grandchildren! I want them to know who I am and where they came from because I believe it is important for every human being to understand his connection to the past. Otherwise, that person is likely to be totally adrift and without a point of reference from which to chart a future for himself and his children. An intelligent person almost by instinct wants to know his personal history, no matter how undistinguished that history may be. I want to save my family some of the trouble I had in trying to discover my ancestors and the various branches of my family. As a result of this effort my four children and ten grandchildren at least will know a large part of who I am.

*   *   *

Being one of thirteen children in a family growing up in the South during the Great Depression may be hard for many to imagine today. However, in a family of that size it would be unusual if more than six or seven siblings were living at home at the same time. At about age 16 the older girls often got married and left home. And boys tended to try to establish their independence from parents at about that same age. One of the more thoughtful things our parents did was to allow about a two-year interval between the births of each of their thirteen children. By the time I was a teenager several of my older siblings had left home. Nevertheless, my entire childhood was spent in a crowded home environment.

In my third year our family moved from the small shotgun house on North Main Street where I was born to a larger house around the corner on Gordon Street. This house had three bedrooms, one for the boys, one for the girls and one for Momma and Papa, as we all called our parents. The only other rooms were a living room (we called it the "front room") and a large kitchen with enough space for family dining. The covered front porch spanned the width of the house, as did the back porch. A path about thirty yards long led from the back of the house to a small structure we called the "out house"—our bathroom or toilet. The rear of the toilet sat on the edge of an alley, a single lane road along the rear lot lines of all the houses on Gordon Street. It thus served the houses facing both on Gordon Street and the next street over. A wooden bench or raised platform about two feet high and eighteen or so inches deep spanned the width of the outhouse. In the center was a hole over which one sat to do one's business into a shallow excavation in the ground below. Periodically, in the warmer months of the year a man in a horse-drawn wagon would come along through the alley at night and remove the human waste, sprinkling the area below the toilet with lime.

The house had no indoor plumbing. Water to the house was supplied from a single hydrant located just off the back porch. We were among the better-off families because we had direct access to a hydrant in our own back yard. Some families in the neighborhood were not connected to the water main. Those families would make agreements with neighbors for their water supply. Given the water supply conditions in our community, bathing and routine personal hygiene were not the easiest habits to form and maintain. We usually took a full bath no more often than once a week. Bathing took place in the kitchen where water heated on the wood cook stove would be poured into a no. 2 galvanized washtub. Usually two or three of us would bathe in the same water before it was discarded. On the back porch stood a small table on which we kept a white enameled pan. This pan served as the basin the family used to wash up before meals.

The house on Gordon Street also was not connected to the electric utility company that served the city of Jonesboro. This too was not unusual in our north side Jonesboro community. At night kerosene lamps provided light for all of our evening activities at home. Each of the rooms in the house had one or more glass lamps, the lower part of which held the kerosene fuel, which we called "coal oil." A fabric wick extended up from the fuel through a small metal device that could be adjusted to raise or lower the wick and the lamp was fitted with a glass globe, once the wick had been lighted. Each week one of the older children was assigned the task of cleaning and maintaining the lamps, seeing to it that each contained enough coal oil to last until bedtime.

While kerosene lamps provided fairly adequate general lighting, they were not well-suited for reading or other close-up work. Consequently, those of the children who were attending school and had reading or other homework to do were better off if they could complete such tasks before dark. But the older children also had assigned chores to do after school. One of my chores, for example, was to chop logs or cut railroad cross ties into lengths suitable for burning in the kitchen range where Momma prepared all our meals; and in winter, for the large potbellied stoves that sat in the living room and the smaller one in our parents' bedroom. These stoves were the heating systems for the entire house in winters. Doing your assigned chores always took priority over school homework. Therefore, it frequently became necessary to do one's school homework by the light of a kerosene lamp.

Papa and Momma lost their firstborn child, a daughter named Luvester, during the great flu epidemic that followed World War I several years before I was born. Izora, their second child, has always been the senior sibling in the hierarchy of the family. My other older siblings in order of their birth were Robert, Esther,

5

Marvella, Ruth and Naomi. Those in my family who came along after me were all boys: George, born in 1932, Jessie about two years later, followed by Charles, Lorenzo and Earnest.

From my earliest childhood memory until the time I went away to college in 1949, every house we lived in had one bedroom for the boys and one bedroom for the girls, no matter how many brothers and sisters there were at home at the time. Privacy for anyone was almost impossible to achieve in our household. Spring and summer were the most cherished times of the year because the outdoors, our backyard and the front and back porches became integral parts of our living space.

In winter the family would congregate around one of the three sources of space heating in the house, the kitchen range or one of the two wood-burning stoves. Fortunately, we experienced extremely cold temperatures only rarely each winter in Jonesboro, but nearly every year we would have one or two episodes of cold weather. The temperature would drop to 10 or 15 degrees, sometimes lower. These were always memorable occasions because the pipes to our outdoor water hydrant would freeze and burst, unless the spigots were left slightly open to allow the water to flow continuously. Overnight the water on the ground in the yard would freeze, forming an area where we could have fun ice-skating.

My father was a cobbler by trade, but ministry or preaching was his main occupation. As a very young man he was ordained as minister in what was then a fairly new religious denomination called "the Church of God in Christ" (C. O. G. I. C.), sometimes called the "Holiness" church. The church also was referred to derisively by some as the "Holy Roller" church because its services were marked by rhythmic, repetitive music, occasional dancing and speaking in unknown languages. My father came to Jonesboro not only to start a new life for his young family, but also to organize and establish in the area a branch of the Church of God in Christ. At the time establishing the new church was his primary goal and mission in life. When he came to Jonesboro the new denomination had no adherents there.

Unlike most other denominations with which blacks tended to be affiliated—the Baptists, the African Methodist Episcopal Church (A. M. E.), the Colored Methodist Episcopal Church (C. M. E.)—ministers of Papa's church believed they were "called" by

God to preach and took upon themselves the responsibility of finding a place to "preach out" their own congregation. George D. McKinney was not sent to Jonesboro by any board of elders or bishops of his denomination. He and others in his family had been "converted" to the denomination while growing up near Hughes, Arkansas. Before their conversion my parents were members of the A. M. E. Church. The C. O. G. I. C. Church in Hughes "belonged" to the minister there who created it. If George wanted a church of his own he would have to form one somewhere else.

Papa founded the C. O. G. I. C. Church in Jonesboro in about 1920. He began by preaching the gospel of salvation on the streets of Jonesboro to anyone who would stop and listen. Leaders in this denomination believed that the Bible was the revealed word of God and interpreted it literally as it is written in the King James Version. The denomination was the epitome of fundamentalism. Those who subscribed to its teaching appealed to those who professed no religious beliefs at all as well as to those who were active members of other denominations or faiths. Attempts to draw persons already associated with other churches to the C. O. G. I. C. message of salvation tended to create hostility or resentment, particularly among leaders and some adherents in other churches. C. O. G. I. C. preachers maintained that theirs was the only true religion; that unless one were saved, sanctified, filled with the holy ghost and strived to live a life free from all sin, one had no chance of going to heaven. And given the conditions under which most blacks were forced to live in America in the early part of the twentieth century, the idea of going to a better place after this life was an attractive reality for many people. But the lifestyle commanded by the teachings of Papa's church and its claims about being the only path to salvation were, to say the least, quite unsettling to those whose allegiance was to the more conventional established faiths. Occasionally the McKinney children would feel the effects of such attitudes in relationships at school and on the playground.

Street ministry on behalf of a relatively new and strange religious denomination in the early 1920s did not pay well. It certainly did not pay enough to support Papa's growing family. To support the family Papa opened a shoe repair business in a little shop on North Main Street a few short blocks from our home. He was a very skilled shoe repairman and soon gained the reputation of being able to fix any kind of shoe repair problem.

The area on North Main Street where Papa's shop was located was the center of commercial activity in our North Side black community. Mr. Bates, a soft-spoken black man, owned a small grocery store two doors down the street from Papa's shop. Next to the Bates grocery was the filling station with the old-fashioned gasoline pump out front. Around the corner on Word Street was the North Side Dry Cleaners owned and operated by one of the few black men in town who owned an automobile. A few doors further east on Word Street Mr. Conley operated a hauling business (using a horse-drawn cart) out of his backyard. On the northwest corner of Main and Gordon Street a white family ran what we would now describe as a convenience store, the owners' family living in the rear part of the building. Another family of either Greek or Italian extraction, I'm not sure which but they clearly were not "American" whites, operated a bodega that sold what to me were strange kinds of fresh vegetables. (I later learned they were eggplants.) On the northeast corner of North Main and Word Streets was the St. John's Baptist Church, by far the largest black church on our side of town. It was a stately red brick building with four tall white columns supporting the portico over the entrance.

Papa drew some business from street traffic in the neighborhood. But he did not rely on that alone. On some days he would walk through various parts of town soliciting business for his shop. If he found customers he would return to the shop with their shoes, returning the rehabilitated shoes several days later. Or he would tell the customer when the shoes would be ready to be picked up at the shop. Except for simple jobs such as attaching steel toe and heel plates, most shoe repair jobs done the old-fashioned way took time. Papa repaired shoes using the same kinds of hand tools his father had used.

The greatest handicap to the development of his business, however, was access to the state of the art power tools of the shoe repair trade. The two white-owned shoe shops uptown on Main Street had better equipment and could do any given repair job much quicker than Papa. They had the latest power driven machines such as stitching, sanding and buffing, and machines that could nail a rubber heel in place in a matter of seconds. Their customers could walk in and have the repair work they needed done while they waited. The power driven equipment the white shops had was very expensive and could only be acquired by small businessmen through bank financing or credit arrangements with the manufacturers. These options were indeed beyond Papa's reach. Papa could not conceive of approaching the Main Street commercial bank in Jonesboro for a loan; banks in Jonesboro just did not do that kind of business with a black person. And the representatives of shoe repair shop suppliers who regularly called on the white shops up town never ventured north of the railroad tracks that separated our North Side black community from the main business district.

Eventually, through his evangelism on the streets of Jonesboro, the contacts made in the shoe repair shop, and the revivals held during the summer in tents and brush arbors on vacant lots in black neighborhoods, a sufficient number of people committed themselves and agreed to establish an organized C. O. G. I. C. Church in the city with Papa (Elder McKinney) as the pastor. In 1924 Papa was ordained as a minister in the Church of God in Christ. His ordination by the senior elders of the church in Arkansas gave formal recognition to work he had done in extending the denomination to a new area. At first there were only five or six families in the congregation, the Conleys, the Eppersons, the Blunts, a few others and, of course, the McKinneys.

The church at Jonesboro experienced modest growth throughout most of the 1920s. However, the general collapse of the economy following the stock market crash in 1929 and the subsequent Depression were especially devastating to people like our family who lived on the margin of the society. The church never became large enough to support the pastor and his family.

By the time I was born in August 1930, our family had grown from the two little girls my parents had when they came to Jonesboro, to include my brother Robert, born in 1920, and four other girls.

My mother, Roseanna Thompson, was the eldest of thirteen children born to William and Annie Thompson. She was very short in stature, less than five feet tall, but well proportioned. She did not appear to have a forceful, strong personality. She smiled a lot. But these attributes of character could be misleading. Whenever any issue would arise with outsiders concerning the well-being of her husband and her children, she would never hesitate to speak up and defend them with utmost vigor.

Momma never worked at any job away from home. But she was a very hard-working woman who considered the care and nurture of her husband and children her first priority. To help out financially when the money was short (and that always seemed to be the case) Momma would take in laundry from certain well-off white families in town. She would do customers' dress shirts by hand, using a washboard and our galvanized metal bathtub. In order to insure that the shirts were sparkling white, she would build a fire under the large cast iron pot in the backyard and boil the customers' laundry, before hanging the items on clothes lines to dry outside in the fresh air. Then she would spend hours in the kitchen ironing the shirts with heavy flatirons that had been heated on the kitchen stove. No commercial laundry could do shirts like Momma. So her laundry services were always in demand.

Momma's customers would bring their dirty laundry to our house and pick it up whenever Momma told them they would be ready. They were thus in a position to see what a large family we were and the conditions we lived in. Occasionally, customers would deliver not only their laundry but bags of used clothing for us that their own children had outgrown or discarded. I remember wearing clothes of a quality that we could never afford because of the generosity of some of Momma's customers.

When they were not in school my older sisters were Momma's helpers in all the household chores, including our own and other people's laundry. But Momma was the main cook. In the kitchen she was a miracle worker. She could create a filling meal for our large family when there appeared to my undiscerning eye to be nothing to cook, except maybe some lard, cornmeal, a few potatoes, a piece of streak-o-lean and some salt and pepper. Somehow she would stretch a little to serve a lot. In the mid-1930s during the depths of the Depression most weekday meals did not include meat, unless some hunter came by with a rabbit or possum. But in summer we always ate well because we kept a large garden where we grew all kinds of fresh vegetables.

Momma to me epitomized the role of "housewife." Unlike

10

many pastors' wives she did not take a leadership position in Papa's church. She was contented to remain in the background, providing help to others, particularly those working with the young children. Papa traveled quite a bit in connection with his work for the church. There was the annual C. O. G. I. C. convocation in Memphis, Tennessee, in November. State and district meetings also were scheduled annually where representatives of local congregations of the church would come together in a revival-like setting to hear stirring sermons and mass choirs perform. Occasionally, Momma would accompany Papa on trips to such meetings, but most often she stayed at home with the children. Momma always packed Papa's bags when he went away on one of these trips. She would carefully lay out his "good" suit, and best-starched white shirt, instructing Papa not to wear that outfit until the day at the meeting when he was scheduled to preach. Momma appeared to me to take great pride in helping Papa prepare for a trip. And Papa relied upon her totally to get him ready.

While growing up we never had a car, so Papa normally traveled either by bus or by train. As a minister, he qualified for and received a discount on the tickets purchased for his travels. One of my earliest memories was a trip to Marianna, Arkansas, to visit Momma's family. Papa arranged to have Mr. Dudley drive us there in his car. I must have been three or four years old as this was the first ride in a car that I can remember. Marianna is about 100 miles southeast of Jonesboro. I don't recall exactly how many of our family made this trip but I do remember one or two of my sisters riding with me in the back seat of Mr. Dudley's four-door black sedan. Even though the distance was a little less than 100 miles, it seemed to me to take forever for us to reach our destination. The main highway south from Jonesboro had been paved for about thirty miles, but beyond that we would hit stretches of gravel road, which not only would cause us to slow down but kicked up quite a bit of dust in the car as well. And when we had to get off the main road to head to Grandpa Thompson's farm which was some four or five miles off the highway, the road became not much more than a dirt trail.

Sitting in the back seat of that car I remember being mystified by the passing scenery. To me the telephone poles along the road appeared to be moving past us in the opposite direction. This was

11

fascinating to me. Of course, there were no fast food places where we could stop for refreshments or go to the bathroom. Realizing the trip would take several hours, Momma had prepared sandwiches for us to eat and filled several mason jars with drinking water. What made the trip even more of an adventure was the fact that we had no map to guide us precisely to our destination. Although Momma and Papa had gone there before, neither of them had driven a car there. If we became lost or otherwise were unsure of which direction to take at a particular road junction we would simply approach the nearest house and ask direction from total strangers. Once we came to a farmhouse where people were sitting on the front porch. They not only gave us directions but also inquired whether we wanted something to eat. Obviously, we appeared to be in some distress with the restless young children Momma and Papa had in tow. They gladly accepted the invitation to have some lunch, whereupon the woman of the house got up, went into the kitchen and made biscuits, bacon and eggs for our family on the spot.

This type of behavior toward total strangers was common in rural Arkansas in the mid-1930s. People extended themselves and shared what little they had with the traveling stranger because it was understood that the black traveler had no choice but to rely on the generosity of others. Perhaps this explains why Papa from time to time would bring home with him a destitute person (we called them hobos) who had come by the shop looking for a meal or some place to stay for a few days. Although our family had little Momma always found enough food to share with the stranger.

Whenever we made the trip to Marianna to see Grandpa and Grandma Thompson, or to Hughes to see my grandparents on Papa's side of the family, it was imperative to leave Jonesboro early in the morning because we wanted to arrive at their place before dark. Finding your way to their house at night posed a serious challenge. There were no streetlights; the back roads were unmarked and very narrow. If your car left the roadway you were in a ditch, perhaps half filled with mud and water. Since one traveled in those days dressed in one's best clothes, you certainly did not want to have to get out of the car and push it out of a muddy ditch.

Grandpa Thompson's house was larger than our house in Jonesboro. It sat on a small rise a hundred yards or so off the road.

To both sides of the house and in back were open fields for planting crops but the house itself was in a clearing surrounded by large trees. There was no manicured lawn, only bare ground and several flowerbeds near the foundation. A barn and fenced area lay at the rear also and this was where the livestock was kept. On one side was a small covered round stone structure, the well that supplied household water needs. Above the well was a contraption that held a pulley to which was attached a large wooden bucket tied to the end of a long rope. One would lower the bucket twenty feet or so down the well and retrieve a full bucket of water. Water from the well was always cool, no matter how hot the weather. The well therefore served as the refrigerator for the Thompson household. For example, after milking the cow, the bucket of milk would be lowered into the well for it to cool.

The time I spent visiting my grandparents was my only experience of living on an actual farm. There is no place on earth as dark as a moonless night on a farm that is many miles from any city and where your house may be miles from the nearest neighbor. We normally would visit grandparents during the summer months. Arkansas in summer usually is oppressively hot and the humidity is about equal to the temperature. Sundown did not bring much relief from the heat or the humidity. The only escape was to be outdoors where one hopefully could occasionally catch a breeze.

William and Annie Thompson also had a very large family—thirteen children in all. Momma was the oldest of the Thompson children. But several of her younger sisters died at a very young age. I do remember, however, that when we visited the Thompsons in 1935 Momma was welcomed as one who had gone away and made a good life for herself and her family.

*   *   *

There were two black communities in Jonesboro in the 1930s. The smaller of these two communities was on the north side of town where I grew up. The other black community was on the east side. The main business and commercial area of the city separated the two communities. The black high school, Booker T. Washington, was located on the east side. Actually, Booker T. Washington

School included grades one through twelve in the same building. The distance from the north side black community to the east side was about four miles. Since there was no school bus service available to blacks in the 1930s the Jonesboro city fathers saw fit to provide a one-room frame school house on the north side for black first and second graders, so they would not have to walk the three or four miles across town at such a young age to go to school.

My first two years of schooling took place in that one room school on the north side of Jonesboro. One teacher taught both the first and second graders. I began school at age seven in September 1937. While I had reached my sixth birthday in August 1936 I did not start school until a full year later because I suffered a tragic accident on the Sunday before I was scheduled to begin school in 1936. That Sunday my closest friends, Frederick "Little Brother" and Mickey Epperson, whose family lived directly across the street from the church, came over to our house that afternoon to play with my brother George and me. Little Brother and I were the same age and we both were excited about beginning school the next day.

The first day of school marked the end of summer, which meant that little boys could resume wearing shoes after having gone barefoot since the close of the previous school year. We also would get to wear the new pants and shirts our parents had put aside for just this occasion. The Epperson boys, George and I were playing hide-and-go-seek. In the course of the game, which involved chasing one another around the house and through the neighbors' yards, I jumped off the porch in my bare feet on to a broken Coca-Cola bottle and nearly severed my right foot in half. I was unable to walk for quite a long time. So my parents made the decision to hold me out of school until my foot completely healed. By that time I had missed too much instruction to make it up in the time remaining in the school year. So my folks kept me home until the following year.

Having to wait an extra year to start school was a big disappointment to me. My schooling would forever be out of phase with that of kids my own age. There were both advantages and disadvantages to this. I was always older and more mature than the kids in my class, which enabled me to grasp the material being taught somewhat quicker than many of my younger classmates. But the kids my own age who were a year ahead tended to think I may have failed a grade earlier. Of course, they were not aware of the circumstances that led to my being a year behind.

The fact that Momma was to deliver my brother Charles less than two weeks after my unfortunate accident in 1936 also may have been a factor in the decision to keep me home for another year. When Charles came along on September 9, 1936 Momma had a newborn and three other sons six years old and under at home at the same time. As the eldest I would be able to help look after four-year-old George, and two-year-old Jessie while Momma cared for Baby Charles.

Baby Charles' arrival in the McKinney household put added pressure on our limited living space. Papa had to find a bigger house, because it would be two years before my oldest sister, Izora, finished high school and left the nest for college. One of Papa's brothers, Uncle Jessie, had left Hughes and moved to Chicago in the early 1930s and opened a shoe repair shop there. Robert, my oldest brother, had been taught how to repair shoes by Papa. He would work in the shop in the afternoon after leaving school and by the mid 1930s was quite an accomplished cobbler. The Depression had reached its nadir by 1936-37 and had taken its toll on Papa's shoe repair business in Jonesboro. Somehow Papa came upon an idea for alleviating our living space problem at home. Whether this idea originated with Papa or was planted in his mind by Uncle Jessie is not clear. It may well be also that Robert himself suggested it. After all Robert turned 16 years old in March 1936. In those days it was not unusual for a boy to begin asserting his independence at that age, particularly if he had a trade that might enable him make a living for himself.

In any event the idea was that Robert would go to Chicago to live with Uncle Jessie and his family and work in Uncle Jessie's shop while completing his high school education in the much better Chicago school system. Robert apparently liked the idea of getting away from home and living in the big city. Papa saw it as a partial solution to our living space problem. On the other hand, Momma was extremely skeptical, having serious reservations as to whether Robert was ready to cope with living in Chicago. The one aspect of the proposition that Momma did consider to be positive was the prospect that her oldest son would have the benefit of a better high school education than the Jonesboro schools could provide. Momma reluctantly gave in to Papa's wishes and Robert left home in 1936 to complete the final years of his secondary education at Englewood High School in Chicago, Illinois.

Although I did not realize it at the time, Robert's leaving surely had an impact on my development as a person. I did not enjoy the benefit of an older brother being around during the critical years of my adolescence. Robert never returned to Jonesboro while I was growing up so I never really got a chance to know him until many years later when we both were grown men. I do remember that he sent us the yearbook from his senior class at Englewood High. The striking thing to me as the family gathered around to look at the pictures in the yearbook was the fact that the Englewood High School student body included many more white students than black ones. I was particularly impressed also with the number of students in the senior class. There were several hundred seniors alone. I surmised that the entire high school student body must have included more than a thousand boys and girls. Alongside each senior's picture they listed the various clubs, athletic activities and interest groups to which each student belonged, along with a brief statement by the student of his life philosophy or goal. Robert's reported goal was "to study life and to be of service to mankind."

It was difficult for me at the time to conceive of a racially integrated school. In Jonesboro in the 1930s there were separate schools for blacks and whites. None of the blacks in my community publicly questioned this arrangement, although there were obvious differences in the two systems. We never got new textbooks at the black schools. What we got instead were books that previously had been used at the white schools, sometime many years before. The system frequently would hire as teachers for the black schools persons with only a high school diploma—no college teacher training at all. It would have been unthinkable to do such a thing in any of the white schools. Jonesboro's Booker T. Washington school had neither a gymnasium nor a science laboratory; offered no courses in chemistry; there were no lockers for students either. The North Side one room school I attended for first and second grade was heated in winter by a potbellied wood stove that sat in the center of the room—the only thing separating the

16

two grades from one another. From third grade until after World War II we would watch the yellow school buses go by as they transported the North Side white kids to their schools across town while we walked the four miles or so to Booker T. Washington School. Teachers in the white schools were paid on a scale that was thirty to forty percent higher than that for black teachers. In Jonesboro in the 1930s and early 1940s this was regarded as the natural order of things.

The Jonesboro schools were segregated when I was a boy but the neighborhoods were integrated. From the time I was born until I went away to college in 1949 white families lived either next door to us or within a block of our house. It was not uncommon for white and black kids in the neighborhood to play together when they were young. But by the time they reached school age they tended to go their separate ways.

By the time I finally was ready to start school in 1937 my family had moved from Gordon Street to a different house at 515 Third Street, which was about three blocks away. Our new place was a little larger than the Gordon Street house, but it too had no indoor plumbing or electricity. Again there was a large front porch with one of those swings that hung on two metal chains that were attached to the ceiling. The water hydrant at this house was in the front yard not far from the sidewalk and street. There actually were two lots—the house sat on one and the second lot was used as a large vegetable garden. Just beyond the house directly north of us was a deep drainage ditch and stream, which divided our part of town from the unincorporated areas to the north populated totally by poor whites. Several peach trees were in the back yard. Also, there were two other structures: next to the back porch was a small wooden shed and out near the outhouse along the alley was a small barn for storing grain, garden tools and other equipment. The shed next to the porch we used primarily as a smokehouse for curing meat at hog killing time in late fall. This house also was closer to the western edge of town near corn and cotton fields.

Papa decided to move on from the C. O. G. I. C. church in Jonesboro in about 1938. He took over an already established church in Malvern, a town in central Arkansas not far from Little Rock. On alternate Sundays he preached at the church in Malvern and one in Pine Bluff, the second largest city in the state, located

40 miles southeast of Little Rock. Notwithstanding the changes in the locale of Papa's ministry, there is no evidence that moving the family to south central Arkansas was ever contemplated. Papa would take the Cotton Belt passenger train to his churches usually on Saturday morning and return Monday evening.

*   *   *

It was about this time that Papa entered into a sharecropping arrangement with an older black man who owned 40 acres of land just west of Jonesboro. The landowner who lived not far from our house had two mules, plows, a wagon and other necessary farm equipment. The deal made was for the landowner to supply all the equipment, the land, seed and fertilizer and Papa would till the soil, plant, cultivate and harvest the crops. In other words, the landlord supplied the capital and Papa supplied the labor for the enterprise. A small plot of the land was set aside for Papa's sole use to raise pigs and plant root crops such as peanuts and potatoes for our own family. When the main crops were harvested and sold the proceeds would be evenly split between Papa and the landowner.

Farming a small plot of land is a very labor intensive activity. Having a large family gave such a farmer quite an advantage if the children could be put to work in the farming operation. By 1938 Papa had four potential male farm hands in Rufus, George, Jessie and Charles, to say nothing of my four older sisters still at home. Working the land to raise your own food also was viewed as one way to offset the problem of acquiring money to buy life necessities during the Depression. I am certain that these factors weighed heavily in Papa's decision to enter into the sharecropping deal. I believe he saw this as the best way to take care of his family. It appeared at that time that the prosperity generally enjoyed during most of the previous decade would not be returning to Jonesboro soon.

But the shoe repair shop continued to operate during the winter months, until Papa sold some of his equipment early in 1940. I remember thinking at the time that selling the shoe repair equipment was a bad move. Although I had not shown much interest in becoming a cobbler, George, Jr. and Jessie did. I was concerned

18

that their opportunity to fully learn the trade under Papa's tutelage, as Papa had under his father, would be lost.

There were perhaps six or eight first graders and about the same number of kids in the second grade at the little North Side school in my first year. Because there were no walls separating the two classes and only one teacher, while one class was reading aloud the other would be assigned work to do quietly on their own. In such a setting it was extremely important to maintain discipline. Any talk was strictly forbidden while the teacher was engaged with the other class. Violation of this rule was severely punished with several raps on the knuckles with a ruler. The school day started promptly at 8:30 A.M. That meant you had to be in your assigned seat at that hour ready to begin work. First graders were expected to be able to read any section of the first grade reader by the end of the year. They had to know about numbers, recognize letters, shapes and colors and how to spell the words used in their textbook. By the end of the second grade we were required to recite the timetables up to twelve.

From my earliest memory I have been driven to excel in school. Momma instilled this trait in me, and she did the same with all of her children. She believed one could not overemphasize the importance of education. She always said education is your ticket to a better life than that of your parents who were only one generation removed from slavery. From first grade on I enjoyed going to school and relished doing the work required to get good grades. However, learning did not come easy for me, except in a few subjects. While I studied hard and got good grades in math in both high school and college, even today I have little understanding of mathematical concepts and the "why" of the right answer to math problems. On the other hand, history, geography and government (we called it "civics" in high school) came easy for me. The subject of English and literature fell somewhere in between. I could never see any logic in many of the rules of sentence structure and parts of speech. Distinguishing adverbs from adjectives and nouns from gerunds still is difficult for me.

But when I was young I was blessed with remarkable powers of memory. It was my ability to memorize and recall information I had read and studied that enabled me to stand at the head of every high school class I was in and to finish with the second highest academic ranking in the class of 1953 at Arkansas A. M. & N. College. (The top rank went to a woman who had transferred to A. M. & N. College in her senior year. Mine was the highest rank of any student who had spent the entire four years there.) This record continued through my first year of law school at Indiana University Law School, where I finished 5th in a class of 105. Obviously, the law school competition was somewhat tougher. It was in law school that I began to sharpen my reasoning powers and to develop more fully the ability to write and speak persuasively in public.

Moving from the North Side school to third grade at Booker T. Washington School in 1939 was quite a change. George, Jr., who started school the year I went to second grade, got a double promotion at the end of his first year. So we were in third grade together, though he was two years younger. I resented being in the same class as my younger brother. His double promotion after first grade also implied that he was smarter than I was and this added to my resentment. But I was very protective of George, "Little Mac" as all our friends called him. They called me "Big Mac", a nickname that followed me throughout high school. The first fist fight I remember ever having on the school playground occurred when Osie Mathis, a boy my age, attacked George while we were out for recess. I left another group of kids and ran over to defend George. I landed the first good blow to Osie's face, causing his nose to bleed profusely. Fortunately, Mrs. Murphy, the fourth grade teacher, observed everything from the window in the fourth grade room and knew that Osie's attack on George had been unprovoked and that I had good reason to come to his defense. My punishment for fighting was not nearly as severe as it might have been because Mrs. Murphy saw the whole incident. That fight that left my opponent bloodied gave me a certain tough guy reputation among my classmates that said, "Don't mess with 'Big Mac'."

Though I never said so until much later in my life, I began to wonder why Papa found only his third son worthy of his own name. This clearly was out of the historical pattern, the father's name usually being given to the firstborn son. The question in my mind about Papa's choice of names for his first three boys was soothed somewhat by the knowledge that I had been honored by being given the names of my two grandfathers: Papa's father was

20

named Rufus and my middle name William after Momma's father. I was always proud to carry both grandfathers' names. I never discussed this subject with Robert and therefore never discovered how the firstborn son felt about not being made a "junior." I have come to believe, however, that Papa had good reason to make George a junior and not me or Robert. From a very early age, in fact as long as I can remember, George had exhibited qualities of serenity that made him seem special. I think Papa knew then that George, not Robert or Rufus, would follow him and pursue a career in ministry.

Booker T. Washington school was for me an imposing building. It was three stories high, including the ground floor, and sat on a hill far above the street. The white trim of its large windows provided a striking contrast with the building's dark red brick construction. One could enter from an identical set of concrete steps on either end of the front of the building. These entrances brought you to the second floor level into a hallway that spanned the building's depth. The ground floor contained classrooms for girl's home economics, boy's shop and agriculture, the kitchen and cafeteria, the boys and girls' bathrooms, and several storage and utility rooms. On the second floor were classrooms for first, second, third, fourth, fifth and sixth grades. The third floor housed the principal's office, the auditorium, which doubled as the homeroom for seventh and eighth graders, classrooms for high school students, a small library or study hall and a nurse's station.

The land sloped gently away from the rear of the building several hundred yards. Some sixty yards down the slope from the building was a clay surfaced tennis court with basketball goals at either end. The outdoor tennis court was the only athletic facility at Booker T. Washington School. This outside open area was where the elementary grade students took recess at staggered times mornings and afternoons, weather permitting. This also was the practice area for our high school football and basketball teams, known as the "Jonesboro Eskimos". We came by this name because our school was the northernmost black high school in the state of Arkansas, and because the weather got much colder in Jonesboro than most other places in the state where our black school competitors were located.

The entire student body of Booker T. Washington rarely exceeded 250. The class of 1948-49, the year I graduated, was comprised of seven students. This was a fairly typical size for senior classes during this period of time. In my graduating class were four girls—Eva Mae Thomas, Clara Mae McCollough, Thelma Lee Park, and Georgia Lee Holliday—and three boys, myself, Frederick Cook and Osie Lee Mathis. A ninth grade class of 20 students usually would dwindle down to less that ten by graduation time four years later. The main cause for the attrition among girls was pregnancy or marriage. For boys, it was restlessness, pressure to get a job to make money, or refusal to accept physical punishment from teachers or the principal for infractions of rules of one kind or another. In the 1940s persons in positions of authority at school were within their rights to mete out physical punishment to students of whatever age. And the community generally condoned the practice.

One of the saddest cases of a boy's refusal to accept physical punishment, leading to expulsion in his junior year, was that of young man named Stinnett who lived on the North Side of town. Stinnett was very industrious. He worked odd jobs after school to help support his single mother. He was a bright student and very proud of the way he conducted his life. The shop teacher, who was also the principal, proposed to spank Stinnett for his failure to do a job in the shop that Stinnett felt was not his to do. Stinnett stood his ground, asserting that he was a man just like the principal and would not submit to a spanking. For this he was told to leave school and never return.

There was hardly any turnover of teachers at Booker T. Washington School, particularly at the grade school level. During my entire time there Mrs. Boone Watson taught third grade, Mrs. E. M. Murphy taught fourth grade and Mrs. Greene taught second grade. Mrs. F. C. Turner, the home economics and science teacher, also my senior class sponsor, was there too throughout my tenure. The changes in faculty that did occur tended to take place at the high school level. Our high school teachers often were drawn from the ranks of recent college graduates who taught school for a few years to earn money to pursue graduate degrees later on. I had the misfortune to draw a high school teacher who had been assigned to teach math, but knew little about algebra and geometry. Miss O'Neil was young, had just finished college, and apparently had very little interest in making teaching a career. Rumor had it that on more than one occasion she dated boys in the senior class. Whether or not this was a fact, the idea that she may have been amenable to such overtures from male high school students was a titillating thought.

For the most part our teachers were excellent. What they may have lacked in the way of formal credentials they more than made up for in dedication to their work and in an intense desire to bring out the very best in students. They knew well the limitations imposed upon them by the racial segregation "system" but did not allow that knowledge to deter them from the task at hand. Every effort was made to provide enriching experiences for my classmates and me.

The tenure of principals at Booker T. Washington School tended to be much shorter than that of teachers. Five different principals served at the school in my twelve years there. Initially there was Mr. F. C. Turner (who was married to Mrs. Turner, the home economics teacher). Next came Mr. J. H. White, who was there for only one or two years. Then came Mr. Herbert Smith, who was principal during my seventh, eighth and ninth grade years. He was followed by Mr. Price and Mr. W. F. Branch.

*   *   *

Every year high school students produced at least one play written by a famous playwright such as Eugene O'Neil or Maxwell Anderson. On the night the play was performed, the school auditorium would be filled with parents and well-wishers from all over town. Being chosen for even the smallest part in such a production was a signal of honor for the student. We would spend hours after school for weeks learning and rehearsing the parts, preparing for the performance under the guidance and watchful eyes of faculty members. My ability to memorize written material gave me the inside track on landing the meatier roles in plays in many instances, despite my deficiencies as an actor.

Spending time at rehearsal after normal school hours for a play my brother George and I were in led to one of the last occasions I remember being administered a whipping by Momma. It was in the spring of the year and the carnival had come to town.

After rehearsal was over that evening several members of the cast decided to go to the carnival and have some fun. I decided to join my friends and George reluctantly went along. However, we knew doing so would cause us to get home much later than normal. We also knew that going to the carnival violated one of our parents' firm rules against attending this type of entertainment event. In our household, going to a movie theatre even, at any time, was considered sinful and against the religious principles of the holiness church. Kids who went to the Baptist or Methodist Church were only forbidden to attend movies and carnivals on Sunday. Nevertheless, George and I went and had a great time at the carnival, eating cotton candy, seeing the freak shows and going on several of the rides. All of this was a brand new experience for us.

Eventually it was time for us to go home so the question was how were we going to explain getting home so late to Momma. I told George to let me handle explaining things to Momma, if that became necessary. There was a chance we could sneak into the house unnoticed, in which case we would be home free. I should have known better. Momma was up waiting for us when we got home, wanting to know what took us so long. I proceeded to tell her that we had run into a problem at rehearsal and the faculty sponsors had kept us much beyond the normal time. This seemed like a perfectly good explanation to me and I think Momma had almost bought it. But George was too honest a person and confessed to Momma precisely what had happened. George got off without punishment but I got one of the worst whippings of my life for telling a deliberate lie.

No course in music was offered at Booker T. Washington School. However, one of the teachers organized a choir, usually during the spring quarter. The choir would perform during the two major events at graduation time: the Sunday baccalaureate services for seniors at a nearby church, and the graduation ceremony itself held later that week in the school auditorium. During the course of the school year the principal would invite some well-known black artist to perform at special events at the school. One year the famous classical singer, William Warfield, came to our school.

Each spring the girls held a mother/daughter banquet and the boys a similar event for the fathers. For the father/son banquet the

24

boys took on as a project each year the task of ordering and raising from baby chicks the chickens that were to be served as the main course at our banquet. The shop class teacher would order the baby chicks through one of the local feed stores in January. The chicks would be delivered a few weeks later. In the meantime, we would build a chicken coop frame with wire netting all around. The new chicks, only days old, would be cared for by the students until they grew to pullet size in May.

The coop was kept in the school boiler room. Every day one or two of the boys would be assigned the dreadful job of removing the soiled newspapers from beneath the coop and replacing it with clean papers to capture the droppings. Another team had the daily job of refilling the feed and water troughs. Raising the chickens gave the boys practical training in animal husbandry, an essential skill to have in any farming community at that time. When ordering we would specify a preference for female chicks, as female chicks yielded the most tender fryers. We learned about the different breeds of chickens, Dominique, Rhode Island Red, Leghorn, their egg laying propensities, and their rates of growth. Although boys in farming communities probably are less squeamish about such matters, we sent the chickens to a slaughter house to be prepared for the banquet, instead of doing that job ourselves.

*   *   *

During Professor Herbert Smith's tenure as principal, he started a chapter of the "New Farmers of America" (N.F.A.). This organization was the black counterpart to the "Future Farmers of America," which was for white school kids in farm communities. The N.F.A. was founded as an organization for youth enrolled in vocational agriculture. It was dedicated to making a positive difference in the lives of young people by developing their potential for leadership, personal growth and career success through agricultural education. Professor Smith had graduated from Arkansas A. M. & N. college, with a degree in agriculture. The parents of most students at Booker T. Washington School were not directly engaged in farming as my family was when Smith became principal. But many of them worked in occupations related to farming. Two of the largest industrial type operations in Jonesboro were the

25

cotton gins and the cotton compressing plant that provided employment for many Jonesboro residents. And quite a few of my classmates would spend time in the nearby fields "chopping" cotton in early summer and picking cotton in the fall to earn money. But for me and my family farming had become the primary source of our income by 1940, though we continued to live in town.

I found the N.F.A. program attractive and was encouraged to participate in the organization by Professor Smith. He took a special interest in the organization's program to develop students' abilities to do public speaking. Each year the N.F.A. held a national public speaking competition. A boy was selected from each N.F.A. chapter to compete against boys from other chapters in the state. The winning contestant at the state level would go on to compete against winners from other states in the region. Regional winners move on to the national finals where the overall national winner would be determined.

In my eighth grade year Professor Smith selected me as public speaking contestant for our school. No doubt my reputation for memorizing materials was a major factor in Smith's decision. He knew that rules of the contest required speakers to recite a prepared text from memory. Another requirement was that the contestant participate in the writing of his speech. When Professor Smith chose me as contestant, however, he also gave me the speech he wanted me to learn and said nothing about input from me as to the content of the speech. As I read and reread the speech in an effort to commit it to memory I gave no thought to how the speech might be improved or changed to reflect my own thoughts. But I was concerned as to what I would say if officials in charge of the contest should ask about who wrote my speech. Fortunately for me the subject of authorship never arose, and of course I was not about to call attention to the subject myself.

I began work on learning the speech early in the spring of 1945. The state level contest was to take place in May of that year on the campus of Arkansas A. M. & N. College at Pine Bluff. A. M. & N. College was the state supported institution of higher learning open to Negroes at that time. The college's agriculture department had oversight of the New Farmers of America program and would conduct the speech competition. Of course, I was very excited about making the 150 mile trip to Pine Bluff, the farthest I had ever been away from my hometown.

I cannot recall exactly the title or content of the speech, but it had something to do with the importance of rotating crops in order for the land to remain fertile and productive over longer periods of time. I do remember that it was several typewritten pages in length and required about fifteen minutes to read aloud before the mirror. From time to time Professor Smith would monitor my progress by having me recite the paragraphs I had committed to memory. Sometimes I would do this in the principal's office; other times he would have me recite before a class, giving me the opportunity to develop a feel for presenting the speech before an audience. Of course, my rehearsal frequently was interrupted for suggestions about gestures and other tips on how to make a more effective presentation. The more I performed before a class, the greater my confidence. This process also led to my becoming one of the better known eighth grade students at Booker T. Washington School.

Two weeks or so before the date for the trip Professor Smith paid my parents a visit. He explained to them everything about the contest and the trip and asked their permission for me to accompany him to Pine Bluff. He told them we would travel in his car; that we would arrive in Pine Bluff the afternoon of the day of our departure from Jonesboro; that I would stay in one of the men's residence halls on the campus, along with my fellow contestants from other places in the state. We would return the day following the contest. On the basis of Professor Smith's assurances about my safety, my parents agreed to my making the trip.

The state contest was scheduled to take place just after A. M. & N's graduation which occurred in mid-May. The college students had left campus but many of the faculty remained, including residence hall supervisors. Professor Smith and the other adults accompanying contestants were assigned special quarters at other locations on campus. Shortly after our arrival all the contestants and their adult sponsors were brought together for a reception, hosted by the head of the agriculture department at the college, Professor S. Alexander Haley. It was at this reception that I learned that the N.F.A. was not just an organization for secondary school students. There were chapters for college level persons as well and one existed on the campus of A. M. & N. College. I got the chance to meet all the other contestants at the reception, as well as several members of the agriculture department faculty who were active in the N.F.A. At 14 years of age I was certainly the youngest of all the contestants. All other contestants were already in high school. Just being on a college campus and, along with my fellow contestants, the center of attention as well was an awesome, unforgettable experience for me.

Professor Haley was a kindly, soft-spoken man who obviously had the respect of my principal and the other teachers present. Many of them had studied under Professor Haley earlier and knew him well. In addition to his reputation as an excellent teacher, Professor Haley was known to have an appreciation for music and a good tenor voice. Toward the end of the evening someone prevailed upon him to favor the group with a rendition of "Danny Boy." This turned out to be the highlight of the evening, sending all the contestants back to the dormitory on a high note.

The following morning all six contestants, each of us dressed in his Sunday best outfit, left the dormitory together for the short walk across the campus to the administration building where the auditorium, called Caldwell Hall, was located. Caldwell Hall clearly was the place on campus where important ceremonies took place. The floor was highly polished mahogany, and sloped gently toward the front to an impressive, velvet-curtained stage. The fold-down seats were anchored to the floor in three sections separated by two side aisles. In the rear of the hall on a raised platform was another seating section, one side of which was configured to serve as a choir loft with a place for the director and a large grand piano. All the contestants were escorted to the stage and seated behind a lectern. The only audience were the adult sponsors and several members of the faculty, including the three judges who had not been separately identified. Professor Haley presided. He spoke briefly about the history and purposes of the New Farmers of America, introduced members of the faculty and the agriculture teachers who accompanied the contestants. He then turned to the contestants on stage, asking each of us to stand and identify ourselves and our school affiliations.

One by one the contestants rose, came to the lectern and gave their speeches. It took a little more than an hour to complete the presentations. After that, three men who had been scattered in the audience taking notes got up and went to the rear of the hall, sat down together and talked quietly among themselves for several minutes. Meanwhile, Professor Haley invited the contestants backstage to relax, have a glass of cool water and await the judges' decision. Having met the other contestants for the first time less than twenty-four hours before, I recall there was little, if any, small talk among us after the contest was over. We all were anxious to know how the judges viewed our presentations. One or two speakers who "messed up" by forgetting some of their lines, or repeating passages of their speech, already knew they could not win. I was not among them as I had recited my speech perfectly, showing some emotion and feeling as well. I felt relieved when we were called back to the stage to hear the results.

The lead judge joined the contestants on stage and was called to the podium to give the judges' decision. He complimented every speaker first, then proceeded to give a brief critical analysis of each of the presentations. Then he finally announced that the contestant from Jonesboro, Rufus W. McKinney, was the winner!

About three weeks after winning the Arkansas State title, I traveled with Professor Smith to Grambling State College in Ruston, Louisiana for the regional finals where I met the winning contestants from the states of Mississippi and Louisiana. We drove from Jonesboro to Pine Bluff where we spent the night again on the A. M. & N. College campus. Leaving the next morning for Grambling, the drive south from Pine Bluff down through El Dorado exposed to me features of the Arkansas landscape that were totally different than where I grew up. I saw oil wells for the first time and was introduced to the foul odor of paper mills, from which one could not escape without driving many miles.

The format for the regional contest was quite similar to the one at A. M. & N. College earlier. Here again we stayed in campus housing, but by this time of year there were even fewer people on the campus. The contest took place the day after our arrival. Again, my speech was judged to be the best of all the presentations in the regional contest. I was extremely pleased at being chosen to represent the entire three-state area at the national finals which were to be held in July at Tennessee State College in Nashville, Tennessee.

On the return trip we again stopped in Pine Bluff. This time Professor Smith took time to show me some parts of the city surrounding the A. M. & N. College campus. I noticed that while Pine Bluff was considerably larger than Jonesboro, the area immediately adjacent to the campus seemed more undeveloped and "country" than even the black communities in my hometown. Jonesboro had paved sidewalks even in the black sections, but Pine Bluff did not. Our streets that were not paved had graded gravel that at least occasionally were treated with oil to keep down the dust. Many streets in the black residential areas in Pine Bluff, on the other hand, were simply unimproved paths. While I was very impressed with the beauty of the A. M. & N. College campus, its buildings and layout, I was quite disappointed to find that Pine Bluff, the second largest city in Arkansas and the home of our state college, was not much more that a sprawling country town. What did impress me about Pine Bluff was the size of the black population relative to that of the whites. It was evident that blacks made up a much higher percentage of the total population of the city than in Jonesboro.

On the final leg of our trip back to Jonesboro Professor Smith and I talked about my experiences so far in the N.F.A. public speaking competition. One subject of our conversation related to some of the inconveniences blacks face when traveling, especially throughout the South. I noticed that Professor Smith always arranged overnight accommodations for us at the black college campuses, and not at any of the hotels at our destinations. He explained that this was done not only to save money but also because people like us were not welcome at hotels and motels along the way. In light of this fact, Professor Smith observed that black colleges throughout the South, if given sufficient advance notice, usually made available their facilities in dormitories and dining halls to persons involved in education as they traveled on business in the area. This too was a way of shielding black teachers and other professionals from some embarrassing encounters and to ensure a welcoming environment. It also helped to sustain a network among the black intelligentsia throughout the South.

He talked also about our visit to the Collegiate Barber Shop a few blocks up North Cedar Street from the A. M. & N. College campus. He asked if I had noticed the clientele of well-dressed professional looking people—that many of them were college teachers, and other successful persons who enjoyed a lifestyle that was the envy of many white people. I think Professor Smith was trying to tell me that a life of meaning and fulfillment could also be mine if I continued to develop my mind and set lofty goals. Going on to college is a necessary first step, despite the limitations that blacks in the South lived with. I have to believe that Professor Smith deplored the segregation system and how it tended to curtail opportunities for young black men and women. But I am not sure he then foresaw the social changes in America that would be precipitated less than twenty years later by the student protest movement at black colleges in the South.

The trip to the national finals in Nashville, Tennessee, seemed to take a long time. It was very hot and uncomfortable in the car, but the roads were better in Tennessee. Professor Smith drove the entire distance, nearly three hundred miles in a single day. We arrived in Nashville late in the afternoon well before dark and found our way to the Tennessee State campus, which is located in the heart of the city. Nashville had the look and feel of a real city, with tree lined, well-paved streets. Tennessee State's buildings appeared to me to be older and more stately than anything I had seen before on a black college campus.

The national finals included a representative from three other regions—Texas/Oklahoma; Tennessee/Alabama/Florida; and Georgia/the Carolinas/Virginia. The format was similar to the other two contests, except that the competition was held in the evening the day after our arrival in Nashville. My presentation was called last and this turned out to be a disadvantage for me because I had heard the others' presentations. Two of them were particularly strong, in my opinion, and that heightened my nervous tension. Having given the same speech twice before in the contest, I thought I was immune to this sort of tension, but clearly I was not. Being again the youngest contestant did not help matters either. In any event, I stumbled over a few of my lines during the course of my presentation. When the judging was announced I was awarded the third place prize. To this day I do not remember which of the other contestants won first and second place. I fully expected to win and was extremely disappointed when I failed to do so.

The formal awards ceremony took place that same evening.

Many more dignitaries and national officials of the New Farmers of America were present. All the contestants and their sponsors were introduced and congratulated on the work they had done in producing such a spirited competition. The first and second place winners received college scholarships. My prize for the third place finish was a gold Bulova watch.

Professor Smith too was disappointed that I did not win, but I could tell he was very proud to have had me enter the contest and that I made my way through to the national finals. The success that we did achieve reflected well upon him and the work he was doing in Jonesboro, Arkansas. I am confident this was the case because a few days after our return to Jonesboro a nice write-up appeared in the Jonesboro daily newspaper, which extolled the fact that Rufus McKinney, an eighth grader at Booker T. Washington School, had won third place in a national public speaking contest in Nashville, Tennessee. Although he never told me so, I am sure that Professor Smith was responsible for getting that story about me into the mainstream daily newspaper. Mine was not the lead story in the newspaper that day. The lead story was that the United States had dropped an atomic bomb on the Japanese city of Hiroshima on August 6, 1945.

*   *   *

Papa's decision to sell his shoe repair equipment and go into the farming business was not one of his better ones from my standpoint. At age ten it turns out that I would become his number-one farm hand. This meant that at certain times of the year I could count on going to school only when the weather was too bad to work in the fields. On weekends Papa went away to his churches in southern Arkansas. Usually he would not return until Monday night. If there were farm jobs that had to be started on Monday morning, it became my responsibility to do that. At a very early age I had to learn how to harness the mules, hitch them to a wagon or other farm implements, and drive them out to the farm.

Farming the way we practiced it was all hard work. We had no tractors or other power equipment. In spring the first job was to prepare the ground for planting by turning the soil over with what was called a broadcast plow. By this procedure weeds and stubble from the previous years growth was buried under the tilled soil so that it would decay and add nutrients to help sustain the new crops. Plowing a field for the first time after it had lain undisturbed over the winter months sometimes turned up surprises, such as the dens of small animals and snakes where they had hibernated during the winter. In plowing a field broadcast fashion, one would start at the outer edges of a square or rectangular area and continue tilling the edges of the area until the whole field had been turned over. I took great pride in plowing a strait furrow, walking behind the single bladed plow while guiding the struggling mules as they pulled the plow through the soil. The next step was to drag the tilled soil with a harrow to smooth it out for planting the corn or cotton seeds.

The forty acres we worked as sharecroppers was quite small, even by Jonesboro standards, and did not take all that long to prepare for planting. About eighty percent of the land was planted in cotton and the rest in corn and the small plot set aside for potatoes, peanuts, vegetables and the hog pen. In the spring I might be required to miss a total of three or four weeks of school in order to help with the planting. Typically I would lose about the same amount of school time at harvest season in the fall.

The lost time in spring created the greatest problem for me in keeping up with my school work and maintaining high academic standards. It occurred near the end of the school year and close to the time for final examinations. There would be very little time for me to catch up on the school work I missed. Some teachers were quite understanding and did what they could to help by sending me projects that could be done at home. Others were not so sympathetic. I was in really big trouble if the teacher decided to base your final grade more on classroom participation than your score on the written examination.

When the school year ended in mid-May work on the farm became nearly a full time job until crops were laid by in late July or early August. At that time my older sisters still living at home and my brothers who were old enough to handle a hoe might be pressed into service on the farm. Cotton and corn are row crops. The rows are planted several feet apart to allow the soil in between to be cultivated, or loosened to facilitate growth. Once the plants break the surface and begin to develop, the farmer faces a constant battle with pests, and with weeds that compete with the crop for the nutrients in the soil. We had plows that were specially designed to help remove unwanted grasses and weeds between the crop rows while at the same time loosening the soil. Some degree of skill is required to do the cultivation work around young, growing row crops. Usually a single mule would be harnessed to draw a multi-pronged cultivator down between the rows. Care had to be taken not to bring the instrument too close and cause damage to the plant roots.

Cotton was planted in such a way as to require it to be thinned out manually once it had reached six to eight inches in height. We called the thinning process "chopping" cotton. This was done with a long-handled tool called a hoe. Unskilled farm hands did this job after being given simple instructions about the amount of space to be left between the plants. As Papa's top assistant it was one of my responsibilities to help supervise my siblings in the chopping activity. (Perhaps being made a straw boss at such a young age partly explains my current propensity for attempting to order my wife and children around.)

Corn, on the other hand, did not have to be thinned. But it did require cultivation, usually at a somewhat later stage in its development than cotton, in order to have a maximum yield. The unwanted growth between the corn rows, therefore, tended to be more mature and tougher. The tool for doing this job had three curved metal prongs with fitted points attached to a plow, also pulled by a single mule. The spring-like action of the tool made it difficult for a small boy to handle and keep the instrument beneath the surface of the ground as it was pulled through tough Bermuda-like grass. The first time Papa gave me this job I complained about my not being strong or heavy enough to hold the tool in the ground. The solution Papa came up with was to find two large rocks that he then placed in the back pockets of my overalls to give my body added weight. After wrestling with that instrument all day I had no trouble sleeping that evening.

Our work on the farm would begin very early in the morning at about seven o'clock. One of the younger children was assigned to be the "water boy." His job was to bring water to the workers so that they would not lose an undue amount of time for water breaks. Keeping the workers supplied with water was an important job because working in an open field under the hot sun without adequate water could lead to heatstroke, a very serious, often fatal illness. Another risk was thunderstorms and lightning. All hands took shelter as soon as signs of a storm or lightning appeared nearby. Appropriate dress was critical also. One needed a broad brimmed hat, gloves and loose fitting clothes. Chopping cotton could be made fun since one could talk with those in rows nearby to take the mind off the work at hand. But all hands were expected to keep pace with the lead chopper and others in the field.

We would work until the noon lunch break, leaving the field to walk the mile or so to our house. There Momma would have prepared our largest meal of the day. Plenty of fresh vegetables—tomatoes, fried corn (my absolute favorite), greens seasoned with fatback, sweet potatoes, and some type of meat, tea or coffee and for dessert peach or apple cobbler. For this meal everyone would be seated around the large dining table in the kitchen. The talk usually was about the work ahead or about some aspect of life in the church. At about two or two-thirty we would return to the field and resume work. The work day ended at six-thirty or seven o'clock. The family kept this kind of schedule for about four or five weeks during June and early July. After that, work in the field was pretty much limited to Papa and the older boys. We had to continue to feed the hogs every day and occasionally do other chores.

Our sharecropping deal ended in the mid-1940s. Thereafter, the McKinneys continued working on farms in the area, chopping cotton for others for wages in early summer and picking cotton (paid by the pound) in the fall. During cotton-picking season Papa insisted that the money earned by each member of the family be put together at the end of the day and treated as family community property. The pool of money would be managed by Papa, but each member of the family had the right to draw from the pool as necessary to buy shoes, clothes and other things that they needed. In addition, we were allowed pocket change if we wanted to buy candy or ice cream. While this system of pooling family revenues worked fairly well, I harbored feelings of envy upon learning that my friends got to keep all the money they earned picking cotton, and did not have to share it with their parents or others in their family. The system of pooling and sharing the money we earned was a compromise that Papa reluctantly agreed to as a result of Momma's quiet intervention. Papa subscribed to the view that money earned by minor children living at home in fact belonged to the head of the house and could be spent by that person as if he had earned the money himself.

Mechanical cotton picking machines were in the very earliest stages of development in the 1940s, and did not come into general use until much later. So the big cotton farmers south and east of Jonesboro had to rely on gangs of temporary laborers to harvest their crops. At the height of the season persons seeking work in the fields congregated early in the morning at certain locations along North Main Street. Farmers would send their trucks to these locations to pick up workers for the day. North Main Street became in effect a hiring hall. Occasionally, a form of bidding would take place; one farmer's offer of $1 per hundred pounds being topped by another's offer of $1.10. However, farmers usually paid the same price. A worker indicated his agreement to the rate of pay by boarding the truck.

There was a certain degree of risk for the farmer involved in obtaining the laborers he needed in this way. Cotton picking abilities tended to vary a great deal from one person to another. Some men could pick five or six hundred pounds of cotton in a ten hour day while others could pick not more than two hundred pounds. And there always were kids who went out primarily for the fun of a trip to the country, having no intention of exerting themselves picking cotton. The farmer had an interest in completing the harvest as quickly as possible because the weather became more and more problematic as time passed in the fall of the year. On the other hand, the non-serious cotton picker faced a risk also. The farmer might fire him and refuse to transport the worker back to town. The threat to refuse return transportation became more serious the greater the distance was from the farm back to town. The McKinney family almost invariably traveled on the same truck. Over the course of the season we developed a certain reputation for reliability. Farmers who knew us preferred our services over some others.

Unlike chopping cotton, which was paid at a certain amount per day, the amount of your compensation for picking cotton depended upon your proficiency and speed as a cotton picker. The greater the weight of the amount of cotton picked the more you were paid. I was the best picker among all the McKinney children, but Marvella was the best among the sisters. Each picker owned his own cotton sack. After arriving in the field the picker would be assigned a particular row and proceeded to remove the cotton from the open bolls on each stalk and place it the sack as he dragged it along the row over one shoulder. A weighing station and large wagon or truck bed was placed at some central point in the field. A picker filled his sack as many times as possible during the day. Each filled sack would be weighed and the amount recorded to the picker's name. At the end of the day the amounts would be totaled and the picker paid in cash.

Cotton tended to weigh more early in the morning when it was damp with dew. Pickers therefore wanted to get started as early as possible to take advantage of the heavier cotton. Occasionally a picker would carelessly put stems, leaves and such in his sack to add weight, but the weight checker could spot such contaminates as the bag was being emptied. The first offense brought only a warning but further attempts usually resulted in a hefty weight reduction penalty.

*   *   *

Prosperity began to return to Jonesboro during the war years. Our house was connected to the electric utility system. At first we had only electric lights. We acquired an electric radio by 1945, and a telephone a few years later. Before we acquired these modern conveniences, reading newspapers, books and magazines was the principal means by which I connected to the world beyond Jonesboro. I followed the progress of World War II through stories in *Readers Digest,* which reported in detail the campaigns of American forces in both the European and Pacific Theatres. These stories and other reports on the war created in my mind's eye vivid pictures of faraway places, people and conditions such that I felt as if I had experienced the events myself. I believe that reading and listening to the written word can stimulate the mind and the imagination greater than any other medium of communication.

I consider myself fortunate to have grown up in a world without television, as it has now evolved. I sense that few kids today know the joy of reading or listening to the radio for entertainment. I discovered major league baseball in 1945 through radio broadcasts of St. Louis Cardinal games by Harry Carey. Through radio a good announcer can make you feel you are actually present at the game. I could be transported to a fantasy world by reading any of several Frank Yerby novels or brought back to the reality of life for blacks in America by reading the Chicago Defender or Richard Wright's *Native Son*.

*   *   *

I never paid much attention to my rate of physical growth and development as a boy during my younger adolescent years. All my friends who were about the same age were similar in stature, although some were better than others at the games we played. For example, I never was good at baseball or softball, being a very poor hitter, and only a fair fielder. I was nearsighted and wore glasses since about the ninth grade. I was a fast runner, however, and excelled beyond all my peers at a game we called "overs." The game was a form of leap frog, a game in which the players would leap over a boy's back as he bent over clasping his ankles. But our game was different from simple leap frog in that we introduced an element of competition. First, a flat object would be put down as a plate and the players would take turns to see who could make the longest leap from the plate after a running start, just as in the track event called the long jump. The boy making the shortest jump had to assume the bent over position and present his back for the players to jump over, while the boy making the longest jump led the competition by making the first leap and determining the distance from the plate for the next leap. He would decide also whether the leap over the back had to be made in one or more bounds, depending on how far the back was moved forward from the plate. The first player who failed to make the required leap would become the next person to present his back.

I did try out for football in my sophomore year of high school. My football career was very short, only one season. I endured the pre-season training OK. Problems began to surface, however, when we began contact drills. The coach thought I might be able to run back kicks. The drill called for me to catch the football and try

38

to elude two defensive ends sent down to challenge the return. One of those ends was a wiry player named Harold Pittman. Pittman was fast, about five feet ten and weighed about 175 pounds. I tried to juke him but he hit me square on at full speed. When I regained consciousness several minutes later I realized that football probably was not my game. The year I played, 1946, was the year that several boys returned to Booker T. Washington School after their discharge from the armed services. Pittman had served in the U.S. Navy and returned to get his high school diploma.

My maximum weight in high school was 120 pounds. And I don't think I grew one inch after reaching my seventeenth birthday. For a while I made a conscious effort to enhance my stature by drinking milk and trying some of the remedies advertised on the back page of comic books. But these efforts all failed. The Thompson/McKinney genes posed an insurmountable barrier to my becoming a 175 pound six footer. I resigned myself to the fact that five feet six inches was going to be my maximum height.

That did not deter me from joining the basketball team in my final years of high school. Because we did not have a gym we scheduled most of our games away from home against schools having access to indoor facilities. During my junior year the Jonesboro school board did agree to our using a gym at the Jonesboro Community Center which up to that time had been available only to whites. There were certain restrictions, however. Our school was permitted access for practice only for certain hours one or two days a week. Also our games could be scheduled there only when whites were not planning to use it. At the time being given the privilege of using a municipally-owned gym seemed like a major advance for the Jonesboro black community. The Community Center gym was far superior to any other gym we played in other towns. Our team always dreaded going to play the school at Marked Tree, a little town about forty miles east of Jonesboro. The gym there did not have the dimensions of a regular gym, being not much more than an elongated classroom. The ceiling was only 12 to 14 feet from the floor, and the baskets were directly attached to the walls at the ends of the room with hardly any clearance. One could not shoot the ball with a normal trajectory even on free throws. Extreme care had to be taken also when going in for a lay-up because of the risk of collision with the wall. Marked Tree never lost a game at home because their team members had adapted to a style of shooting and playing in their non-regulation gym that other teams had trouble adjusting to. It was not unusual for games at Marked Tree to end up with outrageously low final scores such as 8 to 6.

My most memorable high school basketball experience was a trip to a tournament in Cotton Plant, a farming community in the delta southeast of Jonesboro. Our team was put up in a barn in back of the school where we slept on straw mattresses. The basketball court also was in a barn-like structure that was heated by two wood-burning stoves located on either end of the building. Here the big risk was of losing control or being thrown too close to the stoves in going after a loose ball. The real fun was the travel by chartered bus to the away games, especially when the cheerleaders and other students went along. On the bus one would pair off with his best girl and do some heavy petting, at least until one of the teachers that patrolled the aisles came along to enforce the no touching rules.

Beginning about the ninth grade I began to pay a lot more attention to the girls in the neighborhood and those at school. There were three girls in the family that lived next door to our house on Third Street—the Taylor family. The Taylors had three daughters—Mamie Lee, Clyde Lou and Ethel May. Mamie Lee was the oldest daughter and was one or two years younger than I. They were all very cute, brown-skinned girls, but Mamie Lee was the one I liked most. They were in and out of our house a lot, playing with my sisters Naomi and Ruth, whom they tended to regard as their big sisters too.

One or two of the families at our church also had girls about my age that grew up with us. There was Viola and Joanne, both related to the Conleys; the Epperson girls Emma and Jewel, older sisters of Little Brother and Mickey; Goldie Mae Blunt and Tryme, a very pretty girl who had been taken in (adopted) by a family that lived across the street from the church. And then there were the girls who went to St. John's Baptist Church, and the beautiful twin girls who lived across the street from us—Willie Bird and Willie Bee. The twins were about the age of my sisters Esther or Ruth, they had a reputation for being what we called "fast" girls. They wore short, flimsy dresses and red shoes often. They had a Victrola record player at their house which they played so loud that we could hear the music in our house even with the doors closed. Momma called them "bad" girls because they danced with abandon to the Louis Armstrong, Jimmy Lunsford, Billie Holiday and other jazz and blues records they played, sometimes even on Sunday. Older boys and young men visited them frequently and took them out on dates.

Then there were certain special girls who lived on the east side of town whom I came in contact with mostly at school, Eva Mae Thomas, Bette Bew and Freddye Sue Turner. Eva Mae was in my class and competed with me throughout high school to be the number-one student in the class academically. She was the daughter of the pastor of the Colored Methodist Episcopal Church in Jonesboro. Hers was a very prominent large family; her older sisters were friends of my sisters and her brother, Nathaniel, was a very bright student in the class ahead of mine with my sister Naomi. Bette Bew was one of the students who came to Jonesboro from one of the outlying communities where schools for colored kids only went through eighth grade. She was the best friend of the first girl I really loved—Freddye Sue Turner. Freddye Sue was the daughter of Mrs. F. C. Turner, the home economics teacher. She was one class behind me and we were an item throughout high school. We were the original odd couple. Freddye Sue was what one would now call a preppy, a girl who dressed well at all times. She was a good two inches taller than I. I was a poor boy from across the tracks. Certainly there were boys around physically more attractive than "Big Mac." And there were girls more compatible with my short stature whom I might have taken up with. But Freddye Sue always was the one whose affection for me was undeniable and I reciprocated that feeling toward her.

The restrictions on social activity and behavior that were part of the central tenets of our church caused problems and internal tensions for me in my attempts to develop relationships with girls who did not share my family's religious beliefs. We were forbidden to go to dances, the movies, ball games; no smoking, drinking beer or other alcoholic beverages; no engaging in any serious sexual contacts before marriage. A girl who was "saved" would not al-

41

low a man to touch her sexually unless they were married. Girls in the church wore clothes that fully covered their bodies, did not wear lipstick, paint their faces or nails. As long as I can remember my parents taught us that these were sinful practices and those that did them would surely go to hell. I never really believed all of these prohibitions were essential to a committed religious life, but I was not strong enough in my convictions to openly challenge my parents on these issues as I was growing up at home. Except on one issue, that was the question of my participation in high school athletics. Papa finally consented to my going out for the football and basketball teams, and Momma went along.

I never went out on dates and did not learn to dance. I remember going to one party in high school at Eva Thomas' house. I was allowed to go to that party probably because it was held at Rev. Thomas' home and Momma felt that they would not permit any sinful activity to go on there. But it was at this party that I first was exposed to the party game called "post office." Freddye Sue's mother was about as strict on her as my parents were on me. Occasionally I would walk her home from school and we would hold hands and linger on her front steps talking for long periods of time. But things never went much beyond that. At school we would exchange love notes and write poems expressing our feelings for each other, but I never called at her home to take her to a movie or to a school dance.

*   *   *

Arkansas A. M. & N. College had a policy of awarding a full tuition scholarship to the valedictorian of the graduating class at each black high school in the state. I earned that honor at Jonesboro's Booker T. Washington School the year I graduated. I gladly accepted the college's offer to become a member of the freshman class in September 1949. Graduating from high school was a very big event in the black community in Jonesboro. Making it through high school as a black youngster put you in very elite company in and of itself. Most of my friends did not reach that stage of formal educational achievement. Those that did not finish high school were not necessarily viewed as failures. Many of them went on to do well by our community's standards. They got jobs, got married, had families and became contributing members of the community. The few kids who persevered to complete their high school education simply were viewed as having achieved something special. At that time in our history blacks of every stripe and status placed a very high value on education, whether they had the benefit of one or not. The entire black community rejoiced in the graduates' success and turned out in great numbers at graduation to show support and appreciation. Customarily members of the graduating class sent out announcements to family friends and prominent people in the community. Many responded not only by attending the graduation ceremonies, but by presenting gifts to the graduates. Neckties I received as graduation gifts remained in my wardrobe for decades. I just found it hard to part with them because of the sentiment they represented.

The attitude of our community toward high school graduation reflected an understanding of the historical struggle blacks in general faced in American society in gaining access to education. Education for blacks had never been "free" nor universal before or after the civil war. Intuitively blacks knew that powerful forces in society opposed equal access to education on any level and viewed it as a threat to the established order. I sense that in the years since my high school graduation there has been a serious erosion both in the support and the value the black community in general places on education.

Finishing high school was never an issue in the McKinney family. My oldest sister Izora graduated Booker T. Washington School in 1938 and went on to precede me at Arkansas A. M. & N. College at Pine Bluff, graduating in 1942 with a degree in home economics and education. She had a career as a public school teacher in Arkansas, Ohio, Washington State and California. Robert finished high school in Illinois and attended Roosevelt College in Chicago. Esther, upon graduating from Booker T. Washington School, went on to business school in Little Rock. She came to Washington, D. C. during WWII to work for the federal government as a secretary, where she remained until her retirement. After retirement she enrolled at the University of the District of Columbia and earned her bachelor's degree. Marvella became a nurse after graduating high school. Ruth applied to a secretarial school in Jonesboro after finishing high school in 1945. She was deeply crushed when the school refused to honor its commitment to admit her upon discovering her race. She later took a job teaching elementary school in Pocahontas, Arkansas, a town just north of Jonesboro, and at the North Side one room school. Later, after moving to California and raising a family, Ruth too earned her degree from Long Beach State College. Naomi went to Memphis after finishing high school for secretarial training. Four of my younger brothers followed me at Arkansas A. M. & N. College. The fifth and youngest brother, Ernest, graduated Morehouse College in Atlanta.

2

On My Own—The College Years at
A. M. & N.

The 1949 freshman class at A. M. & N. College was the largest in the history of the school at that time, over three hundred in number. They came from every part of the state with the largest groups coming from Little Rock, Pine Bluff and the Marianna/Helena area of eastern Arkansas. A significant number were from outside Arkansas; from Memphis, St. Louis/East St. Louis; Texas; Michigan and Illinois. But the vast majority came from small towns and rural communities like Jonesboro scattered throughout the state. They were young men and women, many leaving home for the first time, seeking a new educational experience.

I took the Trailways bus from Jonesboro to Pine Bluff, a much less pleasant trip than the ones I took four years earlier by car with Professor Smith. The bus stopped at every little town along Highway 1 South—Weiner, Wynne, Forrest City, Marianna, then over to Route 79 through Clarendon, Stuttgart and into Pine Bluff. It stopped to pick up passengers standing along the road as well wherever anyone flagged for a ride. When a new passenger boarded, sometimes an adjustment in the seating arrangements for the previous passengers would be required. If the passenger was white, room for him had to be made in the front section of the bus, even if this meant taking a seat already occupied by a black passenger in the forward part of the back of the bus. The bus would not move until all black passengers were to the rear of the last white passenger. Overall the trip took more than six hours.

By the time I arrived in Pine Bluff my best traveling clothes had become quite sweaty and wrinkled. I quickly gathered my bags and headed for the line of taxi cabs parked on the street outside. As I opened the door of the cab at the head of the line the driver said to me, "Hold on just a minute." Since the cab was empty I thought at first the driver was offering to help me with my luggage. It was then that I got my first lesson in how Pine Bluff differed from Jonesboro. The driver said to me, "Boy you look like you want to go out to the colored college. You want to take one of the black cabs across the street." Sure enough, in Pine Bluff blacks rode in taxi cabs owned by the black cab company—Branton's Taxi Service—and whites were served by taxi cab companies owned by whites. In Jonesboro we had only one taxi cab company and it was white. That company served both races in the town. I presume, however, only passengers from one race at a time. So I went across the street, got into one of the Branton cabs and was on my way out to the A. M. & N. College campus north of town on Cedar Street.

Cedar Street north from the intersection at West Second Street for a mile or so to the campus was lined with dozens of small retail businesses on both sides of the street: Hestand's Grocery, the Duck Inn, the Elite Dinette, Alley's Esso Service Station, Collegiate Barber Shop, College Grocery Store, Johnson's Cafeteria, the Varsity Tavern, Pennington's Liquor Store, Bullards Dry Cleaning, Lomax Rooming House. All of these places were linked to the college through commerce with its students, faculty and administrators. This would be my universe for the next four years.

I checked in with Mrs. E. L. Cooke, the director of men's dormitory 1 and was assigned a room on the first floor. All freshmen were assigned to this dormitory, which was reserved for underclassmen. The second men's dormitory next door was reserved for juniors and seniors. Directly across the quadrangle were the two women's dormitories. My room was set up to accommodate three students with double-deck bunk beds on one side and a single bed on the other. One of my roommates, Nathaniel Guydon from Clarendon, had already checked in and had claimed the single bed for himself. I took the lower bunk of the other bed. Each of the four dormitories had two residential floors with a capacity of about seventy-five students on each floor. On each floor was one large bathroom with latrines, five or six showers and toilet facilities.

The private apartment for the dormitory director who lived full-time in the building was on the first floor. You entered the front of the building into a large lobby area that was set up like a living room, with lounges, chairs and small tables scattered around. There were hardwood floors throughout the living areas and no carpets. It took me a while to get adjusted to living in such luxurious quarters. I had never lived in a place with indoor plumbing and central heating before. Nor was I accustomed to polished hardwood floors and fine upholstered lounges and chairs. This was far different from the linoleum floors and ladder-back cane chairs I was used to.

I think I recognized Mrs. Cooke from my short visits to the campus in 1945, but she did not give any indication that she may have seen me before. She was well-suited to the job of dormitory director—we called her the dorm mother. She was matronly in appearance and had a no-nonsense demeanor. I liked her. Her job was to keep order and enforce the rules of the house—no loud music; no rough-housing in the rooms or public areas; no alcoholic beverages and no girls in the rooms at any time. Mrs. Cooke also was responsible for keeping the public areas clean and neat; the students had to police their own rooms.

From time to time on Saturdays one of the dormitory residents would have to bring the heavy buffing machine from the storage room and a group would be given the task of cleaning and polishing the hardwood floors. Mrs. Cooke never seemed to have much trouble with discipline in her building, unlike the rumors commonly heard about problems Mrs. Ballard had with upperclassmen in men's dormitory no. 2. Residents of our dorm were mostly seventeen- and eighteen-year-old farm boys whose parents had instructed them well about respect for adults in positions of authority. They had not been away from home long enough to feel confident in asserting their own autonomy and independence as young men. The occasional exception would almost always be one of the boys from a big city like Memphis or St. Louis whose upbringing was quite different than that of boys who grew up in Arkansas.

Getting to know the students in rooms near mine did not take very long. My third roommate was a boy from Hope, Arkansas. He took great pride in the fact that Hope was recognized everywhere as the watermelon capital of the state because it held the record for having grown the largest watermelon in history. Next door to us were two boys who grew up together in Marianna, Arkansas—Hanley J. Norment and James Campbell. Also in my first floor wing of the dorm were Herbert Brown from Memphis, Jerry Jewell from West Memphis, Ralph Jones from East St. Louis, Hyman King from Detroit, James Tuberville and George Watkins from Wynne, Leonard Wilborn from Magnolia, and Gordon Morgan from Conway. My circle of acquaintances broadened considerably in the tiresome process of going through the lines to register for classes and at the freshmen's orientation sessions where all of the class assembled in Caldwell Hall.

At the first orientation session the class was introduced to President Lawrence A. Davis and the other top staff of the college. President Davis appeared to be not much older than the students, but he was a very articulate person with the presence and bearing of a leader. He had been chosen by the trustees to succeed the legendary J. B. Watson as president seven years earlier and at the time was reputed to be the youngest college president in the nation. He welcomed the class by pointing to the fact that we set the record for an incoming class. It was on this occasion that I first heard President Davis state the A. M. & N. College philosophy:

"The end of education is to know God and the laws and purposes of his universe, and to reconcile one's life with these laws. The first aim of a good college is not to teach books, but the meaning and purpose of life. Hard study and the learning of books are only a means to this end. We develop power and courage and determination and we go out to achieve truth, wisdom, and justice. If we do not come to this, the cost of schooling is wasted."

We would hear this mantra many more times in the next four years from President Davis as well as others at A. M. & N. College. After President Davis' remarks Dean John L. Wilson took over and conducted the remaining part of the orientation. He introduced first the people on staff that he said we would be seeing a lot of—Mr. Cleveland Christophe, the business manager and person responsible for handling college financial matters, including student tuition and fees; Mrs. Charlie Henderson, the registrar; Mr. Jessie Marshall, director of freshman studies, Mr. J. B. Jones, in charge of personnel and guidance; Mr. Johnnie B. Johnson, dean of men and Mrs. Norma E. Harold, dean of women.

The college operated on a quarter system, with three quarters constituting the regular school year—September through May.

The fourth quarter was mostly for in-service school teachers who came back to the campus to complete some missed requirement or to supplement their training. Registration, which took place in the college gym just in back of men's dormitory 1, was a time consuming and frustrating process. Lines to go through in order to sign up for each class; contending with problems of getting the class you wanted at a time that best fit your work schedule or your sleeping habits, etc.; confirming which fees were covered in the scholarship you held and which fees were not covered. A difference between your understanding about fees and that of the registrar was something one wanted to avoid in the middle of the registration process. But tuition and fees at the college actually were quite small, although the amounts were significant if one had miscalculated the amount of funds needed to register. Full tuition for one quarter in 1949 was $25.00, and room and board including laundry was $30.00 per month.

A very high percentage of the student body was on some kind of scholarship. In addition to those for the athletes, there were scholarships for being in the band; the college choir; cheerleaders; the drama club; the debate team; student government. The college also was quite generous in finding work on campus for students who needed help in meeting their financial obligations, and when all else failed, one could go to President Davis and often come away with a note from him to the business office directing that the bearer be permitted to register on a promise to pay later.

Meals were served in a central dining hall, not in each dormitory as at some of the larger colleges. My first year, the dining hall was located across campus from my dorm. It was only a short walk. In fact, all campus facilities were within a five-minute walk from the bell tower in the center of the campus. Apart from the dormitories and faculty houses, there were only a few other buildings surrounding the quadrangle and the horseshoe shaped roadway that circled the campus from the north entry gate back to North Cedar Street. Most classes for freshmen were held in the administration building. Other permanent buildings included the home economics building, the mechanic arts building, the physical education/gym, the library, the power plant/laundry, and the laboratory school for practice teachers. Several World War II vintage temporary buildings were scattered along the southwestern perimeter of the campus to serve other special needs, including the J. C. Corbin High School.

The most memorable things about dining on campus were that there was no evening meal on Sunday, and the dining hall was presided over by Mrs. Lillie L. Jones, one of the strongest personalities on campus. Because the noon meal on Sunday was the last one for the day, dormitory residents made it their business to try to develop at least one good friend among students who lived at home in the city of Pine Bluff, hoping that such a friend would invite them to their home for Sunday dinner.

If one had money, of course, there were other options available. The Lions Den was perhaps the most popular restaurant nearby. The Lions Den catered to students and younger faculty and staff almost exclusively and was practically on campus property. Next door was Elite's Dinette, and directly across from the campus on North Cedar Street was Johnson's Cafeteria. These were three very distinct eating places. The Lions Den operated like a pub, serving primarily short-order food and all kinds of drinks. There was a long bar with stools as well as cozy booths along the front windows and side walls. The juke box had all the latest tunes and one could get two plays for a nickel. It was a great place to "hang out" after classes and in the evening. "Chief" Mazique and his wife ran the establishment. Elite's was much more subdued, served prepared meals and sandwiches and seemed to attract a more serious clientele. Johnson's Cafeteria was open limited hours, serving lunch and dinner cafeteria style exclusively and no alcoholic drinks. Mr. Johnson himself hovered over the serving process to make sure that portions being dished out to customers were not too large.

The curriculum for first year students was the same for everyone, there being no elective courses. Physical education and English or English composition courses were required in each of the three quarters. There was one quarter of general mathematics, conservation, survey courses in social science, biological science, and physical science, general psychology, and personal and community hygiene. Only in the second year did one begin selecting courses on the basis of his or her field of interest. Presumably, the administration felt that a set curriculum was desirable because the quality of secondary education could vary widely among the various school systems serving its universe of students. It may also reflect a lack of trust in the capacity of these students to make the wisest choices at this stage in their college career.

Being a land grant college the primary emphasis of its curriculum clearly was teacher training and agricultural disciplines. These were the fields of study for as many as half of the students, and I suspect most of the money from state governmental appropriations was allocated to support programs in these areas. Governmental policy makers in Arkansas and most other states having significant numbers of black residents in the 1940s and '50s no doubt believed that the most effective use of governmental dollars for educating blacks would be in secondary teacher training and encouraging use of more scientific farming techniques. The policy reflected and reinforced the reality of what the career opportunities were for most young black men and women who chose to remain in the state. However, from the moment I decided to enter college my career horizon was much broader than teaching school and farming. I always had great respect for teachers—they were my childhood role models. In fact I think my choice of career was somewhat of a disappointment for Momma. She wanted me to grow up to be a teacher. Throughout her life when she wrote me letters she always addressed me as "professor." My voracious reading habits as a child not only entertained but opened up career vistas for me as well. From my experiences as a sharecropper's lead farm hand at age 10 I knew that farming was not what I wanted to spend my life doing. I had no desire to be a preacher and knew that I could not deprive myself of some of the joys of life I thought preachers were supposed to avoid.

While I knew when I came to college that I did not want to pursue a career in teaching, farming or the ministry, I was not certain of what profession I should follow. Having never seen a science laboratory or known anything about chemistry, subjects I assumed the aspiring medical student had to know something about, I quickly ruled out a career in medicine. So my freshman year was spent searching for what I wanted to become in life. For me not having to declare a major in the first year worked out to my advantage. I was able to approach each of my courses without preconceived notions, seeking to find the intrinsic value the subject had to offer.

The required course in conservation that I took that first quarter was taught by none other than Professor Alexander Haley whom I had first met four years earlier at the New Farmers of America public speaking contest. It was only a two-hour course but I had a chance to reintroduce myself to him. This time he felt free to tell me a little bit about his family and its origins in Tennessee not too far from where my own father's people had lived. He told me about his sons Alex and George and how proud he was of them. At the time Alex was in the U.S. Coast Guard and George was planning to become a lawyer. They each would go on to great achievements later in life.

During my first several weeks on campus I did not pay a great deal of attention to any particular girl, but I did notice those that were outgoing and friendly toward me. I was still missing Freddye Sue, the girl I left behind in Jonesboro. We wrote to each other frequently, and I had hoped that she would join me at A. M. & N. College after she graduated from high school in 1950. But things did not work out that way. The Turners were staunch members of the African Methodist Episcopal Church and her mother decided that Freddye Sue should attend Philander Smith College in Little Rock, a school with strong ties to the Methodist Church. My lingering love interest in Freddye Sue no doubt contributed to my ambivalent attitude toward the few girls on campus that I could be attracted to. A girl Freddye Sue visited each summer in Little Rock for years was in the freshman class with me. Her name was Willie Pearl Wisham. I had met her before on one of her visits with Freddye Sue in Jonesboro. She remained one of Freddye Sue's best friends. When I ran into Willie Pearl on campus she would tell me about her most recent letter from Freddye Sue and the news from Jonesboro that I may not have heard.

Willie Pearl also was a friend of Edgar Wade from Jonesboro who had graduated from Booker T. Washington High School a year ahead of me. Wade entered Philander Smith College in the fall of 1948. He and I grew up together on the north side of Jonesboro. Wade was a gifted piano player. He played for the high school choir and for various churches as well. Wade liked to follow major league baseball and so did I so we talked a lot about the game and kept up with the batting and fielding statistics of our favorite players. We were most familiar with players on the St. Louis Cardinal team as it was that team whose games were regularly broadcast on the local radio station.

The fall quarter of my freshman year went by very fast. Carrying 18 hours of coursework left little time for extracurricular activity. I spent many hours preparing for the two most difficult courses that quarter, general mathematics (taught by Mr. Seeley) and English composition. I found my study time in the college library to be more productive than working in the dormitory room in the presence of roommates. In the room we had a tendency to talk too much about things not related to course subject matter. Each roommate tended to have different study habits and I found also that some of my colleagues did not take too seriously the idea that one needed to study at all. In fact, sometimes it was difficult to resist the temptation to join others in a game of dominoes, a game I was introduced to early on by my roommate from Hope, Arkansas.

The two guys in the room next door from Marianna, however, had study habits similar to my own. Hanley Norment and J. D. Campbell not only were very bright young men, but very competitive as well. I could tell right away that Hanley in particular wanted to be "the" leader of the freshman class. He succeeded in reaching this goal by getting himself elected president of the freshman class.

One thing became very apparent to me by the time I completed the first quarter—that there were a number of husband/wife teams on the faculty and staff at the college. I would say that such teams comprised as much as thirty or forty percent of the total faculty and professional staff. I learned later a major reason so many husbands and wives were employed by the college. It was a question of money. While being on the faculty or staff carried great prestige in the community and were coveted positions, the salaries were not commensurate. In order to attract a first rate person to join the faculty or staff it often was necessary to offer the spouse a job so as to maintain total family income at a desired level. No doubt one of the major challenges for President Davis was putting together husband/wife package deals and finding the most appropriate place for the spouse that came along. From my perspective as a freshman student, these employment arrangements seemed entirely appropriate. But when I reflect on it I know that racism played some role in the college's being unable to offer competitive salaries to its faculty. Nevertheless, the faculty and staff I came in contact with initially at the college were first-rate people whose top priority was to bring out the best in students and to prepare them to live fulfilling, productive lives.

I was fairly pleased with my final grades for the first quarter when they were published at the end of November. I earned an "A" in the general mathematics course and a "B" in each of the others, thus qualifying me for the honor roll. My first quarter performance boosted my confidence immensely. I knew then that I could compete academically with anyone on campus, whether they came from big city high schools like Dunbar in Little Rock, or other small systems around the state. While I had done well at Booker T. Washington School, I realized that I had not been up against the best possible competition there. After all there had been only seven kids in the graduating class. Grades were not held in confidence at A. M. & N. College; they were posted on the bulletin boards for all to see. And I believe they also were mailed to parents. Being on the honor roll was a distinction that set you apart from the mass of students. You were identified as "smart" by fellow students.

If you handled it right, being known as a "smart" student could work to your advantage. When I was in college many of the girls had as part of their agenda finding a suitable mate for marriage. Males who were smart were perceived as having the best chance for a successful career beyond college. They were the ones most likely to go on to become physicians, lawyers, college professors and other financially rewarding occupations and professions. So if one were not completely a nerd, and totally unattractive, some female students liked being in your company. My complement of female friends began to expand after November 1949.

Over the years A. M. & N. College developed a reputation for having an excellent debate team. Early in the second quarter debate team coaches announced that tryouts for the team would be held in January. I decided to try out for the team, thinking this would be an excellent way for me to fulfill my desire to participate in at least one extracurricular activity during my college career. The team scheduled debates with several nearby schools annually and in the spring made at least one extended tour to debate colleges in other parts of the country. The prospect of travel was one of the things that attracted me to the debate team. I also saw this as a way to sharpen my forensic skills, in the event I later chose a profession in which such skills were important to have.

The debate program was purely extracurricular and was overseen by professors from different departments of the school. Team coaches included: Tilman C. Cothran, professor of sociology; A. G. Kirby, instructor of agricultural education; and George J. Jones, principal of the J. C. Corbin Laboratory High School. Frank H. Hollis, a fifth year senior, assisted with the coaching duties as well. Frank had been a member of the team for several years. Presumably his undergraduate eligibility had run out. However, he was of invaluable benefit to the team in helping to develop cogent arguments on all sides of a proposition.

Annually a single national topic is selected and that topic is debated by all colleges and universities in the United States and Canada. The debate team at A. M. & N. College might comprise as many as eight or ten students, but the traveling squad was limited to the four or five most highly-rated members of the team. A position on the traveling squad was the prize sought by every member of the team and the competition for those spots was extremely intense. The first hurdle was to survive the tryouts, which took the form of a competition between freshmen and sophomores. Individual contenders for the team would be assigned to debate either the affirmative or the negative of the proposition in the national intercollegiate debate topic. Students seeking a place on the team had to do all the necessary research and prepare the strongest case he possibly could for his side of the proposition. He also had to be prepared to answer or rebut the arguments that might be advanced by the opponents.

The debate tryouts were considered great entertainment by the student body. Students turned out the night of the tryouts in large numbers at Caldwell Hall. There were four or five students from the freshman class, and at least as many sophomores seeking a spot on the team the first year I competed. Usually faculty members not associated with the team were asked to serve as judges. The coaches studied all the performances, closely observing how well each student handled himself in stressful situations, and assessing speaking style, forcefulness, articulation, diction and other similar qualities they believed made the person a good debater.

The national intercollegiate debate topic for 1949-1950 was whether the non-communist nations of the world should create their own international organization as an alternative to the United Nations. The annual debate topic usually related to a current national or international political or economic issue. The topic that year surely reflected the concern that existed at the time about the ability of the Soviet Union and the bloc of nations aligned with it to thwart American world leadership initiatives through the use of its veto power in the Security Council. The mid-point of the Twentieth Century only five years removed from the end of World War II was a time when many people still thought it was possible to settle international disputes by peaceful means through an organization such as the United Nations. Fifty years later the United States appears to have abandoned that hope in favor of using its unchallenged military power to impose its will on other nations.

Debaters spent hours in the library researching the topic, looking for articles written by experts on the subject, or speeches delivered in Congress and other forums about the issue. The coaches helped by gathering information on the subject from various other sources, developing the team's own reference library. I found the process of doing my own research, writing my own speech and brainstorming to anticipate counter arguments to my presentation to be quite exhilarating. The idea of proving a proposition by citing facts, expert opinions and sometimes laws or legal precedents seemed awful close to what I imagined lawyers did in real life courtrooms. I liked this work and impressed the coaches by the way I threw myself into it.

That year the freshmen won the freshman/sophomore debate. My performance earned me a spot not only on the team but on the travel squad as well. Also selected for the travel squad were two sophomore girls who lived with their families in Pine Bluff, Delores Mays and Dorothy Ann Davis. Also chosen was Samuel Kountz, a pre-med major from Lexa, Arkansas. All three were experienced debaters who had been on the team the year before.

Delores Mays and Dorothy Ann Davis grew up together in Pine Bluff, attending Merrill High School. Each of them came from large North Side families. Delores' brother Eddie was scheduled to graduate in the 1950 class at A. M. & N. and her younger brothers would follow her at the college. Eddie went on to medical school and had a distinguished career as an army physician. Dorothy Ann was a very pretty young lady with freckles and a steel trap mind. In fact, she had been the star of the team the year before. Her father was a Baptist minister and her mother looked after her three younger sisters who were not yet of college age. Her brother Carl was away in the navy.

Dorothy too had ambitions of becoming a medical doctor. Samuel Kountz was perhaps the most brilliant person I had met. We always teased him about his unusual name for a black person from a rural community in Phillips County, Arkansas. He obviously had mixed racial ancestry. His skin color was light brown, he had keen facial features, high cheek bones and coal black wavy hair. I always suspected that Kountz was as much American Indian as he was black. Arkansas of course subscribed to the "one drop" theory of racial classification—one drop of Negro blood was enough to identify you as black no matter what you looked like. Kountz spoke with a slight accent and had what appeared to be a natural ability in all things connected to language, science, chemistry and mathematics. He too would finish medical school and become a distinguished professor of medicine at several schools, including the University of California, Berkley, Stanford University, and New York University. Kountz would pioneer the development of procedures for kidney transplant surgery in America. Given the talent we had it is not surprising that our 1949-1950 debate team compiled one of the most successful seasons in the history of the program.

Dr. Cothran and Mr. Kirby functioned as assistant coaches, while "Doc" Jones carried the load of preparing the team for the season as head coach. Most of our practice sessions were held late afternoons and evenings in classrooms near Dr. Jones' office at J. C. Corbin High School. The practice sessions enabled members of the team to get to know each other better as individuals. As the freshman member I never felt the need to act in a deferential manner to upper classmen on the team. Perhaps this was because I was older than the sophomore members of the team and was at least as mature as all the others.

Preparing and delivering a "canned" opening speech is the easiest part of debating. The hard part is the rebuttal speech which requires thinking on your feet and developing spontaneous logical responses to unanticipated assertions by the opponents. During practice sessions we got to know which team members were strong in rebuttal, which could write well, who could best withstand criticism or personal attack, etc.

The team's annual tour in the spring of 1950 would take us to Alcorn State College in Mississippi; Southern University, Dillard University and Xavier University in Louisiana; Marshall College, Wiley College, Texas College, Prairie View A. & M, Texas Southern, and Jarvis Christian College in Texas. We traveled together in Coach Jones' car and invariably were housed on the campus at each college we debated. The debate trips were truly an adventure. Coach Jones (we all called him "Doc" Jones) had a large four-door sedan, but when you piled four or five college students in it with their luggage for a ten day trip the car became quite crowded.

Doc Jones was a most interesting man who himself had been a debater during his student days at the college. He was short of stature and had a congenitally deformed body. He had to walk on the toes of his feet. Both of his arms were shortened and permanently curled forward. Overcoming these physical disabilities and attaining the position he held at the college was a clear testament to his indomitable spirit. He was always in control and radiated confidence despite what appeared to be an enormous handicap. There was nothing wrong with Doc Jones' mind or his command of the English language. Though he may have been outranked by other faculty members on the coaching staff, Doc Jones was without a doubt the head coach of the debate team. Members of the team looked primarily to him for leadership, intellectually and otherwise.

I discovered on that first debate trip in 1950 that traveling by car in the South for blacks had not changed since my earlier travels with Professor Smith in 1945. Bathrooms at service stations on the road still were not freely available when we stopped to buy gas. It still was best to pack your own food because roadside restaurants did not welcome black customers to sit down and refresh themselves in main dining rooms. A group of well-dressed black men and women riding together in a large late model automobile also drew curiosity if not suspicion from white police and other authorities. So one had to be extremely careful and avoid late night travel if at all possible. Everyone knew that these conditions prevailed. Occasionally they were the subject of conversation in the car as we traveled. We deplored having to endure these indignities but we were not obsessed by them. In fact, we frequently made jokes about the absurdity of it all.

The first leg of the tour took us to Alcorn State College in Lorman, Mississippi, a little town located between Vicksburg and Natchez, just a few miles east of the Mississippi River. We could reach Lorman either by crossing the river from Louisiana at Vicksburg and driving south in Mississippi on Highway 61 for about 40 miles or we could take Highway 65 south from Pine Bluff into Louisiana and continue driving in that state, crossing the river some fifty miles south of Vicksburg at Natchez. The latter route was a little longer but it would mean less travel in Mississippi. We opted to take the longer route in order to minimize our time on the roads in Mississippi. More than any other Southern state Mississippi was known for its hostility toward blacks.

Compared to Lorman, Pine Bluff would have to be considered a big city. However, the facilities at Alcorn were not much different than those at A. M. & N. College. Both schools' buildings and other facilities reflected their status as second class higher education institutions made available to black citizens in the segregated South. Alcorn's debate program was still relatively new and did not begin to approach the sophistication and tradition of the program at my college. We spent little more than thirty-six hours at Alcorn before departing for our next destination, Southern University at Baton Rouge, Louisiana.

Southern University was a much bigger school than A. M. & N. College and exuded a totally different atmosphere than Alcorn or Grambling which I had visited five years earlier as a freshman in high school. Being located in the state capitol placed the school in much closer proximity to the source of its financial support, the state legislature, and near its white counterpart, Louisiana State University, where any disparities in financial support for the two institutions could be easily observed. Our schedule, however, did not permit us to spend much time at Southern University, although I found the place to be quite nice. Doc Jones seemed anxious to move on to New Orleans as soon as possible. So our debate at Southern occurred the evening of the day of our arrival. This enabled us to leave for New Orleans mid-morning the following day in time to arrive in the Crescent City hours before nightfall.

It soon became apparent to me why Doc Jones was anxious to get to New Orleans. This was the first truly great city I had ever experienced. The really tall buildings; the wide boulevards; all the bright lights; the hustle and bustle of people on the streets; the noises and aroma of the city; the sense of excitement; the mix of so many different looking people—blacks, whites, people speaking languages I had never heard before. I had never seen so many black girls with long straight hair and fair almost opaque skin. I could not help but recall scenes from some of the Frank Yerby novels I had read in my youth. Were these the real life vixens of Yerby's novels?

We arrived in New Orleans late in the afternoon. Doc Jones and Frank Hollis decided that we should first check in at Dillard University where we would be staying. However, instead of taking the evening meal at the college dining hall as had been our custom at other schools, Doc Jones suggested that we go out on the town and have a nice dinner at a black-owned restaurant that had music and entertainment. Everyone agreed that was a great idea. Besides, we thought it was time for Doc Jones to spend some of the money the college had given the team for trip expenses. Quite frankly we had had enough of cold sandwiches, potato chips and soft drinks out of the bottle consumed in the car or at some roadside picnic table.

We were instructed to put on our best outfits for the evening on the town and to meet Frank Hollis and Doc Jones in the lobby promptly at seven o'clock. Coach Jones obviously knew about a place he wanted to go for dinner and entertainment. Everyone showed up in the lobby looking real sharp, especially the girls, Dorothy Ann and Delores. After we had gotten into the car and headed for the restaurant, Hollis suggested that we first drive to the famous French Quarter area of town. Since some of the team had never been to New Orleans, this seemed to be a good idea, particularly since the restaurant we planned to go to did not take reservations. The detour proved to be a rewarding experience for everybody. We decided to park the car near the French Quarter off Canal Street and to walk over to the French Quarter. The unplanned walking tour allowed us to observe closer up the sights and sounds of life in the area. People walking in the middle of the narrow streets; barkers trying to coax passersby to come in to the various bars and clubs to get a better look at the dancers and musicians inside. I was struck by the way second floors of buildings overhung the sidewalks below with people standing on the wrought iron balconies observing the street scenes passing by. After spending nearly an hour roaming around, trying not to get lost from the others, we finally found our way back to the car and headed for dinner.

The restaurant was not too far from where we were staying. I remember it was on a commercial street in a one-story building with a parking lot on the side. It took a little while for them to set up a table to accommodate our party of six. It was Friday night and business was beginning to pick up. I thought the place was too dark inside, but was assured by the others that the lighting was normal for this kind of business. There was a bar over to one side with ten or twelve stools. Everybody in the place was black. There was a juke box near the bar and a band stand or stage across the back of the room with an upright piano. We had been seated for perhaps ten minutes when the waitress came over to the table to take our drink orders. This was an entirely new experience for me. Judging by the lighted signs outside and those behind the bar advertising various brands of beer, wine and liquor I am sure the waitress assumed we would all order some kind of alcoholic drink before dinner. At least two of our party had never had a drink of liquor before, me and Sam Kountz. I am not sure about the girls in the party. They did not seem to be as awed by the setting as Kountz and I obviously were. They both grew up only blocks from the Duck Inn and the Varsity Tavern in Pine Bluff, each being notorious drinking places frequented by students from the college. Dorothy Ann of course was forbidden to enter either of these establishments, her father being a prominent Baptist minister in town. But I would not put it past her to slip into one of these places with her boyfriend Ed Townsend as he walked her home from the college some evenings. Besides, her 85-year-old grandfather, Papa

61

Brown, lived with them and he was known to drink at least one-half pint of liquor every day. Dorothy Ann inherited much of her grandfather's spirit.

I don't know whether Louisiana had a minimum drinking age law in 1950. Everyone at the table, however, was at least 18 years old and by the way we were dressed the waitress reasonably could have assumed we were all adults. In any event the question never came up. I recall each of the girls ordered a Shirley Temple, Doc Jones and Frank Hollis ordered some kind of cocktail. Although I was tempted to do so, I was not yet free of the injunctions against drinking alcohol drilled in me by my parents over the years, so I ordered a Coca Cola. When the waitress came to Kountz he innocently ordered a strawberry sundae! Needless to say the waitress and everyone at the table were astonished to hear Kountz' order and broke out in a big laugh. The waitress told Kountz that the bar did not carry the ingredients for a strawberry sundae, but she would be glad to bring him a soft drink. For the rest of that trip everyone teased Kountz about his ordering a strawberry sundae in a bar and night club. We had a great dinner of New Orleans style food that evening. The band and singer came on about 9:30 and we all had a very good time.

After New Orleans, the rest of the tour was anticlimactic. All the Texas schools except Texas Southern in Houston were not much different than Alcorn and Southern. Prairie View was a larger institution but its location was quite isolated. The thing I remember most about Jarvis Christian College was that all meals were served family style with diners serving themselves from platters of food in the center of large tables. We all were anxious to return to A. M. & N. College to catch up on classes we had missed and to begin preparing for third quarter final examinations.

I finished the freshman year with very good grades in all subjects, except for a "C" in physical education in the second quarter. I made the honor roll each grading period that year. I was proud of this performance and so were my parents. I rushed home to Jonesboro as soon as exams were completed because I wanted to find a job as quickly as possible. My goal was to work and save enough money to pay most of my room and board for the next school year. There were not that many job opportunities open to me in Jonesboro where I thought I could make that kind of money.

I knew I probably could go back to my old job shining shoes at Jimmy Reeves shoe repair shop downtown, but Alfred, the guy who had the shoe shine concession, probably only needed help on the weekends. Working only on weekends would not produce enough earnings to permit me to save the amount of money I needed to save.

After a few days in Jonesboro I decided to take the bus up to Cleveland, Ohio to visit my sisters Izora, Marvella and Naomi, who had moved there to live. I would stay with them while looking for summer work there. They agreed that job prospects would be better for me in Cleveland than in Jonesboro. My sisters had a third floor apartment in a large detached house on 132nd Street right off Kinsman Avenue. The Skippers family owned the house and occupied the first floor. The second floor was rented to the Mason family. My sisters' third floor apartment was directly accessible from the street through a rear stairway. They put me up in a small Florida room at the back end of the apartment. That way I could come and go without disturbing anyone. I began my search for a job immediately, but I had no attractive leads from anyone. First I scanned the want ads in the newspapers and made a list of the names and addresses of companies I wanted to call on cold each day. This was not an easy task as I did not have access to a car and therefore had to use public transportation. Getting around by public transportation in an unfamiliar big city in search of a desperately needed job enables one to learn the city very quickly. In 1950 Cleveland was probably the third largest industrial city in the country, after New York and Chicago. Many major companies had their headquarters there and many manufacturing and industrial facilities were located there as well. I had hoped to hook up with one of these big firms in a good paying job. I was willing to do almost any kind of work, provided it paid enough for me to meet my savings goal. Several days of cold calling yielded no favorable results with the larger companies.

Either my approach toward finding a job was wrong or there was something I had overlooked. Much later in life I came to realize that most firms in Cleveland were highly unionized and that organized labor had a great deal of control over who got hired and who did not. I also discovered that a referral from an employed relative or friend sometimes is essential. It's not enough simply to be available and willing to work hard. After a while I finally found employment at a restaurant and bar in the west side community of Lakewood. I was a general handyman at the place doing whatever jobs needed to be done—cleaning up, refilling the coolers with drinks, assisting in the kitchen etc. It certainly was not what I had envisioned doing the summer after my first year in college, but the pay was steady, if not much. The bus trip to and from work required me to change buses in downtown Cleveland and took about an hour each way.

I liked Cleveland and found living there very exciting. Terminal Tower was by far the tallest building I had ever seen. I was very impressed with the public transportation system, including the Rapid Transit. One who used the bus regularly could purchase a pass that permitted you to ride anywhere on the system by simply flashing the pass as one boarded the bus. The automat also was fascinating—buying a whole meal out of a vending machine in a cafeteria-like establishment. I learned how the city was divided into various ethnic neighborhoods, beyond simply black and white, and how some white ethnic groups also had trouble getting along with each other.

Being in Cleveland brought to mind something I had almost forgotten. That is how close my father came to moving our family there in the early 1940s. Papa had taken a trip to Cleveland shortly before or right after the war started, to explore opportunities for work there both as a preacher and otherwise. When he returned home I remember he and Momma talking quietly between themselves about the pros and cons of such a move for a family like ours. Had the family been smaller I suspect Papa would have made the move. I believe he did not do so because Momma felt the children's chances for going to college and improving their future life chances were better where we were. She probably was right, but I cannot help but wonder what my life and that of my brothers and sisters would have been had we moved to Cleveland.

The summer of 1950 turned out to be a relatively carefree one for me, despite the ten-hour work days. In the evenings I got the chance to talk and spend time with my sisters, especially Izora who had left home before I got to know her well. She had moved to Cleveland a few years earlier after becoming disenchanted with teaching school in Fordyce, Arkansas. She decided she could do better financially in the Cleveland school system. I suspect also that all three sisters figured chances of finding a good husband may be better there. They had joined Williams Temple Church of God in Christ on Woodland Avenue near downtown Cleveland. The pastor there was Bishop Riley Williams, a nationally renowned leader in the denomination. Williams Temple had a large active membership and worshiped in an impressive building.

Williams knew my father and may have encouraged him to move to Cleveland sometime earlier. On Sunday mornings my sisters and I would take the bus to Williams Temple and spend much of the day there. Morning services tended not to end until after two o'clock in the afternoon. And traditionally in the Church of God in Christ at that time there also was a full service on Sunday evening as well. Sunday evening church activities began with Y.P.W.W. (young peoples' willing workers) something like night Sunday school. Sometimes, instead of going home after the morning services ended we would go downtown to the automat and have dinner. I liked it when some of my sisters' female friends came along.

Bishop Williams had a large family, including three beautiful daughters. The younger one was about my age. I was quite attracted to her and sought out opportunities to talk to her every chance I got. Being the bishop's daughter and pretty as well meant that there were many other young men vying for her attention. I never had much of a chance but we remained friends.

While I was in Cleveland war broke out in Korea and things did not go well for our side throughout most of the summer. I turned twenty years old in August that year. I was in the prime age group that might be called up for military service if the war got worse and dragged on for a long time. Two years earlier when I turned 18 I registered for the draft but I had not thought very much about military service since that time. Now I had to start considering the possibility of my college education being interrupted by a call from Uncle Sam. I soon concluded, however, that it did no good to worry about that.

By the end of July I realized that I would not attain the savings goal that I had set for myself at the beginning of summer. Forty-five dollars a week just does not go very far in Cleveland after taxes, commuting costs, helping out the sisters with household expenses, buying a few new clothes, and the cost of a bus ticket home to Arkansas. As August wore on I noticed that the days were getting shorter and the weather much cooler than I was used to at that time of year, especially at night. I was ready to return home at the end of the third week of August. I wanted to spend a few days in Jonesboro with the family before going on to Pine Bluff. Registration for the new school year at A. M. & N. College takes place right after Labor Day and I did not want to be late.

At some point between the time I left Cleveland and the beginning of the fall quarter I decided what field of study to concentrate on in college. I chose to major in business administration and take a minor in economics. Of all the programs being offered at A. M. & N. College the courses required in these departments appeared to suit my talents best. That combination of courses also seemed to allow the most flexibility in terms of alternative career choices down the road. The programs included several courses in accounting, a profession I might pursue. I thought a career as an owner or operator of a small business of some kind might be possible and that too interested me. And then there was the thought in the back of my mind that my forensic skills could be put to good use in the legal profession.

I did not know any black lawyers personally, but I had always admired the work they did in the South defending black men and women, many of whom had been unjustly accused of criminal law violations of one kind or another. At that time the most famous black lawyer in Arkansas was attorney Harold Flowers, who lived right there in Pine Bluff. I read accounts of the work of lawyers like Harold Flowers in the black newspapers that were often sold door to door and on the streets of our community in Jonesboro. Perhaps more than their legal skills, what really inspired me was the courage such lawyers exhibited by taking on unpopular cases in communities where the white power structure and legal systems were totally hostile to the interests of their clients.

My whole life and that of my family had been spent in an environment in which black men and women were tolerated as second class beings by those who controlled everything. Blacks who asserted themselves as free citizens and insisted on protecting their rights invariably were endangering their lives. My reality had always been that blacks had no rights that whites were bound to respect. If any particular whites behaved otherwise it was a matter

66

of their choice, not something they could be forced to do by the then constituted legal authorities. I often wondered whether I would have the courage to do what Harold Flowers regularly did, i.e., intervening to try to save some young black man in situations where the police, the prosecutor, the jury and the judge constituted in effect a legal lynch mob.

At that time I identified the legal profession primarily with work involving the criminal justice system. Even the few recent cases arising out of challenges to the Jim Crow system by returning World War II veterans often developed in a criminal law context. It was much later that I began to realize the true scope of the practice of law and the potential opportunities a career in that profession offered to serve other important needs of my community.

My second year in college introduced me to two teachers who, along with the debate coaches, would become influential actors in my life. Butler T. Henderson, assistant professor of economics, and Harding B. Young, assistant professor of business administration, both were very good teachers. Young taught courses in accounting and business law while Henderson taught courses in economics. Once they became aware of my interest in law they offered continual encouragement.

I continued to do well academically the sophomore year, receiving an "A" in all courses during the fall quarter. My brother George, "Little Mac," joined me on campus as a freshman. George had already firmly decided to become a minister when he started college in the fall of 1950. In fact, the word had spread to other churches in the denomination throughout our hometown area that one of Elder McKinney's sons had gone into the ministry. On more than one occasion when George and I were together people assumed that I was the preacher since I was older. Usually it did not take long for people to figure out that Rufus was not the preacher. George and I were about the same height and build but we had very different personalities. George was the quiet, soft spoken, contemplative type. I was the more direct, outspoken brother who relished spirited conversation and debate. I found myself going to Papa's church more often after George came to the campus. Before he came I would attend Smith Temple Church of God in Christ, which was located just off the rear of the campus, only when I knew Papa was going to be there. Otherwise, my church going was pretty much limited to attending vespers services held every Sunday afternoon in Caldwell Hall.

While the college clearly was a nonsectarian, publicly financed governmental institution its leadership made a conscious effort to provide some outlet for the religious life of the students living on campus. President Davis understood that religion was a vital aspect of the lives of many families from which his students came. The school therefore operated much like the historically black colleges that were founded or supported by churches. The music department devoted much time and attention to the college choir, which performed religious music for the school's solemn ceremonies, including the Sunday afternoon vespers services. The college choir annually made a tour to major cities around the country, performing fundraising concerts to benefit the school. On Sunday mornings large numbers of resident students attended the John Brown Watson Sunday school held in Caldwell Hall, under the voluntary leadership of college faculty and staff. Every spring the college sponsored "religious emphasis week" during which a prominent religious leader came to the campus to conduct a series of events having a religious theme. Student attendance at these events was strongly encouraged and they responded by turning out for these events in great numbers.

With so much emphasis today on maintaining the so-called wall of separation between church and state I doubt that a state school could engage in or support such religious activities for any length of time without significant legal challenge. I believe, however, that the school's policies with respect to religious values being an integral part of the culture of the institution and insisting that such values are essential to the educational process is what helped to make it a very special place. The school did much to shape the lives of many men and women. Instilling and reinforcing such values contributed to the making of successful and productive men and women and ultimately to creating a better society.

*   *   *

The social fraternities and sororities on campus actively began recruiting students to join their respective organizations

68

shortly after their enrollment as freshmen. However, they were allowed to initiate a student only after he or she had successfully completed the freshman year. Four of the major national black undergraduate fraternities maintained chapters at A. M. & N. College. They all attempted to attract students having the best academic records. Although social fraternities had been on campus for only a few years, each of them had already acquired distinct reputations. Because of my academic record most people assumed I would be inclined to join the fraternity having the reputation for academic excellence and high achievement. I chose instead to accept the overtures from the Gamma Sigma Chapter of Kappa Alpha Psi fraternity. The men in Kappa Alpha Psi fraternity were not always the best students academically. Of all the fraternities the Kappas appeared to represent the best balance between academic achievement, leadership qualities, physical courage, and sociability. Many of the best athletes on campus were Kappas. They were well represented among the leaders in student government and other student run activities. I noticed too that the prettiest girls seemed to be attracted to Kappa men. Men in Gamma Sigma made it clear that they wanted me to join them to help dispel the notion that the chapter did not value academic excellence in its membership. So I became a pledge in the Gamma Sigma Chapter of Kappa Alpha Psi fraternity in my sophomore year.

As a prelude to becoming a pledge I had to attend one of the fraternity's "smokers," a social event put on by members to give them an opportunity to observe how potential members behaved in social situations. None of the fraternities at the college had its own fraternity house so the "smoker" was held off campus in private facilities at a restaurant. It was at a Kappa Alpha Psi fraternity "smoker" that I had my first alcoholic drink. The brothers had gone down to Pennington's Liquor Store a few blocks from the campus and bought several bottles of Four Roses blended whiskey, one of the cheapest brands I later discovered. It was being served at the "smoker" with ice and Coca-Cola so it had a sweet taste. The moment I put the glass to my lips a sense of guilt came over me. Here I was at the age of 20, only a few months from my 21st birthday, being traumatized briefly because I knew I was violating a tenet of the religious faith I had grown up in. Nevertheless, I drank the cocktail, not because I was compelled to do so, but because I

69

saw this as a way of finally freeing myself and asserting my autonomy as a person. I doubt if any of the brothers or other pledges sensed the tremendous internal struggle I was experiencing in the midst of all the frivolity of the party. I tried hard not to show any signs of my personal internal conflicts.

I endured all the silly things pledges were required to do in order to become a member of the fraternity. I also survived the physical pain the brothers felt compelled to inflict upon those that would be members. I saw men who failed the tests, being unable to put up with what some would describe as abuse. For me personally it was worth it all and I was extremely proud when the initiation process finally ended and I was inducted into the fraternity in May 1951. I believe I was the first member of my family to join a social fraternity. Charles, one of my younger brothers, also became a Kappa when he was at A. M. & N. College several years later.

*   *   *

The debate team's tour in the spring of 1951 took us north to St. Louis, Missouri, where the coaches had scheduled debates with St. Louis University and Washington University, two predominantly white schools. Allen Black, a freshman, had joined the traveling squad, which again included Dorothy Ann Davis, Delores Mays, and me. Our presence on these white school campuses frequently drew curious glances from the apple-cheeked white students. However, I found that debating against white students in the final analysis was no different than competing against black students. White debaters had strengths and weaknesses just like we did and our objectives as a team had to be the same as with any other opponent, i.e., exploit the other team's weaknesses as much as possible. We held our own against both northern white schools that spring.

3

From College Student to Family Man

I found myself spending more and more time with my teammate Dorothy Ann during the 1951 debate season. Frankly, I was a little surprised that she seemed interested in knowing me better. First of all she was a junior while I was only a sophomore. Females in the junior class did not often date young men in the classes below their own, although the obverse was not unusual; upperclassmen frequently dated girls in classes below theirs. Furthermore, Dorothy Ann had been dating a very popular young man in her own junior class, a man from Memphis named Ed Townsend. Townsend was tall and handsome, was a member of the dramatics club and sang in and traveled with the college choir. I assumed at first that this very pretty girl who had the advantage of living in town, and therefore was not subject to the strict dating rules that apply to girls living on campus, could have her pick of all the young men around.

Doc Jones asked me to help write opening speeches for other members of the team that year. It was in this process that Dorothy Ann and I wound up working very closely together in the early part of the debate season. After a while I gathered enough courage to ask if I could walk her home after one of our late practice sessions, and she agreed. She lived on King Street, just two blocks off North Cedar Street about a mile from the campus. It took less than a half hour to walk from the campus to her house, which was near the end of King Street, which came to a dead end at the Arkansas River.

Dorothy Ann introduced me to her family. She had three young sisters, Lola, Jo Marva and Gail. Her mother, Mrs. Mattie Davis, was a tall, stately woman who clearly controlled the Davis household. Her father was away but her grandfather, whom everyone called Papa Brown, was there. Right away I decided that I liked Mrs. Davis and I think she liked me. I soon discovered, however, that while Dorothy Ann was not subject to the strict rules that applied to female dormitory residents, Mrs. Davis had her own rules for her daughters that in some respects were even more stringent than those of Mother Harold at the women's dormitory. Mrs. Davis made it a point to know what Dorothy Ann's class schedule was and what extracurricular activities she was engaged in. She had a pretty good idea what time she should be home every day.

By the end of the 1950-51 school year I had made up my mind that I wanted to marry Dorothy Ann. We spent long hours sitting on the bank of the river near her house talking about a possible future for us together. We talked a lot about how we could afford marriage at such an early age and at this point in our college careers. I had two more years before obtaining my degree, while Dorothy was to become a senior that fall. Neither of us was financially secure or totally independent of parental support, but we were young, in love, impatient and full of optimism about our ability to make it as a couple while completing college. We began developing our strategy first for telling her parents of our desire to get married, and secondly of having answers for the inevitable questions about such things as where we would live, how would we support ourselves, would one or both of us continue in school to obtain a degree.

Shortly after the spring semester ended Dorothy and I decided to join her father on his next trip to the Baptist Church where he was the pastor in McGhee, Arkansas, a town about 60 miles southeast of Pine Bluff. I thought being together with Rev. Davis on the trip would be the ideal setting for me to inform him of our plans to get married and to seek his approval. I had hoped that our conversation in the car on the way down would naturally develop an opening for me to raise the subject of our getting married. Rev. Davis was not the kind of minister that avoided small talk with his children or with others he liked. He was a big major league baseball fan as was I. On several occasions we had sat on the front porch swing of the Davis house listening to broadcasts of St. Louis Cardinal baseball games together. He was a heavy smoker too, the one habit he had that I did not like. His interests ranged far beyond the Bible and religious subjects. He had a tremendous sense of humor and had a great relationship with all his daughters. We talked about many things during the less than-two hour drive to McGhee but I had a tough time saying outright why Dorothy Ann and I wanted to come with him on this particular trip.

Finally, as we neared our destination Dorothy Ann nudged me real hard and I knew she was trying to tell me to get to the subject of our marriage. As I recall it, I did not ask permission to marry Dorothy Ann. Instead I told Rev. Davis that I was in love with his daughter, that we wanted to get married later that summer, and would like his blessings. He did not seem startled or in any way surprised by my statement. He looked into the rear view mirror at Dorothy Ann, who was in the back seat of the car, and asked her if this was what she wanted to do. She answered "yes." That was about all that was said at the time. I felt as if Rev. Davis knew more about our situation than we thought he did. In any event, he did not seem unduly concerned about how we planned to take care of the responsibilities of a married couple.

Later on when Rev. Davis and I were together alone I told him more about our marriage plans and how we intended to continue in school. Both Dorothy Ann and I were on full tuition scholarships at the college. We had arranged housing on campus in one of the World War II vintage Quonset huts that were made available to married students and some faculty members at fairly nominal prices. I had made plans to take a job not far from the campus that would permit me to work part-time after classes ended each day and on Saturdays. Dorothy Ann would continue working that summer as she usually did as a nurse's aid at Davis Hospital in the city.

The Davises gave their blessings. We set August 18, 1951 as the date for our marriage. The marriage would take place at Barraque Street Baptist Church, where Mrs. Davis and her family had been members for many years. The Pastor Rev. Knox agreed to perform the ceremony that Saturday afternoon.

When I told my folks about our plans to get married they raised no objections but questioned me closely about the practical issues of how we would support ourselves. If they had concerns as to whether the two of us were mature enough for married life, such questions were left unstated. I sensed that these concerns were

73

there nevertheless. My folks liked Dorothy Ann and thought she was a wonderful person.

Our wedding was probably the biggest social event of the summer in Pine Bluff. Having grown up there Dorothy Ann had no trouble involving her many friends in the wedding. Her very closest friends included Edythe Etherly, Faye Wiley, Lazelle Brown, and Myrtle Brown. Mrs. Davis was an accomplished seamstress and made all the dresses for the bridesmaids and other participants in the wedding. I asked my friend Edgar Wade from Jonesboro and now a third year student at Philander Smith College in Little Rock to be my best man. He not only agreed to be best man but invited the newly wedded couple to spend their honeymoon in his mother's home in Jonesboro. (Which offer we gladly accepted.) Some of my Kappa brothers, including Roscoe Word, served as ushers and groomsmen at the ceremonies.

My acquaintances at the college, students and faculty alike, found it hard to believe that Dorothy Ann and I were married when they returned to school in September 1951. We both enrolled as usual for the fall quarter, but this time Dorothy registered as Mrs. Dorothy Ann Davis McKinney. We were determined to prove to ourselves and to the skeptics that we could continue to excel in school while taking on the full responsibilities of a married couple. I planned my class schedule in such a way as to permit me to report to work at Hestand's Grocery Store by 4 P.M. working about 3 hours each weekday afternoon and a full day on Saturday gave me nearly a 30-hour workweek for which I was paid $45.00. When I approached the owner, Mr. George Hestand, about the job I explained my situation to him fully; that I was a student at the college entering my junior year and had just gotten married. I needed a job that would enable me to support my family while continuing my education. He agreed to these terms and made this clear to his son Joe, the store manager, a young man not much older than myself.

My primary job at the store was to restock the shelves as needed and assist the produce department manager in removing perishable items from display cases to refrigerated storage at the end of the day. Doing this job gave me knowledge about prices of the various grocery items and where they were located in the store. I therefore became a source of information for customers as they

74

shopped and put me in position to be helpful to all the checkout personnel as well. After a few months the store manager occasionally would ask me to fill in at the checkout counter. I therefore became the first black checkout person of any grocery chain store in Pine Bluff. I suspect the Hestands felt it might be good for business to have me work the cash registers and interface directly with customers. After all the store was in the heart of the black community and was patronized by many of the faculty and staff from the college. Still, this was the Deep South that strictly observed customs by which certain jobs were reserved for whites. Working as a cashier in a mainline grocery store was one of those jobs in Pine Bluff. I am not sure Hestand would have put me on the cash register at the second store he owned on the southeast side of town in a predominately white neighborhood, but he might have done so because he was a strong willed, independent, very successful man.

I continued working at Hestand's grocery until I left Pine Bluff for law school in September 1953. When I left Mr. Hestand told me that a job at any of his stores would be waiting for me if I should ever return to the city. I deeply appreciated this gesture but hoped I would never have to accept the offer.

*   *   *

The entire McKinney family moved to Pine Bluff from Jonesboro before school started in the fall of 1951 and took a house on Eureka Street near the college campus. So all my younger brothers except George would spend their adolescent years in a town that was quite different than where I had grown up. I am not sure, however, whether the changed environment for them made all that much difference in their outlook on life and the development of their personalities. Each of them was motivated to further their education beyond high school. Being in the larger city did not diminish their desire to prepare themselves to be more than farmhands or common laborers. I think they made the adjustment to living in Pine Bluff better than I did to having the family again living so close to me after two years of separation. Momma seemed particularly pleased with the move. It meant that she had finally won out in the subliminal contest with Papa over the years as to the direction their children should take in life. Papa at last gave up on the idea of our becoming a farm family. The move in part at least was undertaken to make it easier for the younger brothers to go to a nearby college, thus giving them a better chance of entering rewarding professions or occupations. Momma also made new friends easily, not only at the church but among others in the college community. Some of the women with young families around the campus came to view her as a beloved surrogate grandmother. Momma obviously liked that role.

Papa had challenges as well. The college decided to expand its campus to the south and west to build new dormitories, a new gymnasium and several other new facilities. The land Papa's church stood on had to be acquired in this expansion. So he relocated and built a new church. During this period Papa began to experience health problems, finally culminating with a major operation at a hospital in Little Rock. Papa came from very good stock, however, and survived the operation. He completely recovered after a week's stay in the hospital and several weeks of recuperation at home. It was during the weeks of Papa's recovery that he came to know what a caring, generous person Dorothy Ann really was. She used her nurse's training very effectively, attending Papa's wounds and convincing him that he had many more years left. For the rest of his life Dorothy Ann occupied a very special place in Papa's heart.

*   *   *

The war in Korea continued throughout 1951 and 1952 without either side being able to win a decisive victory. American led forces rebounded after nearly being pushed off the Korean peninsula completely early in the conflict. They regained all the ground they had lost below the 38th parallel, crossed over into North Korea and appeared to threaten to go all the way to the Chinese border. China entered the war with massive numbers of troops, driving our forces back to the original boundary. All of this action created· a great demand for more American soldiers. Many of my fellow students were being drafted into military service. I was not surprised when Uncle Sam came after me with a notice to report to Little Rock for a pre-induction physical in the spring of 1952. I passed the physical and a few weeks later was reclassified 1-A, which meant that I was in immediate danger of being drafted into the army. Fortunately, my draft board was still in Jonesboro, not Pine Bluff, my real residence for the past three years. The Jonesboro draft board apparently was not calling up young men in that area as fast as the Pine Bluff board was because it seemed that some of the men who took their physical with me got their induction notices shortly after passing the physical.

In the meantime, the Selective Service system instituted a new policy with regard to young men who were still in college. They decided to issue deferments to those students who were doing well in college until after completion of their undergraduate training. I took advantage of this opportunity to postpone my military service and was reclassified from 1-A to 4-S, the student deferment category. By the time I graduated in 1953 a truce between the belligerents had been reached. With prospects for ending the war in sight the need for new troops was significantly reduced. I therefore escaped the Korean conflict entirely.

I can only speculate on what might have been had I gone into the army in the early stages of the Korean War. Casualty rates in that war were very high, especially among young black recruits in the first few months of the war. Many of these young men with very little training were in effect sacrificed in the effort to stem North Korea's early advances down the peninsula in 1950. Had I gone in then there is a good chance I would not have survived. On the other hand, if I had served and survived the war I would have been entitled to the benefits that veterans of the war enjoyed. I was envious later when I saw classmates in graduate school who were veterans having the entire costs of their education paid for by the federal government while I struggled to make ends meet by doing odd jobs. I think, however, that those who served in the armed forces fully earned all the educational and other benefits that they received after the war.

My life as a student changed in some important respects after Dorothy Ann and I got married. Managing time became much more critical. My class schedule had to be planned with great care because of my work at the grocery store. I had to factor into my schedule the time it took to walk the two miles to and from my job. Time between classes for study also became critical because often I would be too exhausted to do much studying after dinner, usually around 8:30 or 9 o'clock at night. On Saturdays Hestand's grocery opened at 7 A.M. and closed at 9 P.M. That was the length of my workday. In 1951 nearly all major commercial establishments were closed on Sunday, including grocery and department stores. I very much looked forward to Sunday as that was the one day of the week that Dorothy and I could have quality time to ourselves, and to enjoy visits from family and friends in our nice little Quonset hut home.

The Quonset hut complex was located in the southwest quadrant of the campus. There were perhaps twenty-five Quonset huts in the complex and each one had two housing units, one on either end of the corrugated rounded steel structure anchored to a concrete slab. Each housing unit contained an area of about 600 square feet with two small bedrooms, one bath, a small living room and a galley kitchen with room for a small dining table near the front entrance. A small awning-type window was on each side to allow for cross ventilation, a very important feature because the metal exterior generated a tremendous heat buildup inside during the hot summer months.

Ours was the rear unit of hut 49, the entrance to which was only a few feet from the college's rear property line chain link fence. Our neighbors on the other end of the hut were Mr. and Mrs. James R. Seawood and their infant son. Mr. Seawood was an instructor of industrial education at the college. Next door in the very last unit in the complex was Mr. and Mrs. George Howard. George Howard went on to finish law school at the University of Arkansas, later becoming a member of the Arkansas Supreme Court. From there he was appointed to the federal bench as a U.S. district court judge. Our hut was sparsely furnished but entirely functional for a newly married student couple. Mrs. Mattie Davis made nice café curtains for all the windows. We were proud of the practical wedding gifts of flatware, dinnerware, glassware, linen and other useful household items. We always had plenty of food, which should not be surprising since I worked at a grocery store. Our student friends always knew there would be something to eat at our little place.

I shall never forget the first time Dorothy Ann and I had two of her friends over for Sunday dinner. Dorothy spent much time making a fancy dessert and all the side dishes for our first dinner party. It was only when we all sat down to eat that we realized that the pork chops we planned to have as the main course were still in the refrigerator uncooked. Of course we were embarrassed and everyone had a big laugh about it. Our guests chalked it all up to our inexperience at serious entertaining.

By the end of the fall quarter it became apparent why Dorothy Ann and I were in such a rush to get married. She was pregnant with our first child, a son, who was delivered at home late in February 1952 by Dr. Cleon Flowers, the younger brother of my idol, attorney Harold Flowers. The Flowers were related in some way to Dorothy's family. We named our son Rufus William McKinney, Jr., but from the very first we called him "Rudy." He was the most handsome baby boy I had ever seen, with a full head of hair, a light brown complexion and healthy in every respect. Rudy was the first grandchild in the Davis family and Momma and Papa's first grandson.

The two families competed vigorously for babysitting time with him. So his parents were in the enviable position of deciding which grandmother would have the privilege of keeping Rudy while Dorothy and I were at classes or at work during our final year in college. Neither Dorothy or I fully realized then how lucky we were at the time to have "free," loving baby sitters so near at that crucial time in our lives. We discovered later when we went away to graduate school how invaluable our parents and younger siblings had been in getting us through that time.

I began exploring my options for law school early in my senior year. I explained to every law school that I applied to that I would require some form of financial assistance and a part-time job. The Indiana University Law School at Bloomington, Indiana, made me the best offer, which I accepted with alacrity in the spring of 1953. Their offer included full tuition and assurance of part-time employment on the campus. Also, my family would be able to rent one of the many trailers near the campus until an apartment became available in Hoosier Courts, a large complex of World War II vintage temporary barracks that housed hundreds of married students and their families.

The final two years at A. M. & N. College seemed to go by very fast. I remained a member of the debate team both years and was permitted by my employer to travel with the team on the spring tour. Dorothy Ann rejoined the team for our senior year season as well. On the annual debate tour to compete against the Texas colleges in 1953 a match with the Southern Methodist University team also was put on the schedule. Most of our debates were held in the evening and usually took place in an auditorium before a sizable audience. At S. M. U. the format was quite informal and the debate was held in a large classroom with only a handful of students present. Our team was treated well by everyone at S. M. U. We found the city of Dallas to be more urbane and sophisticated than Houston and all the other Texas cities we had visited.

I completed nearly all the required courses for a degree in business administration with a minor in economics in the fall quarter of the 1952-53 school year. I decided to try to round out my education during the winter and spring quarters by taking courses in subjects that were interesting to me or from professors having interesting reputations. I therefore took courses in art history and appreciation, American government and comparative government, English literature and Negro history. The course in art history and appreciation, which was taught by Professor John M. Howard, was fascinating to me. Mr. Howard, who himself was a renowned painter whose works had been widely exhibited and acclaimed, opened my eyes to an entirely new world. He helped me understand the creative process and how ideas and emotions may be expressed with great force and power without words. I always wanted to take one of Mr. Ray Russell's history courses and to find out for myself whether his reputation for being stingy in awarding high grades was really true.

I waited until my final college quarter to earn the second "C" in my entire undergraduate career, the first having been earned my freshman year for the course in physical education. The second "C" I got in a course called "office machines," where we were introduced to the mechanical calculator, typewriters, and mimeograph machines. In my lifetime all of these machines became totally obsolete and relics in office machine museums. It just goes to show how inexorable technology development is. It demonstrates why education and learning are ongoing processes that should never end. The skills that one learns today can become of little or no use tomorrow. The true value of education then is to condition the body and mind to know how to adjust and be able to make good decisions in an ever changing environment.

Graduation exercises at A. M. & N. College were the grandest and most important events of the year. Every year the college somehow was able to attract a graduation speaker with a national or international reputation. 1953 was no different. The speaker that year was Dr. Mordecai W. Johnson, the president of Howard University in Washington, D.C. The ceremonies were held in the recently completed gymnasium on the east side of North Cedar Street directly across from the campus. Late May usually is summertime in South Central Arkansas, which means that the temperature reaches 90 to 95 degrees with about equal humidity at midday. May 26, 1953, was very hot outside and it was even hotter inside the gym, which was not air conditioned. Of course, I dressed in my best suit with starched white shirt and tie, as was customary for the occasion. The satin graduation robe was put on over the suit for the procession of graduates and dignitaries into the gym, increasing my discomfort level even more. It was important that the graduates looked their best because their parents and families were there to witness the achievement of a lifetime they had helped to produce—college graduation for a son or daughter. Momma and Papa came over to our Quonset hut and walked across the campus with Dorothy and me to where the graduates assembled before formation of the procession. Rev. Silas Davis and Dorothy's mother joined us there. Our son Rudy spent the night before with his Davis grandparents and on graduation day was left in the care of Dorothy's sisters, Lola, Jo Marva and Gail at the Davis home.

I do not remember any of the content of Dr. Mordecai Johnson's graduation address: what I shall never forget about the speech, however, is that it was about two hours long. He missed numerous opportunities to end the speech and some in the audience noticeably became restless as he went on and on. But the college choir sang beautifully the hymn they traditionally performed at solemn ceremonies, and one of my favorites, "God of Our Fathers Whose Almighty Hand." The highlight of a college graduation exercise, however, is not the speech but the awarding of degrees to the graduates. This is the part of the program where parents and families get to inject themselves into the proceedings by exuberant expressions and cheers when their son or daughter's name is called. When I graduated, colleges had not yet abandoned the practice of actually having each graduate come forward and march across the stage to receive their degree certificate from the dean and shake hands with the president of the institution. A group of some 320 that started out four years earlier as freshmen wound up as a graduating class numbering just over 150 persons. Presenting degree certificates individually to that many graduates takes considerable time. With Dr. Johnson's two-hour speech, the introductions of dignitaries, President Davis' remarks and all the interruptions as graduates received their certificates, the entire graduation ceremony lasted nearly four hours. I was filled with a sense of pride when the dean called my name and added the phrase "Summa Cum Laude," meaning a graduate with highest honors.

For more than an hour following the ceremony we milled around campus buildings and grounds saying good-bye to class-mates, signing each other's yearbook or graduation program with expressions of good wishes for the future. We knew we would scatter to the four winds after graduation and for most this would be the last time we would see each other, though we hoped that would not be the case. I would not be surprised if my wife Dorothy Ann felt a little differently about graduation than I did. After all, the class she entered college with had graduated the year before. Her graduation was delayed by our marriage and the birth of our son Rudy. Throughout our life together she never to my knowledge voiced any regret at the choices we made. I certainly felt that we had made a good life for ourselves in the two years we had been married and we both believed that a great though uncertain future lay ahead as we moved beyond the college years.

4

The Law School Years—1953-1956

Dorothy Ann and I took the Greyhound bus from Pine Bluff to Bloomington, Indiana, a 12- or 14-hour ride. We left Pine Bluff about 6 o'clock on Sunday morning, hoping to arrive in Bloomington before dark that evening. We knew we would have to wait until Monday to arrange the move into our new quarters on campus so we called ahead and made reservations to spend Sunday night at the Van Orman Hotel in downtown Bloomington. We thought it best to leave our son Rudy with the Davis grandparents until we saw exactly what our living situation would be like in Bloomington. Rev. and Mrs. Davis were more than happy to oblige. The trip north was long but uneventful. People sitting around us on the bus could tell the two of us were very much in love because Dorothy and I held hands and showed great affection toward each other the entire trip. At that time America was still a segregated society, even in its interstate transportation system. Blacks sat in the back of the bus: whites sat in the front. At rest stops along the way facilities at bus terminals too were completely segregated. At the time all of this seemed quite normal to us; that had been our experience throughout our lives. For some reason though I think we believed that since Indiana was a Northern state things may be different when we arrived in Bloomington, a university town in a state outside the South.

We had shipped our household belongings via railway express to Bloomington earlier so we had only two suitcases each to carry our clothing on the bus trip north. We arrived at our destination at about seven that Sunday evening and took a taxi from the bus terminal to the hotel, which was located in the heart of the downtown area. Hardly anyone was in the hotel lobby. I walked up to the registration desk, told the clerk my name and said my wife and I had reservations for a room that evening. The clerk looked at me incredulously and after a brief moment stuttered that there must be some mistake. I insisted that I had called several days earlier and made reservations, indicating that my wife and I would be arriving at this hotel Sunday evening to stay one night before going out to the Indiana University campus to the housing we had arranged for there. I pointed out that I was to enroll the following day at the university law school. The clerk then said just one moment and went into a room behind the counter to speak with the manager. After several minutes he returned and said that they had found my reservation. I proceeded to register and Dorothy and I took the elevator upstairs to our room.

As soon as we were inside the room Dorothy said to me, "What was that all about at the desk downstairs?" I said I'm not sure but I think we may be the first black couple they have seen as guests at this hotel. Clearly the clerk was not expecting to see a black couple claim the reservation someone calling himself Rufus McKinney made from Arkansas. The significant fact is that the hotel honored our reservation. Beyond that, there is much room for speculation as to why our being registered was not a routine matter. It is possible that the clerk actually did not see our names on the books as persons with a reservation. My later experiences in Bloomington with reference to blacks being served by local restaurants and similar commercial establishments leads me to believe that the hotel management made an exception in our case to a policy of not catering to blacks who are not part of a racially mixed group of customers. Throughout my three years in Bloomington I found that bars and restaurants off the university campus commonly observed a policy of serving black customers only if they were accompanied by whites. In any event, we were too exhausted from our long bus ride to allow the unpleasant incident at the hotel desk to deprive us of getting a good night's sleep in a nice clean room. That initial encounter left little doubt in my mind that North or South, being black in America you were more or less assured of disparate treatment; it's only a matter of degree.

The next morning we had breakfast in the coffee shop of the hotel without incident and after checking out left immediately for the housing office on the I. U. campus. We encountered no problems and were treated cordially there. They gave us a map of the campus and directions to the trailer courts and the unit where we would be staying. I believe we took a university shuttle bus to the area where our trailer was located. We were amazed at both the beauty and size of the I. U. campus. Most of the buildings were of stone or granite construction with a Gothic style of architecture. In the center of the campus was a quadrangle several acres in area crisscrossed by paved paths with stone benches alongside at intervals. The quad was surrounded by very mature trees.

The trailer courts were located beyond the field house and the I. U. auditorium about a mile from the center of the campus. In this vast expanse of land were hundreds of trailers that obviously were no longer mobile, lined row upon row. Interspersed among them were dozens of double-wide trailers that served as communal bathrooms, men on one side and women on the other. Out front of each double-wide was a fueling station for dispensing kerosene. Our assigned trailer was at the far end of the complex. As soon as we went inside I remarked to Dorothy Ann that this was not nearly as nice as the Quonset hut we left behind in Pine Bluff. The trailer was only five or six feet wide and perhaps eighteen feet long. On one end was the sleeping area and on the other the sitting area with a fold down table. Just to the left of the entrance was a kerosene fired heater, an electric cooking stove and a small refrigerator. Across from those was an enclosure for clothes and storage. Clearly our trailer was meant for two people only.

We discovered that our bathroom unit was only a few yards away. There were three shower stalls and toilet facilities in the men's side; presumably the women's side was similarly equipped. Once again, I was to be in a living arrangement that required going outside to a separate little house to go to the toilet. I had much experience at such an arrangement in my years growing up in Jonesboro. As long as the weather was mild and not raining, we got along fine with this arrangement. What I came to dread, however, was going to the bathroom on a cold, wet morning or having nature call in the middle of the night. But we were young and realized that these were temporary living arrangements that had to be endured for three years at most, and probably less time than that. Our main concern was how our one-and-a-half-year-old son Rudy would fare in this environment, since we had planned to bring him back with us when we returned from the Christmas holidays in Arkansas.

*   *   *

One hundred and five men and women enrolled with me as first year students at the Indiana University Law School in September 1953. Three of them were black, including Doris Keyes from Marion, Indiana, and a young man from Florida. First-year law students at I. U., as in most state university law schools in 1953, all take identical courses. It is a curriculum designed to insure that the student is exposed to the fundamentals of the fields or subjects one is sure to encounter in the general practice of law. This includes courses in the law of contracts, property law, criminal law, the law of torts (private or civil wrongs), legal remedies or procedures and legal research and writing. Successful completion of these courses in the first year puts a person a long ways down the road toward becoming a lawyer. In the final two years of law school the student has greater freedom in selecting courses of study that appeal to his interest or desired area of specialization upon completion of training and admission to practice.

The overwhelming majority of the people in the first year class were from the state of Indiana, and most of those had attended I. U. I say "attended" I. U. instead of "graduated," because some of them were permitted to enroll in the law school in the senior year of college and received both the bachelors degree and the LL.B upon graduation from law school. Those who entered law school as I did after receiving the undergraduate degree were eligible for the Doctor of Jurisprudence (J.D.) degree upon graduation from law school. Many of the law students came from small towns all around the state, some from places where black residents are extremely rare. I encountered no problems as a black law student and was treated with respect by everyone. In most of the classes students were assigned to particular seats in the classroom, usually alphabetically. The professor, therefore, could tell whether you were present by looking over the classroom. Naturally, the first persons I struck up conversations with were those seated around me in the classroom.

The I. U. law school faculty, without exception, used the case method of teaching, a system pioneered at Harvard law school decades earlier. The case method is a system of teaching and studying law by examining the cases that have been decided by courts or other competent legal authorities in the past. By reading and analyzing facts and the reasoning of the decision maker in the reported cases (usually but not always cases decided at the appellate court level) students seek to discern the principles of law involved in the case and how they may apply to other situations. So the professor's role in the classroom is not simply to lecture, or tell the student what he knows, but to guide the student toward discovering and understanding for himself the legal rules or principles that may apply in solving a legal problem. The law school classroom, therefore, is a forum for dialogue between the student and the professor and sometimes among the students themselves. The major objective in teaching and studying law is to develop to the maximum extent possible the student's reasoning powers, the ability to think analytically. Rote memory of information is not enough.

After one or two weeks of classes the professors pretty well knew which students came to class prepared to discuss the cases that had been assigned for study. Frequently those students would be called on to get the discussion going, either to summarize the facts in the case or to initiate dialogue on the legal principles involved. Sometimes the professor would call on a student having the reputation of not being prepared just to embarrass the student. I was determined not to be embarrassed and therefore I spent a lot of time briefing the assigned cases and preparing notes on what I believed the case stood for. Class participation did not directly impact the grade one received—grades were based solely on written examination results—but the student's performance in classroom dialogue could influence either positively or negatively the professor's attitude toward the student when grading examination papers. Often there is not a single "right" answer to a legal problem. The professor then has some latitude in giving the student credit if his answer appears to be well-reasoned or points to plausible alternatives to what others might regard as the "right" answer.

My first year professors were all men who were regarded as experts in their field. The criminal law course was taught by Mr. Jerome Hall, a longtime fixture on the faculty, who also taught constitutional law. The course in property was taught by Val Nolan, a young man who recently had graduated from the I. U. law school. The course in contracts was taught by Mr. Autterburn, who later left the faculty to become a member of the Indiana Supreme Court. Mr. Clifford taught the course in torts. Clifford looked the part of a law school professor, a tall white haired man with great bearing and presence. Mr. Bauman taught the course in remedies. The law school dean, Mr. Leon Wallace, did not teach any of the first-year courses but made himself freely available to all the first-year students for counsel and advice. Dean Wallace was a kindly, very fair-minded man who seemed to get along well not only with the students but with the faculty members as well.

It took me a while to realize how intense the competition was among the first-year law students at I. U. Unlike the situation in undergraduate school where many of the students had non-academic reasons for being there, every first year law student had the same ultimate goal, to complete the courses and earn the right to practice law as a profession. There was no time for foolishness. Many in the class were married and had children already as did I. We were under a great deal of pressure to get out of school and begin earning a living to support our families. Some were being supported in large part by working wives. Many had always been high academic achievers accustomed to leading their class in college and in high school. Soon after entering I learned what an honor it was to be selected for the school's law review after the freshman year. That honor was bestowed upon the five or six students with the highest academic rank in the class. Members of the law review usually had their pick of many job offers from the best law firms when they graduated. Every person in the class had an incentive to excel and do well.

The law school was located in Maxwell Hall near the center of the campus. It was a large old building made of stone, perhaps one of the original permanent structures on the campus. The freshman class met in the largest classroom in the building on the second floor. The walk from our trailer to Maxwell Hall took about thirty minutes, so once I was on campus I usually stayed there until all my classes for the day were over. Any free time I had during the day would be spent either in the law school library or in the student union building, which was located just behind the law school.

The student union building was a large, more modern structure that housed a number of facilities, including the bookstore, a cafeteria, a large lounge where students could gather in small groups for cards or conversation, and offices for the student government. A barber shop was on the lower level. All the barbers were white. I was told early on by more than one of the black male students not to try to get a haircut in that shop. The barbers would not directly refuse to serve black customers. Instead they would simply tell blacks that they did not know how to cut their hair. I knew of no black student who was willing to take the chance to find out if this were true or not. After about a month I decided to go into the town, find the black section and locate someone who could cut my hair. I had been accustomed to getting a haircut every two weeks, so I was beginning to look pretty shaggy. I later discovered after talking to other black students that several of them had developed enough skill to cut each others hair and they did so at their residence on campus, usually on Saturday morning. I found this to be a more convenient alternative to the long bus trip into Bloomington to find a barber every two weeks or so.

We did not do a great deal of socializing with our neighbors in the trailer courts as everyone was so busy attending classes, studying or working. We did get to know the couple in the trailer right next to ours, Johnny and Janet, their infant son and Janet's cat. Johnny was of Polish extraction from Gary, Indiana, and his wife was from a little town in South Dakota. Johnny had served in the army and came to college late on the G. I. bill. Janet had already finished college elsewhere and now spent her time taking care of their baby and the cat. They were quite friendly and Dorothy and I enjoyed their company. Janet obviously had had the cat long before their baby was born and she seemed to care about as much for the cat as she did for her baby. In fact we noticed that the cat seemed jealous of the baby. Janet told us that she did not like to leave the baby in the trailer alone with the cat because she feared the cat might try to harm the baby.

The game of canasta was all the rage at that time and Janet especially encouraged us to learn the game so we could play it with her and Johnny whenever we had spare time. In the fall we would get together to play canasta and to talk about ourselves and our families. Johnny soon told me that he grew up in a neighborhood in Gary populated almost exclusively by people who had immigrated from Poland or were of Polish descent. He told me that his father in Gary would strongly disapprove of his becoming friends with Dorothy and me. He said that the Polish and black communities in Gary did not get along well with each other and that where he grew up it would be unusual for a black man and a Polish man to become friends. He also explained that Poles often had similar attitudes toward other ethnic groups who were white, so the antipathy toward other groups was not necessarily based on their racial identity. His wife Janet, on the other hand, said she had never been around any black people until she came to Gary with Johnny. Where she grew up in South Dakota the only people of color she had seen were American Indians. Recalling the summer I spent in Cleveland a few years ago I remembered vaguely how the city was divided into various ethnic neighborhoods, but this was the first time I really understood how deep some of these ethnic divisions could be. I said to myself the black-white divide I was used to dealing with as a Southerner can be even more complex in large northern cities where other ethnic groups may harbor ancient animosities against each other.

Dorothy Ann found a job on campus working in the dental research lab of one Dr. Joseph Muhler. Dr. Muhler was doing work in the area of tooth decay prevention and was experimenting with the use of fluoride in tooth paste. She seemed to find working in the lab to be interesting as it kept her in touch with the science field, which had been her major in college. The income Dorothy Ann earned enabled me to concentrate on my law school studies that first year. I now realize that I did not tell her often enough in words and deeds how much I appreciated the sacrifices she made for me. I thought the bargain Dorothy Ann and I had reached was for her to help me get through law school and I would thereafter take care of her while she nurtured our children. I would discover much later that the bargain I thought we had lacked mutuality. Dorothy Ann had always dreamed of becoming a medical doctor. At some point during the early years of our marriage I thought she had abandoned that dream in order to help me put myself in position to make a good life for our family. It turns out, however, that Dorothy Ann merely postponed her dream of having a career in medicine. I now think she believed it possible for her to go to medical school after my law school graduation, despite the fact that we had two boys under five years of age at the time. The unfortunate thing is that we did not discuss the bargain I thought we had openly, frankly and completely. I continued operating on one set of assumptions while she had an entirely different set of assumptions on this matter of ultimate importance. Had we talked we might have avoided two tragic events that later struck our family.

A fellow student whose family lived in Texas placed an ad in the college newspaper seeking a couple to share expenses for his drive home for the Christmas holidays. We responded, telling the driver we would accompany him as far as Pine Bluff, Arkansas. He accepted and agreed to pick us up on the return trip to Indiana as well. We were anxious to get home to see Rudy and the rest of our families. We left Bloomington in late afternoon, drove in bad weather through the night and arrived in Pine Bluff the following morning. Rudy, now nearly two years old, hardly remembered his mom and dad. Four months is a very long time in the life of a less than two-year-old boy. He had adjusted to our absence and had conferred his affection upon the grandparents and aunts who had taken care of him while his parents were away. Since he no longer saw us every day he had good reason to think that we may have abandoned him. Of course, Dorothy Ann and I were deeply saddened to find that our son had nearly forgotten about us in the short space of four months. Although our living situation in Bloomington was not well suited for a two-year-old boy, we were now convinced that we had to bring Rudy back with us when we returned to Indiana from the Christmas holiday in January 1954.

First semester final examination results were posted on the bulletin board at Maxwell Hall not long after we returned from the Christmas holidays. I recall feeling good about how I had done on the examinations, but there was an element of uncertainty because I had not had examinations like these in undergraduate school. There were no multiple choice or true or false questions on any of the examinations. Instead, we were presented with a series of factual situations involving disputes between one or more parties. The student's challenge was to ascertain what the legal issues were in the case and to sort out what the rights and remedies may be for the parties involved. Thus an essay was required in expressing your response to every problem on the examination. Writing skills were at a premium, and equally important was the ability to manage the amount of time spent on each question. I was pleasantly surprised when I saw my first semester grades: an "A" in contracts, a "B" in each the torts, criminal law, remedies and property courses and a "C" in the one-hour freshman research course. These results confirmed in my mind that a graduate of Arkansas A. M. & N. College could compete academically with graduates of more prestigious colleges and universities in other parts of the country. I felt good about myself and about the undergraduate institution from which I had graduated. I knew then that I would not be among that percentage of the freshman class many professors predicted would not make it through the first year.

*   *   *

The entire state of Indiana goes a little bit crazy when basketball season rolls around. We found that out early in 1954. I had never been a big basketball fan before, but it is hard not to become one if you live in Indiana. Indiana university stands at the apex of a vast basketball pyramid in the state. The base of that pyramid is comprised of the hundreds if not thousands of towns and hamlets in the state, each with a well-developed high school basketball program. Every one of these high schools has a legitimate chance at fame by winning the state high school basketball championship, no matter how small the school.

The season before I came to Bloomington, I. U. won the national championship of college basketball and some of the enthusiasm from the previous season spilled over to the next year when coach Branch McCracken had several players returning from the championship team. A new addition to the team that year was a black player from Indianapolis named Hallie Bryant. Bryant was an all-state selection from Crispus Attucks High School, an all black school whose team had made it to the state tournament finals a few years earlier. Finally, black students at I. U. had a chance to cheer one of their own at the sold out games at the I. U. fieldhouse. In the 1950s it was rare to see black basketball players at any of the big time colleges and universities. There were none at any level among the Southern schools. Hallie Bryant was among the first black players to play for Indiana University and it was in-

92

teresting to observe how this breakthrough developed during the 1954 season. In high school Bryant played under Ray Crowe, a coach who employed a wide open system of play that allowed the especially talented player to display his virtuosity on the court. Branch McCracken's teams played a different style that emphasized defense, positioning, set plays, outside shooting and total discipline and control of his players. From the very beginning it was apparent that Bryant's talents could not be exploited to the fullest under the McCracken system and Bryant became increasingly frustrated as a player as the season went on. Whenever Bryant would make a brilliant individual play he would be pulled from the game and scolded by coach McCracken. The McCracken system of basketball obviously had been a successful one. Not many college coaches could boast of having won the national collegiate championship as McCracken could.

The way Coach McCracken handled Hallie Bryant and the system he used probably discouraged some of the top black players in the state from coming to I. U., despite the program's historical success. Oscar Robertson, another outstanding alumnus of Crispus Attucks High School, chose to play for the University of Cincinnati and led that school to national prominence in basketball. While attending a game in the 1954 season I sat near another outstanding black high school player being recruited to play for I. U. He was the tallest person I had ever seen. It was a boy named Wilt Chamberlain from Philadelphia. He chose to attend the University of Kansas instead.

*   *   *

The spring is tornado season in many parts of the Midwest and Southern states. They strike without warning and the most vulnerable type of dwelling or place to be in when a tornado comes up is a house trailer. At the time I never thought much about the tornado risk, except when reading stories about the destruction wreaked upon some other unfortunate place. However, every time we experienced high winds in the area I was reminded of the need to speed up the process of getting into larger, more secure quarters next school year.

In the meantime, things continued to go well with my law

school studies. As second semester final examination time approached I felt more confident than before. I completed all but one examination when on the night before the last examination I began to experience intense abdominal pain. No matter what I did the pain would not go away. We left Rudy with a neighbor while Dorothy Ann went with me to the college infirmary to seek medical help. They quickly came to the conclusion that I probably was experiencing an appendicitis attack that may require surgery. They sent me immediately to the Bloomington Hospital as an emergency case. As we had no private physician I was entrusted to staff doctors who performed surgery the following morning. The doctors told us later that I came very close to having a serious problem with a ruptured appendix. The hospital stay was short and I recovered at home without complications. I was concerned, however, about missing the scheduled final examination. Dorothy called the law school on the day of my surgery to let Dean Wallace know about my situation. He and the professor in the course were very considerate and agreed to allow me to take a make-up examination as soon as I was well enough to return to Maxwell Hall.

My second semester grades were even better than those I got the first term. Again I received an "A" in contracts and an "A" in legislation, the course in which I had to take the make-up examination. I earned a "B" in all the remaining subjects. My overall performance the freshman year put me in the top ten percent of the class and earned me an invitation to become a member of the law review staff. Needless to say, I was extremely proud of these accomplishments.

In the spring of 1954 the United States Supreme Court announced its decision in the *Brown* v. *Board of Education* case, finding that the policy of "separate but equal" school systems in the nation violated the U. S. Constitution. That decision therefore outlawed a fairly common practice in the Southern states among state-supported colleges and universities under which states, in order to avoid admitting blacks to their professional and other graduate programs for which the state offered no training at state supported black institutions, would pay the tuition of black residents to attend graduate programs in schools outside the state. It would be years before the impact of the Brown decision was felt throughout our educational system. Even before that decision came down some Southern state universities, because of legal challenges and other pressures, had already undertaken to desegregate their graduate school programs. The University of Arkansas was among those universities. As soon as he had heard about the Brown decision my freshman black colleague from Florida told me he would not be back at I. U. the following year because he now had the right to continue his legal studies at the University of Florida. I wished him luck.

Dorothy's father drove up to Bloomington to bring my family home to Pine Bluff for the summer. By mid-June I had fully recovered from the surgery. I decided to take Mr. Hestand up on his offer the year before and went back to work at Hestand's Grocery Store. Dorothy Ann was now about five months pregnant and very much needed the time to be with her family and relax as much as one can with an energetic two-and-a-half-year-old son. The closing weeks of my second semester of law school had been very stressful on her. Fortunately her younger sisters, Lola, Jo Marva and Gail, took turns making sure our son Rudy was entertained. They would take him exploring along the banks of the river just a few yards from the Davis' back yard. The Davis' large back yard had several mature pecan trees which Rudy liked to try to climb. They also raised chickens, which ran freely around the house and Rudy enjoyed chasing them. Mrs. Davis kept pretty busy all the time. When she was not sewing or making some item of clothing for a neighbor or friend, she was cooking or orchestrating the girls' work doing other chores that needed to be done. With such a crowded household, there was plenty of washing, ironing and cleaning to do.

Second year students selected for law review were required to report two weeks before school started in the fall of 1954. I therefore left Pine Bluff a few days before the end of August to return to Bloomington. Dorothy Ann and I had decided that she should remain in Pine Bluff the first semester of my second year because our second child was due to be born sometime during the month of September. I very much wanted to be present, but it was highly unlikely that I would return to Pine Bluff for the event. Our first child Rudy was delivered at home, in Quonset hut No. 49 on the campus of Arkansas A. M. & N. College and I was there in the bedroom when Dr. Flowers delivered him. This time we were determined to have our second child delivered at Davis Hospital, the

95

main hospital serving Pine Bluff and the southeastern part of the state. Dorothy Ann had worked as a nurse's aide at Davis Hospital for several summers while in high school and during her college years. So she was well known there among the staff.

The first semester of my second year of law school was difficult for me. First of all, I missed my wife and son, and did not enjoy living in Mom Mayes' rooming house with a large number of undergraduate students. Secondly, I found that being on the law review was very hard work that took a great deal of time that otherwise I would have spent studying. I took the course on constitutional law that semester, which was taught by Professor Mann. This was the course I had most looked forward to taking. I envisioned delving into the great legal issues that largely determined what we had been and were becoming as a nation. Much of our constitutional law history was made during my lifetime in the struggles between Congress, the President and the courts over Depression Era legislation, the limits on the powers of the federal government and the role of the U. S. Supreme Court in defining these limits. From a historical perspective I was anxious to know more about how and why the Supreme Court could arrive at the decisions in the *Dred Scott* and *Plessey* v. *Ferguson* cases. To my untrained mind these decisions on their face seemed to be in conflict with the plain language of the Constitution and fundamental principles of justice that that document represented. Studying the landmark cases in a classroom setting with twenty or thirty bright students from many different backgrounds and a wide range of views on social and political matters one begins to understand the fine distinctions and the complexities of constitutional law. The layman tends to make judgments based on his notions of what is "right" and what is "wrong." In the constitutional law context, what is right and what is wrong are not absolutes, but functions of one's life circumstances and experiences. Sometimes there may be more than one "right" choice so the difficulty is in determining between them. Moreover, concepts of "liberty," "freedom," "justice," and "equality," mean fundamentally different things to intelligent human beings from other cultures and backgrounds.

As a black person growing up in a society that not only was totally segregated along racial lines but also one that officially and unofficially denied or restricted the exercise of many of the rights of citizenship to people of color, I had not understood that my cry for "freedom" was at war with the "liberty" demanded by my white counterpart. The dominant group in society, those with the power and control want minimum interference with their right to exercise that power or control. They call that "liberty." Members of the oppressed group want most to be released from the constraints placed upon them by the dominant group. They call that "freedom." To the town leaders about to lynch the wretched black soul accused of ravishing the flower of white womanhood, the deed is done in the name of administering "justice." We mete out "justice" when the court pronounces a long prison sentence to the man found guilty of stealing a loaf of bread, or the drug addict found in possession of a forbidden substance. To me "justice" meant fashioning a punishment to fit the circumstances and the severity of the crime. To the dominant group "equality" is meant for those similarly situated. That is, all property owners are entitled to be treated alike. Those not qualified by ownership of property have no standing to demand the same rights.

The course in constitutional law opened for me new vistas on politics in America. Politics pervades every aspect of society. Constitutional law is politics being practiced at the very highest level. I came to understand that the greatest Supreme Court justices throughout our history first and foremost were politicians who later became justices.

I was one of ten classmates selected as new members of the *Indiana Law Review*. Of the ten one was a woman, Shirley Abrahamson, who led the class in academic standing. Shirley was from New York City. All the others, except me, were from various cities and towns in Indiana; Paul Arnold, Robert Bush, Miles Gerberding, Russell Hart, Ralph Lafuze, Robert Miller, Vern Sheldon and Charles Tiede. Shirley Abrahamson went on to become chief justice of the Wisconsin Supreme Court. Most of the others eventually returned to their hometowns to practice law.

Each new member of the law review was asked to pick a subject and write an article for publication in the law journal. Published pieces written by law students were published as "notes" without being attributed to the author; those written by legal scholars, lawyers and other experts were published as "articles" and the authors were identified with their published work. In selecting a subject we would consult with one of the senior members of the student editorial staff, but once a subject had been chosen each writer worked more or less independently to do the necessary research and decide what it was he wanted to say in the note. Producing a note for publication helped to develop certain of the essential skills needed to become a good lawyer. The lawyer's stock in trade is "words," effective use of the English language to communicate ideas. Lawyers need to be able to distinguish between important facts and other nice to know but not important facts. Knowing what other respected authorities may have said about the subject is important but not conclusive. There is always room for interpretation or putting a different slant on things out of your own experience.

For my first note I chose to write about municipal self-government in the state of Indiana and the role state government plays in determining the extent of powers that may be exercised by cities and towns in the state. At the time this was an issue before the state legislature and a matter of great importance to many localities throughout the state. But this was not an issue having national significance or one that an aspiring civil rights lawyer would be expected to choose to write about. Doing research for the piece did, however, bring me into contact with local and state governmental authorities. That could be helpful, I thought, if I should later decide to practice law in the state of Indiana. Much of my time in the spring semester of the 1954-55 school year was spent writing and rewriting my note about local self-government in Indiana. All the hard work paid off because the final product was published in the winter issue, *30 Indiana Law Journal 265* under the title "Local-State Relations in Indiana: Proposed Charter Making Powers for Municipalities."

I had barely gotten settled in my room in Mom Mayes' rooming house just off the campus when the call came from Pine Bluff that Dorothy Ann had given birth to our second son. The date was September 4, 1954. My wife and the baby were fine; it was an uncomplicated delivery. We earlier had discussed names but had not reached an agreement on what the name should be. I had expressed an interest in honoring my favorite college professor, Harding B. Young, by giving our son the professor's first name as a middle name. Dorothy Ann did not like the name Harding, saying it conjured up memories of the corrupt and discredited 29th President of the United States, Warren G. Harding. I had not thought of that. Dorothy Ann made the final decision herself at the hospital, naming the boy Frederick Warren McKinney. I think she may have misinterpreted something I said in our telephone conversation about names because "Warren" was not the middle name I had in mind. But I liked the name she chose. For some reason though we started calling the boy by his middle name and continued to do that throughout his childhood. Only when he went away to college did he predominately become known as "Fred."

Without a working wife things got a lot tougher from a financial standpoint. On weekends I sought out and occasionally found odd jobs in the city of Bloomington to earn money for living expenses. I worked pretty regularly for an older couple that lived in a large frame three-story house that they no longer could adequately care for. I did odd jobs for them around the house, cleaning floors and making minor repairs. As winter approached I was asked to retrieve the heavy wood-framed storm windows from the basement and install them at a dozen or so windows and doors of the house. I always dreaded doing the rear third floor windows because it required me to climb three stories up outside on an old wooden ladder with the storm window in tow. It was hard but honest work that helped pay my room and board. I would continue doing odd jobs after my family returned with me to Bloomington in January 1955. Later that spring I learned of a part-time job opening on campus which I gladly took because it was near the law school. The job was cleaning classrooms and laboratories at the school of psychology building when the school day ended at about 5 P.M. The job took about two hours and paid enough to get us through until Dorothy Ann could go back to work at the dental school and we found someone to look after Rudy and Fred during the day.

The grades I got during the second year reflected the changes in our family situation. Two kids instead of one. More part-time work for me, including work as a research assistant for Professor Mann. Much more time spent doing law review work. Less time for study, and perhaps some degree of overconfidence as a result of my good first year grades. For the first time also I received a grade much lower than the grade I think I deserved in the course. The course was business organizations and it was taught by an adjunct

99

professor who was a lawyer in private practice in Bloomington. I do not recall the professor's name. I thought I performed quite well on the final examination and was extremely disappointed with the "C" the professor gave me on my examination paper. In fact, I thought the grade was so unfair that I made an appointment and went to see the professor to discuss my exam blue book answers with him. The bottom line was he refused to change the grade, even though our discussion clearly demonstrated the unfairness of how he had graded my paper. To this day I believe he was the one professor I had in law school who believed that no black person could be of more than average intelligence and therefore could not earn any grade higher than "C" in a course he taught.

I earned one "A" the second year, in the course in trusts which was taught by Dean Wallace. I got a "C" in all the other courses I took that year, including the course in constitutional law. I was happy with the "C" I got in constitutional law. The final examination in that course was by far the most difficult one of my whole law school career. It was an open book examination where the problems were given to the students on Friday and they had until the end of the day the following Monday to turn in their answers. That was truly one lost weekend for me. I got less than eight hours sleep from Friday until Monday afternoon as I struggled to identify the issues and answers in the problems the professor had posed for us. The problem with such an examination is that the student tends to try to find the answers by reading and rereading the cases and materials, thus wasting a lot of time that could be more productively spent thinking about the problem and relying on what you knew or learned about the subject earlier.

In January 1955 we moved into better living quarters than we had the previous year. Hoosier Courts were just across the street from the trailer courts. They were World War II type two-story barracks with eight two-bedroom units in each. We soon found a lady who lived in one of the nearby Hoosier Courts units to care for our two boys while Dorothy Ann returned to her job at the dental school. The babysitter, whose name was Madaliane Abner, was the wife of a graduate student named David Abner. Dorothy's return to work greatly improved our financial situation and permitted us to buy our first television set in the fall of 1955.

We decided to remain in Bloomington the summer of 1955.

That enabled me to take the commercial law course during the summer semester, which lightened the course load I would face in the final two semesters. The wives of several graduate students operated a co-op nursery school near Hoosier Courts and we thought it would be a good idea to enroll Rudy there for the summer months. We thought he needed to spend more time with other kids his age. After all he was now three and a half years old and could benefit from the experience of interacting with people outside his family. He was very excited about being in nursery school and could hardly wait to tell us about the activities and new friends he made there. One day in early June he ran home so excited that he could hardly contain himself, exclaiming as he ran up the street to our apartment "Daddy! Daddy! the 'nigeroes' are here!" It turns out that two or three other black kids had been enrolled in the nursery school that day by school teachers from the South who had come up to Bloomington for the summer to continue pursuit of graduate degrees at Indiana university. We had thought little about it before but then realized that Rudy had been the lone black kid at the nursery school until then and he was glad to see someone there who looked like him.

Just as the demographics of Rudy's nursery school changed when the summer semester began, so did the profile of the Indiana University student body. As you walked around the campus you would see many more black students. When the regular school year ended Indiana University became a destination for many black teachers and educators working in segregated secondary schools and historically black colleges in the South. They came to I. U. to study for post-graduate degrees. There was a great demand throughout the South at colleges like Arkansas A. M. & N. for black teachers with advanced degrees, especially the Ph.D. degree. Usually pay scales of black teachers and administrators were directly linked to the level of your post-graduate education—the higher your degree, the higher your pay. Also, the black colleges' accreditation somehow was affected by the number of persons with terminal degrees on its faculty. If a high percentage of the college's faculty had the Ph.D. degree, that fact would be used to promote the school in its efforts to attract students and other support for the school. Being at I. U. in the summer therefore presented opportunities for networking among black students far greater than during the regular school year.

*   *   *

The top editorial staff of the law journal in the senior year is selected from among those who had been chosen as junior writers at the end of the first year of law school. The top job on the law journal, editor-in-chief, for the year 1955-56 went to Vern E. Sheldon from Ft. Wayne, Indiana. The second most important position, article and book review editor, went to the academic leader of the class, Shirley S. Abrahamson. I was fortunate to be selected one of four note editors. The other three were Paul Arnold from Evansville, Robert W. Miller from Anderson and Charles R. Tiede from Wabash, Indiana. Again, I had reason to be proud of the honor of being in such a select group of my third year classmates. As a note editor and a published writer, I would be responsible for assisting the new class of junior writers in their efforts to prepare a publishable note for the journal.

In the meantime I had, myself, chosen to write a second note. The subject was a more controversial one, dealing with constitutional law issues associated with criminal prosecutions under the Smith Act, a law passed by Congress to proscribe subversive activities and threats to national security. The law's primary targets were members of the Communist Party. In 1951 the United States Supreme Court had held the Smith Act was a constitutional exercise of Congressional power, notwithstanding the fact that it clearly prohibited conduct that might be protected under the freedom of speech provisions of the First Amendment. The law prohibited "advocacy" or "teaching" the overthrow of government by force or violence, and "membership" in organizations engaged in such activities. In upholding the validity of the Smith Act in the Dennis case the court obviously had great difficulty in reconciling the statute with principles it had announced in previous First Amendment cases involving free speech issues. In my note I undertook an examination of the government's cases against defendants charged with Smith Act violations subsequent to the Supreme Court's decision in the Dennis case. My note was pub-

102

lished under the title "Post-Dennis Prosecutions Under the Smith Act" in *31 Indiana Law Journal 104.*

I earned better grades in my final year of law school than the year before. I got one "A" in the seminar in titles; a "B" in the domestic relations, wills, anti-trust and labor law courses; and a "C" in the courses in taxation and procedure. As time for graduation approached I increasingly devoted attention to what I should do after law school. First, of course, was the matter of successfully completing the bar examination and gaining admission to the bar. I decided early on that I would take the Indiana bar examination. Taking the Indiana bar clearly was the most prudent thing to do since I knew more about the law of that state than any other. In all the classes at some point we learned about the rules of law followed by the courts in Indiana, which occasionally differed from rules followed elsewhere, either procedurally or substantively, on a particular point of law. The earliest opportunity for taking the Indiana bar examination after graduation in June would be the following October. I figured I would need the intervening time to study my law school notes and prepare for the ordeal of taking the examination.

My greatest immediate concern was finding a means of earning a living. Paying the rent and putting food on the table had been a struggle throughout the past four and a half years, and the size of the family had doubled in that period. I strongly felt the need to earn money right away. That made the option of setting myself up in private practice somewhere not a very attractive one because of the time it would take to get established. There was a real risk of not earning income in the initial period of private practice, and there would be up front out of pocket costs as well. Nevertheless, I felt compelled to explore the possibilities for private practice.

Many of the top students in the class, especially my colleagues on the law journal editorial board, received offers for employment from the leading law firms in the state, or from lawyers practicing in the cities and towns where they grew up. Some of my classmates had family ties or other connections that more or less naturally opened up job opportunities. My situation was quite different from that of nearly all of my classmates. I had not grown up in Indiana and had no family there. Besides, I knew no one of any consequence in the state. I realized that my chances of joining one of the major white Indiana law firms were not very good. To my knowledge no white firm in the state had ever hired a black associate. I did think, however, that one of the really big firms in Indianapolis like Ross, McCord, Ice & Miller might take a chance on hiring someone like me—a person ranked high in the class academically, a member of the law review, and a published note editor in the Indiana Law Journal. Just maybe one of them wanted to break new ground and be a "first" to do something for the cause of equal opportunity. Therefore I sent my resume to several of the top firms shortly after the start of my last semester early in 1956. Not one of them gave me the courtesy of a reply. My inquiries about employment to major companies in Detroit and New York did produce responses but no favorable results. The responses from each of the firms were nearly identical; "We have no vacancies in our law department now but will keep you in mind if something opens up in the future."

I knew of two fairly prominent black lawyers in Indianapolis and made appointments to see them both. Neither of them was in a position to take on a newly minted lawyer and an obligation to pay that person some kind of salary while he got himself established in the practice. I continued discussions with one of these lawyers about a possible arrangement for more than a year, but we never could come to a definitive agreement. Also, I looked briefly into a possible arrangement with an older lawyer who was contemplating retirement in the small town of Richmond in eastern Indiana. Here again, my need for immediate income because of my family situation, soon ruled out that prospect.

Throughout this period I did not seriously consider going back to Arkansas and opening a practice in the state where I was born and reared. Even today, after nearly fifty years, I have trouble justifying in my own mind why I did not consider more thoroughly the idea of returning to Arkansas. Unlike Indiana, I was known to many people in Arkansas and so was my family and my wife's family. Perhaps it would have been a struggle for a short while, but the demographics of Pine Bluff or Little Rock were much more favorable for me than any place in Indiana at that time. Furthermore, I had been inspired to enter law school by the example of Pine Bluff native Harold Flowers, a champion and fighter for the rights of black people in the South. Having been equipped with a law degree to enter that battle along side individuals like Flowers, I found myself obsessed with the immediate need to fulfill my obligations as a husband and father. I still regret my failure to assess fully all my possible options to enter private practice upon graduating from law school.

With the benefit of 20/20 hindsight 1956-57 was an ideal time for an ambitious, courageous, and bright young black lawyer interested in advancing the cause of racial justice and equality to enter the practice of law in the South. We were yet in the very early stages of implementing the Supreme Court's decision in *Brown* v. *Board of Education* in school systems throughout the South. Agitation for equal access to places of public accommodation was spreading throughout the South. Pressure was building for Congress to enact new civil rights laws to ensure voting and other citizenship rights for black citizens. The federal courts were busy issuing desegregation orders in interstate transportation systems. Indeed, as a nation we were on the threshold of the biggest revolution since the Civil War. The need for trained and committed black lawyers had never been greater.

I chose instead to follow a different career path and sought work as a lawyer in the federal government. Dean Leon Wallace clearly understood that my prospects for employment with Indiana law firms were not good and agreed to introduce me to several of his acquaintances who were lawyers with federal departments and agencies in Washington, D. C. I sat down with Dean Wallace in his office one afternoon and he went over a list of persons I should contact in Washington. He identified contacts at the Department of Justice, the Department of Agriculture, the Department of Labor, the Federal Communications Commission, the Federal Trade Commission, the National Labor Relations Board, the tax court and individuals on staff at the U. S. Senate and the U. S. House of Representatives. Dean Wallace agreed to write letters to each of these contacts apprising them of my plans to come to Washington to seek employment.

I decided to travel to Washington, D. C., during spring break the first week in April, 1956, so as to lose as little time as possible from classes. My sister Esther Smith kindly invited me to stay with her family while in Washington and I gladly accepted. The bus ride from Bloomington at this time of year was quite a scenic journey, especially that part through West Virginia and Pennsylvania. I had never been to this part of the country before. The twelve- to fourteen-hour ride gave me time to think about how I should approach the various people I was coming all this way to see about working as a lawyer in the federal government. I already knew that applicants for jobs as lawyers were not required to take the federal employment entrance examinations that persons seeking professional jobs in the regular civil service were required to take. Legal positions in the various government agencies were part of the excepted service. Your training in law school, successful bar examination and admission to the bar of a state, were considered sufficient qualifications for federal legal work. I decided to approach each interview as a challenge: how to convince a total stranger that among all the other interviewees I should be chosen to fill the position. That meant putting emphasis on my most favorable attributes—my excellent college and law school academic performance, my selection for law review, my published notes, my stable family situation (having a wife and two young children), the latter also being evidence of perseverance. I recalled also the advice my father gave me years ago when I was a young boy growing up in Jonesboro: he said, "Son when you talk to someone, no matter who it may be, stand tall and look them straight in the eye."

Dean Wallace told me that he knew some of the men on his list of referrals better than others and those may offer the best opportunities for job offers. His contacts at the Federal Trade Commission and the Federal Communications Commission were people he knew best. Naturally, I would try to schedule appointments first at these agencies, but I wanted most to go to work at the Department of Justice. Late in 1955 I got word of a Justice Department honors program. The honors program was a recruitment vehicle the department initiated to attract the top law school graduates of the major law schools around the country. I had submitted an application under that program earlier but was not selected. I assumed that my class ranking was not high enough or it may have been because the Indiana University law school was not among the schools the department chose to work with. Nevertheless, I set up interviews at the Department of Justice since the honors program was not the exclusive avenue to work there.

My sister and her husband Milton lived with their two chil-

106

dren, Milton, Jr., and Patricia, in Mayfair Mansions apartments in northeast Washington. Esther was on maternity leave from her job as an executive secretary at the Federal Trade Commission. Her husband, "Smitty," was a career postal employee. Their apartment was small but very well furnished. Mayfair Mansions was a very large complex of sturdily built brick buildings, each three stories high with twelve apartments in each. It was widely regarded as the finest apartment complex available to blacks in Washington, D. C. Many very prominent people lived there at the time, including some who went on to become quite famous leaders in business, government and the arts. It was an ideal place for families with young children. There were well-kept lawns between the apartment buildings where children could play under the watchful eyes of parents or babysitters. Each building had its own modern laundry facilities in the basement for tenants to use, and a large well-lighted parking area in the back. For those blacks who were not ready to buy a home of their own in Le Droit Park, Brookland/Woodridge or one of the other upscale areas that were beginning to open up for blacks in northwest Washington, Mayfair Mansions was the place to live.

Esther's husband, Milton K. Smith, was short in stature just like the McKinneys. He had a great smile and a kind and gentle manner. He too was from a large family and was a native Washingtonian. He loved his work as a mail sorter and supervisor at the main post office down by Union Station. He also had quite a reputation as a catcher for one of the softball teams in the post office amateur softball leagues. Esther had met Smitty a few years after she came to Washington during the war to work in the federal government. She had been recruited for secretarial work in government when she finished Johnson's Business School in Little Rock. They were married in 1950, about a year before my marriage to Dorothy Ann.

I was more impressed with Washington, the federal city, than I had been with Cleveland, Ohio the first time I saw it. The cherry trees along the tidal basin were beginning to blossom but had not reached their peak. Spring flowers were everywhere, and the streets were filled with tourist groups, many of them high school students on field trips to see the nation's capital. I had not seen streets as wide as Constitution and Pennsylvania Avenues before.

The capitol building is even more impressive when you see it live than on the picture postcards and news photos. The Sunday before I started my interviews the Smiths drove me around downtown to see all the magnificent government buildings and monuments. It was a damp and overcast day and I noticed what to me seemed to be a pink cast to the color of the stone of the Mellon Art Gallery on Constitution Avenue. The Smiths noted that that comment is made by most of the tourists seeing that building for the first time. They pointed out all the buildings along Constitution Avenue housing the agencies and departments I would visit that week. The Labor Department then was located on Constitution Avenue at 14th Street. Next door was the departmental auditorium and the Interstate Commerce Commission. In the rear of that building on Pennsylvania Avenue was the Federal Communications Commission. A few blocks down the street was the imposing Justice Department building, and at the corner of 6th Street and Constitution Avenue was the Federal Trade Commission.

Not all the government buildings along Constitution Avenue, however, were grand structures. From Seventeenth Street west on the south side of Constitution Avenue were several "temporary" World War II vintage barrack-like buildings that were totally out of character with neighboring buildings. I was told that these structures had been erected hurriedly in the early 1940s to house the huge influx of government workers to staff new bureaus and agencies that had been created for the war effort. They were still standing eleven years after the war ended, and were still in use. There were many vacant lots along the mall between the Capitol Building and the Washington Monument. The area along the south side of Constitution Avenue from Third Street to Fourth Street was filled with perhaps a dozen clay-surfaced tennis courts that came alive with players every afternoon around 4 o'clock. At that time there was no Air and Space Museum, no Museum of History and Technology, no Hirshhorn Museum and Sculpture Garden. The north side of Pennsylvania Avenue west from Fourth Street to Fourteenth Street was nothing but a string of low-rise small commercial establishments selling souvenirs and fireworks, photo shops, restaurants and similar businesses. The development of Pennsylvania Avenue as the corridor for grand inaugural parades would come years later.

I quickly realized that it is not a good idea to schedule job interviews at different government agencies too close together. Often Dean Wallace's contacts who had agreed to see me were not persons having the authority to make a hiring commitment. Usually they were supervisory lawyers looking to fill a position in their organization and were screening several applicants in an effort to identify which in his opinion were the best two or three of the entire group. The initial screener would make his recommendation to his superior who may still need to obtain approval from someone higher up in the chain of command. This meant that if your interview went very well and they were definitely interested, you probably would be asked immediately to see one or more higher ranking individuals. Given this favorable scenario one would be well advised to take advantage of such an offer right away. Having a conflicting appointment somewhere else put you at risk of giving the impression of not being terribly interested in the job by asking to come back later, and calling to reschedule your next appointment might offend your contact there as well. So the more people you were asked to see at a particular agency was a good sign that you made a favorable impression. I also found that if the first interview concluded with a simple referral to someone in the agency's personnel office with the suggestion that you fill out an application form, it probably meant the agency was not interested in hiring you.

My interviews at the Federal Communications Commission on Monday morning went very well, although I knew very little about what the FCC actually did. I got the impression the FCC might be interested in hiring me, but they were not prepared to make a decision right away. My next appointment was at the Federal Trade Commission, whose mission I knew more about as a result of the course in antitrust law I took the fall before. Here again, I think I made a good impression in the interviews. However, they too would require some time to decide whether to make me an offer. Time was something I felt I did not have a great deal of. I would be graduating in less than two months and very much wanted to have a definite job offer in hand by that time. I had not yet become discouraged, however, and remained confident that one or more of the subsequent job interviews would lead to an offer.

My optimism was rewarded when the very next interview I

had, at the Labor Department, went extremely well. Clearly the Department of Labor was looking to hire someone almost immediately. The person I saw first obviously had read about or had been briefed on my qualifications and liked what he saw. He spent most of the interview time probing my personal philosophy about the law and society, about my family, and my attitude about the prospect of living in the nation's capital. He escorted me down the hall to the office of his boss, the assistant solicitor of labor in charge of interpretations and opinions, a courtly looking gentleman with white hair and a thin mustache. He was the spitting image of someone whose picture I had seen often in the newspapers, the former Secretary of State Dean Acheson. His name was Harold Nystrom. The assistant solicitor explained to me why the department of labor's lawyers were in the "office of the solicitor," whereas their counterparts in most other agencies were in the "office of the general counsel." He assured me the functions of both were essentially the same. He instructed his subordinate to make sure that I completed all the necessary paperwork before leaving so that I would not have to make a return trip to Washington for that purpose at a later date. Although I had not received a job offer, I still felt like celebrating when I returned to Esther's apartment that evening.

After dinner the Smiths decided it would be a good time to show me one of the jewels of northwest Washington, Meridian Hill Park on 16th Street. We all got in Smitty's big Buick sedan for the drive across town. Their apartment on Jay Street Northeast was only a short distance from Kenilworth Avenue, which we took west to Benning Road past the large coal fired Pepco electric power generating station and the historic Langston Golf Course, where black golfers in Washington came to play. A few blocks beyond, Benning Road intersected with Florida Avenue which took us through another densely populated black area of town toward Howard University. From Florida Avenue we drove through the heart of the black community in Washington, U Street, perhaps the most famous street associated with blacks on the east coast outside of New York City. From Seventh Street all the way over to Sixteenth Street, U street was alive with people. Small black businesses were everywhere; movie theatres, restaurants, night clubs, beauty shops, book stores, jewelry stores, liquor stores, and other retail establishments of all sorts. In addition, there were offices for doctors, dentists, lawyers, the NAACP, Masonic lodges and fraternal orders of one kind or another. I was a little bit awed by the sight of U Street in the evening and continued to look back as we turned right at Sixteenth Street and headed for Meridian Hill Park.

We parked on the street near one of the entrances. At night the park was an enchanting place. It really is a large formal garden with fountains and wide paved pathways among all kinds of shrubs, flowers and small trees. From the southern entrance the park gently ascends from one level to the next for two or three city blocks. The retaining walls and park benches provide convenient places to sit while enjoying the surrounding beauty. All the foliage tend to muffle the sound of nearby traffic on 15th and 16th Streets, the two busy thoroughfares forming the eastern and western boundaries of the park. It is an oasis in the midst of the city, surrounded by tall apartment buildings, embassy chanceries and offices. The visit to Meridian Hill Park was a fitting end to what had been a very good day for me. I decided I could enjoy living and working in Washington, D. C.

My third day of interviews began with my appointment at the Department of Justice. I was directed to the office of Robert Aiken where I thought I had an appointment. When I got there they had no record of any appointment for me and knew nothing about my plans to see anyone there. I was totally baffled as I was certain that Aiken was the name of the person I had been referred to by Dean Wallace's contact at the Department of Justice. Obviously, there had been a mistake. It turned out to be my own mistake as I had written down in the notes of my telephone conversation with the Justice Department contact the name "Robert Aiken" when it should have been "Robert Aders." I was able nevertheless to set up appointments at the department for later that day with several persons in the civil division. Unfortunately, the civil division had already filled its quota of new recruits for the year. They did, however, refer my application papers to the internal security division which was strongly interested in having me in their appeals and research section. The bottom line, however, is that I came away from my appointments at Justice without a definite commitment for a job.

I returned to Bloomington and told Dorothy Ann all about my

trip to Washington and that I was fairly confident of receiving a job offer soon from one or more of the federal government agencies I had contacted. She seemed relieved and happy about the prospect of living in Washington. Early in May I received the offer from the Office of the Solicitor, U. S. Department of Labor, that I had anticipated. They wanted me to report for work in Washington on June 18, 1956, one week after graduation. Although I thought I would eventually get an offer from the Justice Department, and probably also from the FTC and the FCC, Dorothy and I agreed that I should not delay responding to the firm offer from the Solicitor of Labor. I accepted that offer immediately, and began planning for the move to Washington.

The last few weeks of law school seemed to go by very quickly. There were many things to do besides preparing for and completing the final examinations. I decided to send out announcements about my graduation only to a few relatives. I had not purchased any dress clothes for years and badly needed a new suit for graduation and to wear the first day on my new job at the Labor Department. We needed to get rid of most of the household items we had accumulated. The small amount of furniture we had was suitable for student living on campus but hardly acceptable for apartment living as professionals in Washington D. C. It was hardly a problem, however, to dispose of our household items. There always were plenty of recently married students moving up in class from the trailers to Hoosier Courts who needed more things for their larger new quarters.

Although she had not seen the place, on the basis of my description of Mayfair Mansions and its reputation, Dorothy Ann agreed that we should take a two-bedroom apartment there as soon as one became available. With my sister Esther's help the Mayfair Mansions management informed us that a two-bedroom unit would be available July 1, 1956. We made a deposit to reserve the apartment on Hayes Street right away. This meant, however, that Dorothy, Rudy and Fred probably would have to remain in Bloomington until the end of June, rather than travel with me to Washington shortly after graduation on June 11. Esther and Smitty again generously welcomed me to stay with them until we could get into our new apartment. Dorothy Ann was not at all pleased with having to stay behind and do all the last minute things that

112

are required to move the family out of Hoosier Courts. Although we had no furniture to move, we did have kitchen utensils, dishes, linens, clothes and other small items that had to be packed and shipped via railway express to Washington. Of course it would not be easy getting herself and two small children packed and ready for travel. It was small consolation to her that we decided she and the kids should travel first class by train from Bloomington to Washington, rather than by the much cheaper Trailways bus.

Graduation day was hot and sunny and the campus was filled with visiting parents and families. The commencement occasion generates mixed emotions, both for the graduates and for parents and family members. As a graduate I was elated to be over with classes and examinations, and felt great pride for having accomplished another important goal in my life—earning a graduate degree from a very good school. A tinge of sadness crept into my consciousness when I realized that many of the persons I had come to know as students I would never see again. For many parents the graduating son or daughter thereafter would establish their independence and separate identity and enter a different kind of relationship from the one that previously existed. Being relieved of the expense of college tuition and other costs would be like getting a raise in pay for many parents, and that indeed was something to be elated about.

I was somewhat disappointed that none of our relatives from Pine Bluff were able to come to the law school commencement ceremonies. At one point it appeared that my oldest sister Izora, who was then living in Cleveland, Ohio, might come but she called a few days before graduation to say she could not make it. But Dorothy Ann was there looking radiantly beautiful in her best spring outfit, with Rudy and Fred in tow.

Although several of my law school classmates were married, none of them had more that one kid at the time. So mine was the largest family among all the graduates. Having the largest family was a distinction I would have among my contemporaries throughout most of my career. In fact, the year before we had gone to church on Father's Day and the minister sought to identify first the youngest father in the audience. I won that honor hands down. He next asked fathers with the most children present to also stand. I won that distinction as well.

5

Getting Started in Washington

Obviously, Dorothy Ann and I had taken the biblical admonition "be fruitful and multiply" quite literally, but it was becoming more and more apparent that we soon needed to pay more attention to what was causing the frequent pregnancies and take more effective preventive measures. Two weeks after graduation Dorothy Ann broke the news to me that we were expecting again, early in 1957. I took the news quietly, with a sense of resignation and the feeling that like my father before me, I was to be "blessed" with many children. For some reason I did not then see any connection between family size, poverty, and economic success. Here we were with two children and another on the way just five years after getting married. If we continued at this rate Dorothy Ann and I would have almost as many children as Momma and Papa had by the time I was 40 years old. Because we both wanted to have a baby girl in the family and were hopeful that that wish would be fulfilled this time around, we were not too upset about the expected new addition. I was totally confident of being able to take care of my family, now that I was about to launch my career as a lawyer.

However, birth control methods increasingly became a matter for public discussion, not just a subject discretely to be explored in private between a woman and her physician. "The pill" had not been fully accepted in the American market in the mid-1950s and was surrounded with many uncertainties related to dangerous side effects as well. Dorothy Ann and I had no religious objections to any of the various methods of contraception, but were concerned about doing anything that might jeopardize her health. And so we felt compelled to take the added risks associated with the less reliable birth control methods. With this third pregnancy, for the first time we would not have the support of nearby close relatives that we enjoyed with the first two children. Moreover prenatal and postnatal care in Washington, D. C., certainly would be more expensive than what we experienced in Pine Bluff. Despite the prospect of better economic circumstances as a result of my working on a professional level for the first time, I began to realize that we simply had to do a better job of family planning than we had done in the past.

Completing an accredited law school does not by itself entitle one to all the privileges of being an "attorney." One becomes an attorney when he or she has been admitted to practice before the bar of one of the states or territories of the United States. One qualifies for admission to practice only after successfully completing the state's bar examination, a written test usually administered over a period of several days by a panel of lawyers under the authority of the state's highest court, and upon proof of the applicant's moral character and fitness to practice law. When I reported to work at the Office of the Solicitor, U.S. Department of Labor on June 18, 1956, I was not yet an attorney. The solicitor hired me as a "legal assistant" with the understanding that I would be converted to "attorney-advisor" status immediately after I passed the bar of some state. The pay of legal assistants was considerably less than that for attorney-advisors. My initial pay was at the rate provided for the first step of a Gs-5, at that time about $3,600 a year. Starting attorneys were classified at the Gs-7 level and commanded pay at the annual rate of $4,500. It turned out that our family income improved very little, if at all, in the first months after I took the Labor Department job. I had a tremendous incentive to pass the Indiana bar as soon as possible in order to qualify for the higher pay.

I was assigned initially to the Division of Interpretations and Opinions headed by C. Ira Funston. My immediate boss, however, was Vahan Moushegian, a Harvard graduate of Armenian extraction. The solicitor at the time was a man named Stuart Rothman, a presidential appointee from Madison, Wisconsin. The big boss, the Secretary of Labor, was James P. Mitchell from New Jersey. Mitchell and Rothman had been appointed by President Eisenhower; the lower level lawyers were career people who had served in the department for years under previous democratic administrations. The Solicitor of Labor was the official the secretary turned to when he needed legal advice in carrying out his responsibilities as the top man on labor matters in the administration. He also served as counsel to all the various administrations, offices and bureaus of the department that had been charged by Congress to administer the programs assigned to the department.

The principal "client" of the Interpretations and Opinions Division was the Administrator of the Wage and Hour and Public Contracts Division. This was the office responsible for enforcement of the Fair Labor Standards Act (FLSA), a law requiring employers engaged in interstate commerce or the production of goods for interstate commerce to pay minimum wages and a premium for work over 40 hours a week to their employees. The FLSA was a Depression Era law designed to help working men and women. The department maintained a network of regional offices throughout the country staffed by lawyers, investigators and other department officials, to ensure that employers complied with the law. My initial assignment was to prepare legal opinions in response to questions about how the law should apply in a given situation. Such questions came from a variety of sources, including employers, department personnel involved with enforcement, members of Congress on behalf of constituents, labor unions and others representing the interests of employees.

The FLSA had been on the books for twenty years when I joined the department. Nevertheless the issue that came up most frequently in litigation involved questions of coverage. Was the person doing the work an "employee" or an independent contractor? If the relationship between the person doing the work and the person for whom the work is done is that of an employee, then the employer can be held responsible for paying for the work in accordance with the requirements of the law. If instead the worker is held to be an independent contractor, the entity for whom the work is done may avoid the obligations the law imposes on employers. In the early days of the law small businesses especially went to great lengths to structure their operations in such a way as to avoid having to pay minimum and overtime wages.

Some of the most troublesome cases involved people working at home to make items that are sold by others. Also, in 1956 questions as to whether a business or commercial activity was "in interstate commerce" and thus subject to federal regulatory authority still could be raised legitimately. In a fairly short time I became quite proficient in the law relating to what constitutes an employer-employee relationship. I also got the chance to immerse myself again in the Supreme Court cases which delineated the boundaries of Congress' authority under the interstate commerce clause of the Constitution. I had to do this in order to write opinions, for example, as to whether some small sawmill in Kentucky that cut logs from a local forest and processed it into lumber to supply the surrounding area builders was engaged in interstate commerce within the meaning of the FLSA.

The division maintained an extensive library which included opinions that attorneys had written in previous years under the program. It was imperative to review these precedents in preparing your own opinions. In my research I learned that many distinguished lawyers had preceded me in the division as their names showed up on many of the old opinions—names like Archibald Cox and Joseph L. Rauh.

The work of doing research and writing legal opinions the summer of 1956 fit in well also with what I needed to do to prepare myself to take the Indiana bar examination in October. I tried to set aside a little time every evening to review the notes I had prepared for all my law school classes. Often on Saturday I would go down to my office at the department and spend several hours studying for the bar examination. My bosses in the Solicitor's office were very understanding and did everything they could to be helpful. The solicitor had a habit of coming to the office on Saturday and Sunday or checking the log-in sheets one had to sign for admittance to the building on those days. He was from the old school of lawyers who believed that young lawyers especially could not possibly do the work they had to do in an eight-hour day or a forty-hour week. So if you were frequently seen in your office after normal working hours, you were Rothman's kind of lawyer and he remembered that when evaluation and promotion time came around. Although I did not realize it at the time, the hours I spent studying in the office on evenings and weekends registered with Rothman as extra working time on my part. Perhaps that is one reason why the paperwork on my promotions were promptly approved in the front office.

The unit I served in had six to eight attorneys working under Vahan Moushigian. One of the older, more experienced lawyers in

117

the unit, a man named J. Douglas Carmack, was assigned to be my mentor and help orient me to the work. I shared a large office with Carmack and another newly hired attorney from Scranton, Pennsylvania, named John Schrankel. The entire unit operated out of four adjacent offices that overlooked Constitution Avenue on the fourth floor of the Labor Department building. While the work we did was in support of the program having perhaps the broadest national impacts of all Labor Department programs, our unit was not the most prestigious one in the Solicitor's office. Two other units were in fierce competition for that honor—the Division of Legislation and the Division of Litigation. Each of these divisions was headed by a woman—Edith N. Cook in legislation and Bessie Margolin in litigation. The legislation division was the so-called policy shop of the Solicitor's office. Their lawyers tended to come from the best law schools and had the reputation of being proficient at conceptualizing programs and coming up with new policy ideas for the department.

Bessie Margolin had a well-deserved reputation as an advocate in cases before the U. S. Supreme Court, having argued successfully many of the department's cases that reached that ultimate stage of litigation. She had assembled a team of lawyers trained and experienced in appellate advocacy. The nuts and bolts work of putting cases together and conducting trials in the district courts was done by the regional attorneys and trial lawyers in offices throughout the nation.

A fourth unit of the Solicitor's office handled matters concerning prevailing wage determinations on federally assisted construction projects and federal procurement contracts. Prevailing wage determinations were activities which were of great interest to organized labor, especially in those parts of the country that were not highly unionized. The head of this unit had perhaps the most politically sensitive job in the office because his decisions usually brought him into conflict on a very practical level between powerful union and construction industry forces. Lawyers assigned to this division tended to be more akin to the small town general practice attorney, accustomed to dealing with real world legal problems. They were likely to be graduates of law school evening programs, obtaining their law degree while working full time at some other job.

During the first few weeks after going to work at the Solicitor's office I was introduced to most of the key people, but there was no formal orientation program. I noticed two other black lawyers on the staff. James E. Jones came on board shortly before me and had been assigned to work in the legislation unit. I soon discovered that he too was from Arkansas. He was a graduate of Dunbar High School in Little Rock, had gone to college at Lincoln University in Jefferson City, Missouri, obtained a masters degree in labor relations and later a law degree from the University of Wisconsin law school. James E. Jones was hired as an attorney, not a legal assistant, as he had already been admitted to the bar, I believe in Wisconsin. The other black lawyer was Howard Jenkins, a native of Colorado. Mr. Jenkins, who appeared to be ten or twelve years older than I, had been a professor at Howard University law school before coming to the Solicitor's office a few years earlier. I believe he was the highest ranking black lawyer in the office. He too worked in the legislation division. Both Jones and Jenkins became very close personal friends and remain so to this day, though our careers eventually took very different paths.

I never developed a close personal friendship with other lawyers who were in my unit at the time I joined the Solicitor's office. Our relationships were quite cordial, but did not extend beyond our interactions in the office. Men in my unit in addition to Schrankel, Carmack, Moushegian, and Funston, included a very bright young lawyer named Eli Bernzweig, and a very reserved older lawyer named Harry Tuell. I was able to learn a lot about some of the lawyers just from our casual conversations in the office. Schrankel came from a devout Catholic family in Pennsylvania, but he appeared to harbor grave doubts about some of the teachings of that faith. For example, he said many times that he did not see the need to observe the injunction against eating meat on Fridays, as his parents had done before him. He was married to the daughter of a very prominent elected official from Tennessee and had briefly practiced law in that state after completing law school. He insisted that he would continue practicing birth control methods that were forbidden to Catholics, until such time as the church agreed to help pay the costs of raising children born as a result of accidental or unwanted pregnancies.

Schrankel got a big charge out of telling the story about one of the first clients that came to his law office in a small Tennessee town. The man wanted to file for bankruptcy. When Schrankel inquired about how the client planned to pay for his services and was told he had no money, Schrankel advised him to go to the bank across the street, borrow enough money to pay his legal fees and then to come back to see him.

Moushegian did not talk much about personal matters. I did learn that he had a young family and maintained a summer house at Bethany Beach, Delaware. Some thirty-five years later I had occasion to meet his son while visiting my youngest daughter and her husband at Fort Stewart, Georgia. My son-in-law, who was an army officer in the judge advocates corp stationed at Fort Stewart, told me that his commanding officer was a lawyer, a Colonel Moushegian from the Washington, D. C., area. I told my son-in-law I was willing to bet the colonel was related to my old boss at the Labor Department because that name is not very common. The moment I saw him at a base party I knew I was right, even though I had not seen or heard from Vahan Moushegian in over twenty years. It was a pleasure for me to tell the colonel about how his father and I had met at the start of my legal career in Washington in 1956.

*   *   *

In setting up and furnishing our new apartment in Mayfair Mansions I felt like we were establishing a permanent residence for the first time in our marriage. This was reflected in the type of furniture we shopped for. No more milk crate coffee tables and make-shift beds. We chose to buy our things at the William E. Miller furniture store over on Pennsylvania Avenue southeast, not far from the Capitol Building. We had no trouble establishing our credit with the store, which we definitely would need in order buy all the furniture we required. Real furniture is expensive and there was no way we could pay cash. Having a government job and the promise of a steady, if not large, income was sufficient security for the furniture store. Our apartment had two large bedrooms, one bath, a large living room, a separate dining room and a small galley kitchen complete with refrigerator, gas oven and range. We felt there was plenty of room for our family of four. When the new baby came our bedroom provided adequate space for her crib, which later could be moved to the living room if necessary. The two boys therefore would have a bedroom for themselves. Most importantly, we got the apartment for an affordable price. The monthly rent was only $85.00, including heating, water and electricity. The one inconvenience about it was there was no air conditioning. However, it was designed with large double hung windows on opposite sides so that by opening windows on each side you created a gentle breeze through the apartment. This breeze could be enhanced in summer by the addition of a large electric fan in the dining room window.

We were surrounded by very friendly neighbors in Mayfair Mansions. The Chappelle family lived directly across the hall. They were an older couple whose teenage son attended Spingarn High School. Mr. Chappelle worked at one of the hotels near Capitol Hill. His wife worked at the Bureau of Standards. I came to know a lot about the Chappelles because I helped them do their income tax returns each year. Tony and Dorothy Duncanson lived with their two young sons, Tony, Jr., and Eric, in the apartment above ours. Big Tony was an engineer who worked for a firm in New York involved with developing machines called "computers," which did miraculous things with numbers. His was a very good job that paid well above what most government workers earned at that time. His wife Dorothy was from a large North Carolina family and had graduated from Bennett College in Greensboro, North Carolina. She did not work outside the home. The apartment below ours was occupied by Wilber and Thelma Griffin, a young recently married couple with an infant child. Wilber had ambitions of becoming a dentist but had not yet been able to negotiate the rigorous academic training that was required. Thelma was a very attractive woman with a friendly manner. Whenever she stepped outside their apartment to lounge on the front steps, men both young and old emerged from nearby apartments to catch a breath of fresh air also, or to cast an appreciative eye on all the natural beauty around.

We got acquainted early on also with two other families who lived in the building across the parking lot from our apartment. John Goins, a lawyer who worked for the Internal Revenue Service, lived with his wife Joyce and two children in the apartment near Mr. and Mrs. Williams, an older couple from Jamaica. John Goins was a golfer who went to the Langston Golf Course up on Benning Road nearly every afternoon after work. Mrs. Williams took to Dorothy Ann right away, offering advice on everything from child rearing to tips on dressmaking. Mr. Williams was a master tailor who worked in the alterations department of one of the finest men's clothing stores downtown. Another couple we met were Hosea and Maudine Taylor. They lived in the building that faced ours across the expanse of well-kept lawn with their two daughters about the same age as our sons. Mr. Taylor was a scientist who worked at the National Institutes of Health. The Taylors were avid bridge players, but kind and patient enough to teach the game to Dorothy Ann and me.

It was largely through Dorothy Ann's initiative that we met most of our neighbors that summer because I was not home that much. I usually left home to catch the bus at Kenilworth Avenue and Hayes Street Northeast around eight o'clock in the morning and did not return until six in the evening. Nearly all my spare time in the evening and on weekends was spent studying for the bar examination. During the day Dorothy Ann found interesting things to do with Rudy and Fred. She was not deterred by the fact that we had no car. She would not hesitate to go exploring with them on the bus around the city. One week it would be a morning at the National Zoo. Another it would be an afternoon at the Smithsonian or Rock Creek Park. Occasionally, other young mothers and their children would join her in these excursions. I felt good about finally being in position to support my family from my own earnings, but there still was a problem in that there were so many things we needed and wanted that still were beyond my reach from a financial standpoint. With two young sons we badly needed a car to get around. While it did not seem to bother Dorothy Ann, I was embarrassed to have to take my family everywhere on public transportation. But I was determined to finish paying for our new furniture before buying a car. I did not like it that I could not simply tell my wife to go shopping for a new outfit whenever there was a special occasion we had to attend, such as a wedding or a fraternity party. I knew Dorothy was a good seamstress and could make almost any fancy dress she wanted, but as a new attorney I felt deep down that I should be able to afford such things myself. However, I remained hopeful that things would be better as soon as I passed the bar and was admitted to practice law.

A couple we had known in Bloomington, Jim and Hattie Brown, called to say that two of their relatives would be visiting Washington a couple of days in August and needed a place to stay. We told Jim and Hattie that we would be pleased to have them stay with us. They were coming mainly to see the monuments and other tourist attractions of Washington and just needed somewhere to sleep. They came and we all had a very good time in the crowded McKinney household. For the life of me I cannot remember the names of our visitors from Indianapolis. Like so many other things in my life, something unexpected turns out to be a stroke of good fortune. I had to return to Indianapolis early in October to take the bar exam and would need a place to stay those three days. Paying for hotel accommodations was out of the question so my only option was to find a friend who would put me up. When this matter happened to come up in conversation, our visitors from Indianapolis offered to let me bunk with them when I came back for the bar examination. Their house was in the heart of the black community near downtown Indianapolis and it would be no problem getting to and from the state government building where the exam was to be administered.

One other member of the I. U. Law school class of 1956 took a job in Washington that summer. Bob Miller who had served with me on the law review took a job at the Federal Communications Commission. Bob was from Anderson, Indiana, he had a car and planned to drive back to Indianapolis to take the bar exam. Bob also was a good friend. Occasionally we would study together for classes and during the summer of 1956 we sometimes met and discussed the subjects we thought would come up on the bar examination. I offered to share car expenses and he welcomed me to come along with him on the drive back to Indianapolis. Bob was one of the few unmarried members of the class of 1956. Although I did not know them, his family seemed to be fairly well to do and ran a small manufacturing business in Anderson that made playground equipment.

We decided to leave Washington for Indianapolis in the evening and make the trip at night. Driving at night avoided heavy traffic on the highway, but it also meant we would miss one less day of work. In 1956 we were in the very beginning stages of planning and building the interstate highway system. At that time the best route to Indianapolis from Washington was to take Highway 70 north through Frederick, Hagerstown, and Hancock, Maryland, picking up Highway 40 west. We followed Highway 40 all the way to Indianapolis, driving through Cumberland, Uniontown, Pennsylvania, Wheeling, West Virginia, across Ohio and on into Indiana. Highway 40 was not a limited access road. Over much of the 560 mile distance it was only one lane in each direction. The trip to Indianapolis took us about fourteen hours, which meant reaching our destination mid-morning the following day. Bob dropped me off at the house where I planned to stay and drove on to his parents' home in Anderson, only a few miles northeast of Indianapolis. From where my hosts lived, I believe on Northwest Street, one could see the downtown section of the city where the state office building was located.

Throughout my three-year stay in Indiana I had visited Indianapolis only two or three times. We had visited Jim and Hattie Brown once after they became teachers in the Indianapolis public school system in the summer of 1955; I had gone there to buy the suit I was to wear for graduation at the William H. Block's Department Store; I had gone there for my pre-employment interview with attorney Robert Lee Brokenburr, a prominent black Republican whose endorsement I needed to obtain as the final step of being hired by the U.S. Department of Labor. I was not that familiar with the city, but did not anticipate having any problem getting to where I needed to go from my hosts' house.

The bar examination was a two-day affair, eight hours each day. I don't recall seeing any other blacks in the room where we took the examination. I was quite nervous at first but overcame it as soon as I started trying to sort out my answers to the first set of questions. Nearly all of my classmates were there, having made the same decision I did to take the Indiana bar first, even if their first legal job was in another state. While nearly everyone from the class of 1956 was there for the bar exam, we did not do much socializing with each other. The bar exam really is a kind of competition among all the examinees. In most states a fairly high percentage of all the persons taking the bar examination fail the test the first time they take it. In Indiana the failure rate was not that high, around twenty to twenty-five percent. In states like California and New York the failure rate is much higher, as much as fifty percent in some years. So each person taking the exam tends to cast a wary eye on everyone else as a competitor, hoping to avoid becoming one of the minority of candidates who surely would fail the examination. Unlike some who had the luxury of working in their father's law firm where failing the first time was not necessarily a disaster, I had to pass the first time. My family situation and my job depended on the results. These were indeed great motivators; much like the motivations I had had all my life to succeed in school or face the prospect of following behind a mule, picking cotton or being relegated to some other menial work for the rest of my life.

As I look back, failure to pass the bar exam that October may not have been the catastrophe I imagined at the time. Almost certainly, the Solicitor would have given me a chance to take the bar again either in Indiana or in some other state. I did not allow myself to make any contingency plan because I thought it would indicate I had some doubt about my ability to succeed the first time. I never considered other possible career options in the event I failed to gain admission to practice law in some state. Since 1956 I have met many men and women who finished law school but never could pass any state's bar examination. Others only succeeded after several attempts over many years. Some wound up being successful in other fields, but most viewed their failure to pass the bar to be a stain upon their record that was difficult, if not impossible, to forget.

On our way back to Washington Bob Miller and I talked about the bar exam experience. We each tried to recall how we handled certain questions. If I could not recall identifying what Bob thought was an issue hidden in one of the exam problems, this would heighten my anxiety about how well I had done on the test. Bob would feel the same if his answer did not encompass something I thought the examiners were looking for. Pretty soon we decided it was best to put the exam behind us and not discuss it further. There was nothing either of us could do after the fact to change anything. We would just have to wait to see the letter from the board of bar examiners telling us whether we passed or failed.

We promised to call each other as soon as we got the results, whether the news was good or bad.

My letter from the Indiana Board of Bar Examiners came in the mail six weeks after the examination. Dorothy Ann called me at the office to say an official looking letter was there and asked whether I wanted her to open and read it to me over the telephone. I said "yes" without any hesitation. I knew the result as soon as she began to read the first line of the letter, "We are pleased to inform you . . ." I had passed the Indiana Bar Examination! The exhilaration I felt at that moment was overwhelming. It was a feeling almost like what I experienced when Rudy was born. There was a mixture of pride and relief; pride in having reached another important goal in my life; relief in knowing that I would not have to face the embarrassment of explaining failure to colleagues and friends. The newspapers of record in every state publish the names of every person who passes the state's bar examination as soon as the results are announced. I did not want to have to take calls from people I knew in Indiana or elsewhere about not seeing my name on the list. Now I didn't have to worry about that anymore. I called Bob Miller right away. He had not seen his mail that day so he didn't know what his results were. He promised to call me at home that evening if his letter from the bar examiners had come. He told me later that he too had passed.

Of course I told all my supervisors the good news and inquired as to when I could expect the raise in pay associated with passing the bar examination. I was reminded that that would come as soon as I was formally admitted by the courts in Indiana. I had completely overlooked that part of the letter from the examiners that described the next steps in the process of admission. First I had to appear in person in Indianapolis for an interview with an official of the Indiana bar. That interview was for the purpose of assessing my character and fitness to practice law. If the bar official found me to be of good moral character I would then be certified to appear before the Indiana Supreme Court for admission on December 5, 1956.

The following day I called the board of examiners to see if I could schedule my character and fitness interview a day or two before December 5 so that I could take care of everything on one trip back to Indianapolis. I was much relieved when he agreed since there was nothing in my background to indicate there might be a problem. Again I rode with Bob Miller on the automobile trip to Indianapolis. The character and fitness interview came off without a hitch and on Wednesday, December 5, I, along with all the other successful candidates, was sworn in before the Indiana Supreme Court. Unfortunately, no one from my family was there to witness this important milestone in my life. The celebration was postponed until my return to Washington, where Esther, Smitty, Pat and Milton joined Dorothy Ann, Rudy, Fred and me, along with a few neighbors to mark the occasion.

*   *   *

Dorothy Ann was well along in her third pregnancy in the fall of 1956. She enrolled in a class for expectant mothers at Georgetown University Hospital all the way across town because that is where we decided our new baby would be delivered. She would go to Georgetown University Hospital for medical checkups and to receive information about the latest child care practices every three or four weeks.

Soon after Christmas and New Years holidays her mother came up to Washington to help take care of Fred and Rudy when the time came for Dorothy to go to the hospital. That time came somewhat sooner than I expected. Just before bedtime on Thursday, January 17, Dorothy Ann said she was experiencing slight pains at irregular intervals. Nevertheless, we went to bed thinking that since, according to our calculations, she was not due for another week or ten days the pains probably would subside. I was hoping that she could hold off at least until a more convenient time the next morning. She woke me up at about 1 o'clock A.M. to say we should head for the hospital. I got dressed and called a taxi for the journey across town. We arrived at Georgetown Hospital shortly after 2 o'clock A.M. After the doctor on duty in the maternity ward had examined Dorothy he said she was quite a ways from being ready to deliver and strongly suggested that we return home as it might be days, rather than hours before she was ready. I was not about to question the doctor's judgment on such a matter, so we decided to save money and took the bus rather than a taxi back to Mayfair Mansions.

127

As the two of us sat quietly on the bus Dorothy Ann observed how beautiful the night sky was. It was indeed a crisp, cold and clear January evening. Then she said something about feeling as Mary and Joseph must have felt as they traveled to Bethlehem the night before Jesus' birth. I did not think that last remark was funny. We rode the rest of the way home in silence.

We had not been in bed more than thirty of forty minutes before Dorothy Ann again awakened me to say it was time to go and this time there was great urgency in her tone of voice. So at about 4:30 A.M. we went through the whole process again, except that it took longer this time for me to get a taxi to come to our apartment. We arrived at the hospital before daybreak and I was determined not to leave until after the baby was born. It was not a false alarm. Dorothy Ann delivered a healthy, good-looking, bald-headed baby girl at about 9 o'clock Friday morning, January 18, 1957. Our fondest wish had been granted.

Dorothy Ann and the baby were released from the hospital on Sunday. When we arrived home Fred and Rudy were quite excited and curious about this new baby girl coming into the household. Rudy wanted to hold her right away but Fred was more reluctant. I think he sensed that he was about to be displaced. We had decided before that if it was a girl we would give her the name "Anne Marie," the Marie to honor one of Dorothy Ann's aunts on her mother's side. I could hardly wait to get back to work on Monday to show off pictures of Anne Marie that were taken before leaving the hospital. She was really an alert and beautiful baby and I was extremely proud of becoming a father for the third time. At that time it was customary for the new father to give a cigar to each of his friends and office colleagues. This was a luxury I could now afford.

*   *   *

1957 was one of the most difficult years of my life. It started on a very high note with the birth of our first daughter in January. There were other positive things as well that occurred that year. I got my first paycheck at the higher Gs-7 grade the first week in January. Nine months later the solicitor promoted me again to the Gs-9 level, indicating that my work had been more than satisfac-

128

tory and they wanted me to remain with the office. My father came to visit for the first time in July. We had not seen him for over three years. His visit allowed him to spend quality time with Dorothy and the kids. I too had a chance to relax with him for hours in the evening, talking about his family and what it was like for him growing up in the early 1900s.

That year Congress decided to address the racial problems that were threatening to split the country apart by passing the first civil rights bill in decades. I was so caught up in reports of the political struggles in the House and Senate to keep the bill alive in the face of the most intense opposition from many Southern lawmakers that I was moved to write a letter to the editor of the Washington Post. In my letter I decried some of the compromises the Senate majority leader, Lyndon Johnson, made concerning voting rights protections, but said even a watered-down bill would be better than no bill at all.

My spirit was lifted most of all at Father's Day that year by a handwritten note my wife gave to me, which she had Rudy and Fred scribble their names to also. The note reads:

Father's Day

Dearest Mac:

This day marks the end of the happiest year of my life. You've been everything I could possibly desire of the father of my children: loving, fraternal, a good provider. Especially the little things I hold dear and I know in later years they will appreciate all the more. Walks on Sunday afternoon, worship together, the picnics, zoo and watching television, too. The rough play, how they have loved that and the times you carried them shopping and cutting their hair, polishing their shoes, bathing them. Thank you! You've been a grand Dad to your children. Our lives revolve around you. You are the vortex of importance to us. We are proud of you and love you dearly. Happy father's day.

Signed,
Dorothy, Rudy, Warren & Anne

When I read the note I felt reassured that ours was an intact family. My career seemed to be on track. Dorothy Ann seemed

129

happy. The kids were developing nicely in every respect. I felt blessed. A month later our blissful life suddenly fell apart. Dorothy Ann lost control and fell into a state of deep depression. On August 3 she was admitted to Freedmen's Hospital where she remained for a month. Hers was an illness I did not fully understand. Physically she appeared to be fine. There was no fever, no trauma, nothing that could be fixed by surgery or medication. She seemed to become a different person almost overnight. She seemed to lose interest in the kids, especially the baby who was barely six months old. I was totally devastated. I was fearful that all the plans we had about the future may have to be changed. Suddenly I realized that all was not lost. Dorothy Ann had always been there for me in crisis situations that I personally faced. It was now time for me to be strong and there for her in this crisis in her life. I had to continually tell myself that she was ill with a different kind of sickness; that she could recover with proper love and care from me and our families. Throughout the six years of our marriage we had been extremely fortunate to have a family support system that was second to none.

My first move was to put Dorothy Ann under the care of Dr. E. Y. Williams, the leading psychiatric practitioner at the Howard University medical school. Next her parents consented to bring Dorothy Ann's younger sisters, Jo Marva and Gail to Washington to stay with me for the remainder of the summer to help with the kids. This was a godsend as otherwise I would have been forced either to take extended leave from work or to pay someone locally to come in during the day to take care of the kids. I was particularly concerned about the impact of Dorothy's absence on Anne Marie. Rudy and Fred I felt were old enough to cope with the situation much better, although I knew being deprived of their mother's everyday attention could have damaging effects on them as well.

After Jo Marva and Gail arrived I was able to return to work. However, my heart was not in it. Throughout the month of August, 1957 I would leave work and go directly to the hospital to spend time with Dorothy Ann. At least once a week I would meet with Dr. Williams to discuss Dorothy Ann's therapy and get his assessment of her progress toward recovery. Things went very slowly the first couple of weeks. By week three she was permitted one 12-hour visit at home on Sunday so that she could see the kids and begin reconnecting with our home environment. At the end of her hospital stay we decided it would be best for her and the kids to go to Pine Bluff in September when Jo Marva and Gail returned home to begin school. While this would mean having to miss several days of follow-up therapy with Dr. Williams, she would be in familiar surroundings with family. Hopefully this would speed up her recovery.

My family remained in Pine Bluff for two months. During their absence I usually put in twelve-hour days at the office because I found being immersed in work seemed to make the days go by faster. Being alone allowed me time to try to figure out what I might have done to precipitate Dorothy's illness. More importantly, I wanted to know what I needed to do to remove whatever cause there might be and to take the necessary corrective measures. Dr. Williams tried to reassure me by explaining that women frequently experience depression in the weeks and months following childbirth and that her illness may not have been preventable.

I took leave for two weeks at the end of October and went to Pine Bluff to see my family, hoping that they would be able to return with me to Washington. Soon after returning to Pine Bluff, Dorothy Ann got involved with the A. M. & N. Alumni Association and other organizations and these activities seemed to speed up her recovery. She decided to run for "Miss Arkansas A. M. & N. Alumni" during homecoming that year. That primarily involved raising money to support the school; the person raising the most money becoming Miss A. M. & N. Alumni for that year. She worked hard and raised a lot of money but did not win the contest.

While I was home Professor Harding B. Young invited me to come and speak to his accounting class about my law school experience and budding legal career. I was delighted to do it. I wanted to see what the new crop of students at A. M. & N. was like, to find out if they were as well motivated as students were when I was there. They had lots of questions and seemed interested in the things I had to say. I remember quite clearly one question and my response. The question was what undergraduate course did I find to be most essential to success as a law student. My answer was the course in English and English composition. Most students seemed surprised by my answer. They apparently had expected me to say political science or government courses. I explained to them my view that being able to communicate ideas well is of overriding importance, especially in the practice of law. I also told them that my debating experience had been very helpful and I highly recommended that students participate in that program as well.

I had learned earlier that my law school friend and classmate Vern Sheldon had gone into the army shortly after our graduation and was then stationed at the Pine Bluff arsenal. I got in touch with him and his wife Libby. Dorothy Ann and I made a date for them to join us on the A. M. &. N. campus for the "stunt night" program during the homecoming festivities. We were delighted to see them and we had a good time talking about past experiences together and what we saw for ourselves in the years ahead. Vern said he would at the end of his tour of duty go back to his hometown in Indiana to practice law. That is exactly what he did, becoming very successful at the practice and later a superior court judge.

Dorothy appeared to be almost fully recovered so the entire family along with her sister Jo Marva boarded the train in Pine Bluff on November 4 for the return trip to Washington. Our party of six, including an infant and two boys under six years old, took seats near a restroom for the thirty-hour journey. I was glad to get home, although I was not entirely confident about Dorothy Ann being ready to handle the full responsibilities of taking care of the kids. Fortunately Jo Marva was there to help for a week or two before she had to go back to Pine Bluff.

My concerns about Dorothy Ann and the family made it difficult for me to concentrate on my work at the Solicitor's office and to do some of the things I thought were necessary to advance my career as a lawyer. I put on hold the discussions I had undertaken earlier that summer with a lawyer in Indianapolis about establishing an affiliation there in private practice. When I took the job at the Labor Department I planned to remain in government service for two or three years at the most. After that I figured opportunities would open up for me either to enter practice with a law firm or a company in private industry. The immediate outlook for me had now changed. My priority now was to have Dorothy Ann returned to good health as soon as possible and to stabilize and restore our family situation.

The year I had spent doing legal work for the Department of

Labor convinced me that government work could be very satisfying from a personal standpoint. I felt that what I was doing made a difference and helped to produce changes that improved the lives of ordinary working people. I soon realized that in the 1950s the Labor Department was at the very center of nearly every domestic policy initiative undertaken by the federal government. The central role the department played in federal domestic policy making would continue throughout the 1960s as well. It was a great place to be for a young lawyer with ideas and ideals about the government's proper role in achieving a just society. Of course, as a lowly Gs-9 staff lawyer I was not at a level to directly participate in making policy. But I did have a role in the process. For example, perhaps the greatest single public works initiative of the last half of the twentieth century was President Eisenhower's program to build the interstate highway system. This project did more to bring the American people together and to link the different parts of the nation into an integrated whole than anything since the establishment of the postal system. As a lawyer at the Labor Department I was involved in deciding the applicability of federal prevailing wage laws to contractors and workers who would build that multi-billion dollar system. Likewise, I was involved on behalf of the department in the government's efforts to establish and ensure democratic rights for union members. The main impetus for the government's movement into the area of union governance grew out of disclosures of corruption and mob influence in the teamsters union in the mid-1950s. These disclosures led to an investigation by a Senate committee chaired by Senator John McClellan, a Democrat from Arkansas. I was assigned to cover some of the Senate hearings and prepare reports of the proceedings for the Solicitor's office. As a result of the McClellan investigation Congress finally passed the Labor-Management Reporting and Disclosure Act of 1959, commonly known as the Landrum-Griffin Act.

The Department of Labor became the federal agency with principal administrative and enforcement responsibilities under Landrum-Griffin. I had the honor of serving as one of an eleven member legal task force assigned to write the regulations and interpretative guidelines needed to fully implement that legislation. My work on the task force focused primarily on regulations to implement provisions of the act relating to election of union officers, provisions that went into effect only ninety days after enactment. So the task force had to operate under severe time pressure. For a job well done under difficult circumstances Secretary James P. Mitchell presented the task force the Group Honor Award for notable achievement on March 4, 1960. I believed the work I was doing was important and valued within the department. However, it was not the kind of work that was likely to bring me to the attention of anyone outside the government.

*   *   *

No matter where one goes in this country if there is a large black community in the area quite likely you will find a number of people there who have come from the state of Arkansas. That certainly was true in Washington, D. C. During our first year in Washington we discovered that there were several Arkansas A. M. & N. alumni here, and a sizable number of others who had attended but did not graduate from the school. We decided to organize an Arkansas club centered around our college alumni, but inclusive also of others from the state who wanted to associate with us. We started, however, with the people we knew who had gone to A. M. & N. College. The alumni association gave us some help in identifying graduates now living in the Washington area. At first there were six or eight of us. They included Bertha Neal, Raye Jean and Weldon Means, Maggie Bell Trotter, Margie Coleman, Liston Leggette, and Jewell Young. Or first meeting was at the McKinney apartment early in 1958. Our primary purpose in organizing the club was to create a vehicle for social interaction among ourselves from time to time. Secondarily, we wanted to raise funds to support the school and to strengthen our bonds with the institution that had played such an important role in our lives.

The black community in Washington, D. C. that considered itself to be middle class had a much deserved reputation for being a difficult one for outsiders to penetrate and be accepted in. This was especially true if you were not a graduate of Howard University, or from an old-line black Washington family. Yet the vast majority of black people living in the city had come here from other places, mostly from the southern states. Those who found them-

134

selves outside the favored social circle wound up establishing their own clubs and groups and organized their social life and entertainment around them. In my early years in Washington the Arkansas club fulfilled this need for us. Whenever an official of A. M. & N. College came to town on business for the school, usually we would be notified and one of the members would host a party for him.

The club always threw a big party at Christmas time where each member would invite one or two other friends. Invariably the Christmas party would be held in someone's basement. The members all chipped in money to buy the drinks and food. The host did appropriate decorations and everyone had a very good time. The club eventually would become too large for house parties and graduated to bigger public facilities, such as church social halls and military base officer's and enlisted men's clubs. I never enjoyed the parties at such facilities nearly as much as I did those in the basement at a private home.

*   *   *

Dorothy Ann and I had not actually joined any church since we were married. Before leaving Pine Bluff we occasionally attended services on Sunday morning at Barraque Street Baptist Church where we were married. Sometimes we attended my father's church near the college, Smith Temple Church of God in Christ. While I was in law school we would go to a Baptist church across town in the black neighborhood in Bloomington. Once a student friend of ours in Bloomington named Sam Johnson took us to a white Presbyterian church he regularly attended. That was my first experience of attending any church that was not predominately black. Dorothy Ann and I both knew that we could not continue very much longer without establishing an affiliation with some church, now that there was a degree of permanence about where we were going to live. Church had been part of both our lives from the very beginning, our fathers both being ordained ministers and each of us having grown up in devout Christian homes. While neither of us were what I would call intensely religious persons, we did want our children to have a religious upbringing in the tradition of both our families.

135

Many times we discussed the question of what church to join in Washington. My sister Esther Smith was a very faithful member of Kelsey Temple Church of God in Christ, which I attended several times with her. Although I had been raised as a member of that denomination and attended their services throughout my youth, I was never comfortable with many of the tenets of that denomination and felt I could not live the kind of life that appealed to me and be true to those tenets. I had similar feelings about the Baptist church. So we were searching for a church we both could accept, and one that appeared to engage itself in the significant social and political issues of the day.

In the news stories and commentaries about the struggles being waged by blacks to be accorded their full citizenship rights, the leading spokesperson for one Protestant denomination stood out above most others. That spokesperson was Eugene Carson Blake of the United Presbyterian Church. From my perspective as a black American, on nearly every issue that came up in the battle for civil rights Blake came down on the side of the need for radical change in the way my people historically had been treated in American society. That denomination more that all the others seemed to be committed to the idea that the church had a vital role to play in bringing about social change, in addition to its traditional mission of saving souls. While most other mainstream protestant denominations were urging caution and gradualism, Blake was saying now is the time to take bold actions to make the nation live up to its promises.

When our neighbor in Mayfair Mansions Mrs. Dorothy Duncanson, invited us to visit her church in northwest Washington, Tabor United Presbyterian Church, I was eager to do so. Tabor was a small church, about 200 members, located at 2nd and S Streets Northwest in the very heart of the black community. Its building had been designed and constructed for use as a place of worship, not a converted storefront or renovated residence. Its pastor had finished college and been trained in seminary as a Presbyterian minister. It counted among its members black people from all walks of life ; school teachers, janitors, tradesmen such as barbers and beauticians, lawyers, physicians, dentists, architects, government clerks, postal workers, maids, nurses and short order cooks. Its services were orderly, its music inspiring, the minister's sermons provoked thought as well as appealed to one's emotions and spirit. It was a great little church that was concerned not only about the souls of its members but about the quality of life in the surrounding neighborhood as well. We had found our church home.

We proceeded to become active in various organizations at Tabor. I joined the men's council and the men's Sunday school class. Eventually the men of Tabor elected me as their president, quite an honor for me, a man still in his twenties among a group of men the average age of which was much higher. Every year the men were in charge of morning services on Father's Day and were responsible for obtaining a guest speaker. During my tenure as president we attracted several outstanding people as speakers for men's day services, including the Rev. Samuel D. Proctor, then president of Virginia Union College, Rev. Edler G. Hawkins, pastor of St. Augustine Presbyterian Church in New York City and an early black leader in that denomination and a young black congressman from Michigan named John Conyers.

Tabor Church took an active role in the surrounding community. The men took the lead in organizing a baseball team among the young boys who lived near the church. As a father of two boys and a longtime baseball fan I believed playing baseball was one of the indispensable activities a boy participated in while growing up. So one of the first gifts I gave to each of my sons was a baseball glove. They both were taught how to catch and throw a baseball by the time they were three years old. We discovered that many of the boys in the neighborhood had no male adult living in their homes and most of them did not understand the rudiments of the game of baseball. I wanted to make sure the boys around Tabor Church experienced baseball. We would recruit a team in early spring and enroll it in one of the many little league-type baseball leagues in the city. At least once every year the men would prepare and sell dinners out of the church kitchen in the basement. Although the ostensible purpose of selling dinners was to raise money, the real value of the activity was in bringing a group of men together before daybreak on Saturday morning to get to know each other better by cooking chicken, ribs, turnip greens and making potato salad; and by organizing teams of men to take telephone orders and make deliveries in the neighborhood. It was hard work but we all had fun doing it.

For the annual Father's Day service an ad hoc men's choir was organized to provide the music. Freddye Sue Davy, my childhood sweetheart, moved with her family to Washington shortly after we did and joined Tabor immediately. She played the piano and directed the weekly rehearsals for the group beginning a month or so beforehand. As an aside, Dorothy Ann always was curious as to why Freddye Sue decided to move to Washington. I think she suspected that she had not completely gotten over our childhood relationship in Jonesboro many years ago. After graduating from college in Little Rock Freddye Sue had married a tall, handsome, successful photographer there named Earl Davy. They had two children. Earl Davy took a job at the U. S. Government Printing Office and Freddye Sue became a public school teacher. For some reason it seems that our paths continued to cross throughout our lives.

*   *   *

By mid-1958 Dorothy Ann decided to work again. I think she had become bored with the role of full-time housewife and caregiver to three kids. She took a job at the National Institutes of Health as a physical science aid in chemistry in one of the pathology laboratories. While I hated to see her leave her job as housewife and primary caregiver, I welcomed the additional income. When we netted out the difference between her salary and the costs associated with her not being home the additional income amount was very small indeed. But the principal value of her going back to work was the immediate boost to her ego and feeling of self worth. In September of that year Rudy entered first grade at Nevel Thomas Elementary School. We had to find someone to come in and care for Fred and Anne and be there when Rudy came home from school.

The additional income from Dorothy Ann's job, and my steady movement upward in pay grade at the Solicitor's office convinced us that we could now afford to buy our first car. A man we met at a house party was a salesman at one of the Plymouth dealerships in town. His name was Monk Miller, a garrulous, fun loving salesman type. As soon as he learned that we were in the market for a car he was on the case. Having never purchased a car we were extremely cautious and wanted to be certain that the car we bought was the right one for our family. Monk showed us mostly used cars. We wanted a new car. We were impressed with the Chevrolet ads we saw every night on television. Finally we settled on a new 1958 Chevrolet Biscayne. This was a four-door model and quite a departure from the style of the 1957 model which later became a classic. At that time I was looking only for basic transportation at an affordable price, but having the car greatly enhanced our lifestyle.

The car was not the only improvement. That year we decided to expose ourselves to more of the cultural outlets Washington had to offer. We purchased one of the season ticket offerings for National Symphony concerts at Constitution Hall. We both knew little about classical music but felt we needed the exposure to find out whether we liked it or not. Over the 1958-59 season we had good seats for six or seven concerts, with Howard Mitchell conducting the National Symphony Orchestra. At that time the National Symphony was not considered to be one of the top orchestras in the country. To my not too discriminating ear, however, they were just great. Reading the music critics' negative review of the concert in the next day's *Washington Post* always puzzled me because I thought the orchestra had done a good job. Going to the concerts piqued my interest in several of the classical composers and so I wanted to hear more of their works in the comfort of my home. Until then I had been a fan of jazz and popular music only. Naturally, one wanted to have the very latest in high fidelity equipment to play the LPs on. We therefore invested in a Bogen receiver, a four-foot high custom-made cabinet for a University speaker system, and a Garrard record player and changer.

I opened an account at one of the upscale clothing stores downtown that catered to both men and women. It made me feel real good to know that Dorothy Ann could go shopping for a nice outfit for herself every now and then. We even drove to New York City for a brief vacation as neither one of us previously had spent any leisure time there. On the drive back to Washington we decided to stop off in Wilmington, Delaware, where our old friend Frank Hollis had set up his law practice after graduating from Temple University law school a few years earlier. We dropped in on Frank without notice as we did not have either an address or telephone number for him. We had no problem finding Frank. All we had to do was mention his name to almost anyone on the street and they gave us directions to his office and to his home. Frank was that well known in town. We had a very pleasant impromptu reunion. Frank Hollis introduced us to his very beautiful wife Janice and their three children. I had lost direct touch with Frank when he left A. M. & N. College for the army at the end of my sophomore year. Butler T. Henderson, my major professor in college, made it his business to follow the careers of his more successful students. It was he who told me that Frank had gone to Temple law school in Philadelphia after his army stint and settled in Wilmington. We had always admired Frank Hollis for his intellect and wit and were pleased to have our friendship ties reestablished.

6

Venturing into the Civil Rights Arena

The Washington, D. C. branch of the National Association for the Advancement of Colored People (NAACP) had more than 5,000 members in 1959 when I began my service on the executive board of the branch. Its President, Dr. Jackson, was pastor of one of the largest Baptist churches in downtown Washington. Serving on its executive board at the time were a host of prominent people in the city from both the black and white communities. They included attorney Patricia Roberts Harris, Charles N. Mason, Jr., Dr. William E. Greene, Flaxie Pinkett, Rev. Charles Webber, attorney John Shorter, attorney Tilford Dudley and attorney H. Carl Moultrie. The branch was without question the most powerful civil rights organization in the city. It was the organization black residents considered to be most capable of responding when they had complaints about discriminatory treatment either at the hands of government or powerful forces in the private sector. It served as ombudsman for the poor and the powerless in the city of Washington from its lowly office at 14th and U Streets Northwest.

Service on the executive committee or any leadership position in the D. C. branch was not just an honorific title. Instead, branch leaders though volunteers for the most part, were expected to bring whatever skills or talents they had to bear on the human problems that flowed into the branch office on a daily basis. I saw this as my opportunity to directly contribute something to the civil rights struggle then being fought on so many fronts throughout the nation. Although it was the nation's capital and was commonly viewed as a liberal, progressive community, Washington had its share of the same kinds of problems that were being experienced in Little Rock, Richmond, Birmingham, Atlanta and other places on the frontlines of the civil rights revolution taking place in America in the 1950s and '60s.

The city was governed administratively by a board of commissioners appointed by federal authorities answerable only to Congress and the President. The people living here had absolutely no say in how their government was selected or run. Though blacks formed a substantial majority of city residents, the police force, the fire department, the city school board and all other major city services were run by white people. City neighborhoods were essentially segregated. The local public transportation system was privately owned by a for-profit company headed by a white businessman. It was rare to see black men and women employed at any level above menial service jobs in the hotels, restaurants and major retail establishments in the city. The same was true also for many federal government agencies.

The branch president and executive committee realized the difficulty it faced in trying to handle strictly by the use of volunteers, the volume of problems being brought to the organization. A search for a paid executive director for the branch was undertaken. In the meantime, the various committees, each headed by a member of the executive committee, were relied upon to carry out the work of the organization. I was made chairman of the branch's employment committee. I firmly believed that the key to improving the lot of black men and women in the District of Columbia was to expand the range of employment opportunities. One of the first major tasks the committee undertook was to do a survey of the major private employers in the city. We had several objectives in mind. First, we wanted to ascertain employer attitudes toward the idea of equal employment opportunity. Also, we wanted to identify those employers who had a policy with respect to recruitment and promotion without regard to race. Finally, the survey requested statistical information to show where blacks stood in the hierarchy of job classifications the employer had in his organization. Beyond these finite objectives, however, we hoped that mere knowledge of the NAACP's investigation might spur some employers to move in the direction we wanted them to go.

Initially we targeted the major retail stores such as Sears, Peoples Drug Stores, and the grocery chains. Although we spent a great deal of time developing our survey instrument we had no

142

professional help in doing so. Certainly it was an imperfect one, which when it was received by employers was quickly recognized as the work of amateurs, but it was adequate for the job we had in mind. The cover letter, which was signed by branch president H. Carl Moultrie, branch executive secretary Edward A. Hailes and myself as chairman of the employment committee, read as follows:

As you are aware, the National Association for the Advancement of Colored People is intensely interested in improving and expanding employment opportunities for Negroes in Washington, D. C. We believe that equal employment opportunity and fair employment practices are keys to the solution of many other problems facing the Washington community.

"While many Washington employers in recent years have opened new doors of opportunity to Negroes seeking employment, others, for varying reasons, have either refused or have been extremely reluctant to employ qualified Negroes in certain occupations. The district branch of the NAACP believes that the attitude of some employers in this regard may be changed if they were reliably informed of the experience of the more progressive and forward looking 'equal opportunity' employers in the community.

"Furthermore, we feel that many Negroes are unduly hesitant about seeking employment or even preparing themselves for employment in certain occupations which historically have been closed to them, because of lack of accurate information about recent developments which indicate that a number of employers no longer follow old patterns of discrimination based on the color of a man's skin.

"For the purpose of launching an educational program in this area, we have prepared the enclosed questionnaire which we ask you to complete and return to this office at your earliest convenience. your cooperation in this will be most appreciated.

Two weeks passed and we had not received any responses to the survey. We decided to begin making telephone calls to ascertain whether the companies had received our request for information and planned to respond. It did not take long for us to figure out which companies were disposed to cooperate and which were not. Because our resources were limited it made sense for the committee to concentrate its efforts on the larger companies that were willing to have us come in and talk about what we were trying to do. Sears was one of those companies. We made progress also with Dart Drugs and with Peoples Drugs. The committee met with local store managers and sought to impress upon them the urgency of the need for expanded employment opportunities, especially for young black men and women, and what this could mean in terms of a positive image for the companies in the black community.

Our second campaign in the employment area involved the hotel industry in Washington, D. C. In challenging the hotels we acted in concert with several other civil rights groups, including the Washington Urban League headed by Sterling Tucker, and the Congress of Racial Equality, led by Julius Hobson. The hotel industry in Washington employed more people than any other single private sector employer in the city. Like so many others it too was plagued by patterns of segregation in its employment practices. Sterling Tucker and the urban league early on had taken the lead in calling attention to the problem. The industry was well organized. All the leading hotels and most of smaller motels and hotels as well were members of the Washington Hotel Association. That trade association coordinated the actions of its members, who tended to follow similar, if not identical, policies with respect to hiring and promotion practices. At the time the association was represented by a prominent Washington lawyer named Joseph Danzansky.

The facts about the hotel industry's segregated employment practices were undeniable. No blacks whatsoever were employed in front of the house white-collar jobs. Furthermore, most waiters and bellmen as well were white. The only jobs available to blacks in significant numbers were as maids, janitors and in laundry services.

Through the coordinated efforts of the NAACP employment committee, the Washington Urban League and the Congress of Racial Equality, the hotel association agreed first to meet with representatives of the civil rights groups at Joseph Danzansky's offices on Connecticut Avenue in downtown Washington. At the first meeting a representative of each civil rights group presented a formal statement of position and demands. My statement on behalf of the Washington branch of the NAACP said:

The NAACP, along with all other civil rights organizations represented here today, is very much concerned with the employment situation of Negroes in the hotel industry in Washington, D. C. We are pleased to have the opportunity to meet with representatives of the industry to discuss this situation, to attempt to reach agreement with members of the hotel industry and to develop a program of action to immediately alleviate any existing discriminatory hiring or employment practices.

We are aware that the Washington Urban League already has alerted the hotel association to the need for action to improve employment opportunities for Negroes in the industry. However, our review of the recent employment statistics provided by the hotel association would indicate that little if any real progress has been made in expanding employment opportunities for Negroes in the industry and in eliminating long existing discriminatory practices. For example, the statistics show that in those occupations in which Negroes are usually predominant, such as waiters, waitresses and bellmen, among the Washington hotels, Negroes are not even getting their fair share of those jobs, to say nothing of higher office, clerical and managerial positions. The need for immediate corrective action in this area is really apparent and the NAACP calls upon you to take steps now to correct these conditions.

The NAACP associates itself with and endorses the fair employment policy proposals that have been made by the Congress of Racial Equality. We believe these proposals are reasonable and embody the very minimum program of action that is required to accomplish a fair and just employment program for the industry.

The NAACP pledges to cooperate fully with other organizations and with members of the industry who are genuinely concerned, in all concrete constructive actions to desegregate employment in the hotel industry. We also stand ready to use whatever means and resources that are necessary to accomplish this end.

After several negotiating sessions the civil rights coalition reached an agreement with the hotel association. First, the association on behalf of its member companies made a commitment to a policy of non-discrimination in future hiring and promotion of hotel employees. Secondly, with respect to all new hires in front of the house clerical and managerial jobs for the next year, a fixed percentage of such positions would be filled from the pool of black and other minority applicants until such time as approximate parity had been achieved. Parity was defined to mean a workforce that reflected the racial demographics of Washington, D. C. Third, the association agreed to provide each member of the civil rights coalition regular periodic reports showing the hiring and promotion activity of association members for the previous period so that progress toward the goal of fair employment practices could be measured.

We considered the agreement to be a significant step forward in the quest for equal employment opportunity in the city. But it must be acknowledged that the general political climate in which we were operating at the time was quite favorable to what we were trying to accomplish. The Kennedy/Johnson administration came to Washington in 1961 and, after much agitation and prodding by many national civil rights leaders, began to understand the enormity of the racial problem in the country. The historic "March on Washington" on August 28, 1963, made it clear that things could not continue down the same path as before. Blacks and their allies had shown by their protests and other actions an unwillingness to accept a business as usual approach. By the time Lyndon B. Johnson became President after the tragic event of November 22, 1963 in Dallas, it was clear we had a President who was determined to change the federal government's approach to dealing with the question of racial justice and equality. More than any president before or since, Lyndon B. Johnson demonstrated a profound understanding of the need to take seriously the demands black people and their allies were making to change their status in America to that of full and equal rights as citizens.

I recall one incident that occurred shortly before Inauguration Day in 1965. We were in intense discussions with representatives of the hotel association concerning whether a major hotel in downtown Washington was in compliance with the commitment it had made to hire black front of the house personnel. This particular hotel happened to be one of the main venues for an inaugural ball. The civil rights coalition spokesperson went to the media, identified the hotel involved and stated the coalition's determination to enforce its demands by direct action if necessary against that particular hotel. Upon hearing of this developing crisis President Johnson sent a strongly worded message to all parties involved that they must settle their differences before January 20 because he would not want to see his inaugural festivities exposed to any disruption by picket lines or other forms of protest. The matter was settled to our satisfaction forthwith and inaugural balls went on without incident.

As the point man on EEO matters for the D. C. branch of the NAACP during the 1960s I frequently was called upon to represent the branch in public forums to discuss developing EEO law and policy. Many such forums were held by federal agencies as they struggled to understand and implement the clear national policy enunciated in executive order 11246 issued in 1965. One such forum took place on June 22, 1966, billed as a meeting for managers and supervisors on equal employment opportunity. It was held at a navy department facility on Nebraska Avenue in northwest Washington. Among the sponsors were the naval security group headquarters, the naval communications systems headquarters and the naval security station. Some 100 mid-level managers and supervisors employed in these federal agencies were gathered to hear a talk on "prejudice" by a professor of psychology at George Washington University and my speech on behalf of the NAACP on "Equal Employment Opportunity in the Federal Government."

My talk to the group stressed the point that the new federal EEO policy goes beyond the mere injunction against discrimination and requires every executive department and agency to establish and maintain "positive action" programs of equal employment opportunity. It is no longer enough for the agency to have a procedure for handling individual complaints of discrimination. The new order puts the burden of rooting out discriminatory practices squarely upon the agency itself. It must take steps to correct the effects of past discriminatory policies. I told the group that the NAACP takes the position that the best evidence of compliance with the new EEO policy is the presence of blacks in representative numbers at all levels of jobs in the agency.

Throughout my tenure as chairman, the employment committee held regular sessions at our office at 14th and U Streets Northwest, sometimes weekday evenings and occasionally on Saturday, where individual members and any others from the public at large could come in and present their complaints about acts of employment discrimination. The ones we found to have merit we would attempt to handle by informal mediation. Others required us to take more formal action.

One of my most rewarding experiences involved a case against the U. S. Department of Agriculture. The complainant was a middle aged Gs-7 chemist employed at the agricultural research service in Beltsville, Maryland. He had been discharged from his job on the basis of alleged unsatisfactory performance. He had held the job for 10 years and received good ratings over all except for the last few months of that period.

Our interviews with the complainant convinced us that the man had contracted some type of illness that affected his ability to perform certain tasks. We felt the man had been unfairly treated and set up to be fired. At the least we thought disability retirement would have been the appropriate remedy. So we filed a complaint under the appeals procedures provided by agency regulations in July 1966. After a full day of hearing, and upon the recommendation of the hearing officer, the Secretary of Agriculture eventually sustained the discharge action. I appealed that decision to the Civil Service Commission in March 1967. In early 1968 the Civil Service Commission upheld our appeal and ordered the employee be retired with full disability benefits from the date of his discharge.

The employment committee had similar success in a case against the National Institutes of Health during this same time period. These results could not have been achieved without the hard work and dedication of members of the employment committee such as Reginald Webb and Frank Hollis, and the support of the branch executive director Ed Hailes. Nothing I have done in my entire legal career gave me more personal satisfaction than winning cases like these. The committee took all such cases on a pro bono basis. The greatest reward of all for me was to see the tremendous sense of gratitude on the faces of the clients on being informed that their rights had been vindicated after months or years of struggle.

*   *   *

The Department of Labor established the Bureau of Labor Management Reports (BLMR) shortly after the Labor-Management

Reporting and Disclosure Act and the Welfare and Pensions Plans Disclosure Act were enacted in the late 1950s. The Office of the Solicitor followed suit and set up a new unit to provide legal services to BLMR. I was chosen as one of the lawyers to staff the new Solicitor's Office unit, which was headed by James Beaird, a young lawyer from Georgia. The BLMR set up shop in a new commercial office building on Georgia Avenue in Silver Spring, Maryland. The Solicitor decided that his unit responsible for servicing BLMR also should move to the Silver Spring location in 1961. From a professional standpoint, I was not at all pleased to have my office relocated from department headquarters at 14th and Constitution Avenue. I enjoyed being close to all the action at department headquarters and the proximity to all the senior department officials. I also would miss the opportunity to just drop in on lawyers in other shops doing entirely different work than I was doing and the informal lunches in the department cafeteria with colleagues from other disciplines.

There were other problems associated with moving large numbers of Department of Labor personnel to suburban communities as well. The pace of desegregation proceeded much more slowly in the suburbs than in the city of Washington. By mid-1961 few restaurants, hotels and other places of public accommodations in Washington followed a practice of refusing service to blacks. The same was not the case in many suburban communities, including Silver Spring, Maryland. A significant percentage of Department of Labor employees were black and some were concerned about having their jobs moved to locations that were inhospitable to blacks. Secretary Goldberg certainly was aware of this problem and took steps to alleviate it as best he could. His representatives sought to identify first the restaurants and other businesses that were willing to serve blacks and communicated that information to employees. The recalcitrant businesses also were identified and not so subtle forms of pressure were brought to bear on them to change.

One restaurant in particular was quite adamant about its refusal to serve blacks. It was located on East/West Highway near the intersection with Georgia Avenue. Along with several other black employees and a few white colleagues we would gather from time to time at this establishment during lunch hour, seek service and be refused. We finally filed a complaint with the Maryland commission on Human Relations, whose executive director at the time was Parren Mitchell. Eventually a court order was issued to compel the establishment to serve all orderly patrons without regard to race. The owners finally decided to sell the place rather than to comply with the order.

*   *   *

In 1959 my sister Esther met a young woman who had recently come to work at the Federal Trade Commission. Her name was Lillian Twine. Esther told me that Lillian was married to a young lawyer from Chicago who had just gone to work at the Justice Department and she thought Dorothy Ann and I should meet Lillian and her husband. Soon thereafter we met Lillian and Edgar Twine. Edgar had graduated from the law school at the University of Illinois earlier that year and had been employed under the honors program by the Justice Department. That told me Edgar was a very bright young man who had an outstanding record at the University of Illinois. Our families liked each other right away. The Twines had two young children, a girl named Debbie and a son, Eddie, Jr. They had an apartment in southeast Washington at a place called "Parkland Apartments." which was not too far from our more prestigious location in Mayfair Mansions. The Twines had met as undergraduates at the University of Illinois. Lillian and Edgar were a fun couple to be around. She was a very beautiful and vibrant young woman, rather petite in stature; Edgar was tall, dark complexioned with prematurely grey hair which seemed unusual for a man still in his early twenties.

Through the Twines we were introduced to several other young couples who had known each other while attending the University of Illinois. They were Bob and Barbara Bates who were from Washington originally; Sallie and Eddie Williams, who had gone to Illinois from Memphis, Tennessee; Jennie and Eugene Hamilton, the latter a classmate with Twine at the law school; and Cathy and Buford Macklin. Throughout my life I have maintained close personal friendship ties with the men in each of these couples. We have endured many life transitions, including death, divorce, relocation and remarriage. We have rejoiced in each other's

150

personal and professional triumphs; we have shared grief and sorrow. Yet we remain friends and are still in frequent touch with each other.

Meanwhile, I was making steady progress up the professional ladder at the Solicitor's office. By 1961 I had reached the Gs-13 grade level. The year before Dorothy Ann and I began looking to buy a house as our family had outgrown the two bedroom apartment in Mayfair Mansions. Dorothy's youngest sister Gail finished high school in Pine Bluff, Arkansas in 1959 and came to live with us in June of that year, planning to enroll in college in the Washington area the following year. In the spring of 1961 Dorothy's father died suddenly while he and his wife were on vacation in Chicago. Reverend Davis' death was a tremendous blow to everyone, but Dorothy Ann took his passing especially hard. They were extremely close and he always seemed to accord his special favor on his eldest living child. In every crisis in my family Reverend Davis had been there for us. I loved and admired him; he was a great father-in-law. I made a solemn promise to Dorothy's mother that I would care for Gail as my own daughter, now that her natural father had died.

Our search for a house intensified early in 1961 when Dorothy Ann became pregnant for the fourth time in the tenth year of our marriage. I was determined to be in a new house before the new baby came sometime in the fall of 1961. I met a black real estate salesman named William (Bill) Fitzgerald, who worked for a firm that handled sales in the changing neighborhoods of upper northwest Washington. He found a house at 1310 Locust Road just north of Walter Reed Army Hospital about one block from the district line. The area was called "Shepherd Park," named after one of the early "mayors" of the District of Columbia whose large manor house occupied nearly one square block around the corner on 13th Street N.W. Bill Fitzgerald later became the founder and president of Independence Federal Savings and Loan Association. The house was owned and occupied until recently by a prominent white family, which like so many others at that time, were selling their residences in the city and moving to nearby suburban areas. Shepherd park was in the heart of an area that was undergoing rapid change—whites moving out, blacks moving in.

An organization called "neighbors incorporated" also was operating in the area. They were trying to control panic selling and "block busting" practices of unscrupulous real estate salesmen and firms. The organization encouraged the idea of an integrated community where blacks and whites lived in harmony together. If that concept could be made to work anywhere there was no better place than Washington, D. C. to make the effort in the early 1960s. The city had a very large well-educated black middle class. It had more than its fair share of affluent black professionals. What the black community lacked most, however, was a significant number of business owners and entrepreneurs. (The city still has the latter deficiency more than forty years later.) Neighbors Inc. had modest success for a while, and Shepherd Park remained an integrated neighborhood much longer than most.

We liked the house on Locust Road. By today's standards it was a small house, but when it was built in the late 1930s or early 1940s it was considered large. It was the typical all-brick construction colonial style house with a center hall plan with a full unfinished basement. The living room took up the right side of the first floor; the dining room and small kitchen occupied the left side. And in the rear was a small library or family room and half bath. On the second floor were a master bedroom with its own full bath, two other bedrooms and another full bath. There was a semi-finished attic with good headroom, hardwood floors and good-sized windows for light and ventilation. There were hardwood floors throughout the main living areas, but no central air conditioning.

The house sat on an irregularly shaped lot that was elevated a few feet above street level. It was bordered on one side by an alley that curved around the rear where there was a small separate one-car garage. It was well landscaped with a huge forsythia bush on the front right corner of the lot as you faced the street.

The purchase price in 1961 was $23,000. The mortgage interest rate was 6%, which at that time was considered quite high. We got a conventional mortgage; many new homebuyers got FHA or VA mortgages at a much lower interest rate. I remember the principal, interest and taxes monthly payment was less than $150.

We decided to buy a house in Shepherd Park for a number of reasons. First, we wanted to live where good public schools were available for our children to attend. I have always been a strong supporter of the public school system, believing that without good public schools the society eventually will fragment and disintegrate, leading to chaos. Our three children in 1961 were ages 9, 7, and 4. Shepherd Elementary, the school that served the neighborhood, had a reputation of being one of the best in the city. It was just two blocks from our house at the corner of 14th Street and Kalmia Road. The junior high was Paul Junior High about two miles back toward town near Georgia Avenue and Military Road. Coolidge High School was even closer. These too were good schools, but their school populations were rapidly changing as whites and more affluent blacks opted to send their children to private schools, particularly at the high school level. In 1961 the Shepherd School student body was still predominately white, the blacks comprising less than twenty percent. Most of the teachers and administrators were also white, which was a matter of some concern to me.

What I found most appealing about Shepherd School was the fact that the parents played a vital role in nearly all school affairs. The school had a surfeit of volunteers available to fill almost any need that was not being adequately met by school authorities. It had a very strong PTA whose budget was large enough to supply many deficits that Principal Dorothy Lewis might identify.

Shepherd Park also was a beautiful neighborhood with lots of trees, well-kept houses and grounds, nearby walk-to small shops and service establishments, convenient public transportation access at either Georgia Avenue or 16th Street. Above all there were interesting people of many races and cultures. Many of the people that came to town with the new Kennedy/Johnson administration took up residence in the area. It was a fairly safe and secure part of town. All of my children spent much of their adolescent years in Shepherd Park. They tell me even now that those were some of the best years of their lives. I too enjoyed those years in Shepherd Park. An added bonus for me was being within walking distance of my new office in Silver Spring, Maryland, when my Solicitor's office unit moved there later in 1961.

When we moved to our new house in early summer 1961 there were very few black families in the neighborhood. The area was predominately Jewish and many residents worked at Walter Reed Army Hospital a few blocks away. Dr. and Mrs. Tuckson and their two sons Reed and Wayne lived less than a block away on 13th Street. Dr. Tuckson was head of radiology at the Howard University Dental School. Dr. and Mrs. Melvin Jenkins and their three daughters were three doors up the street on Legate Road. Dr. Jenkins, a pediatrician, also was at the medical school at Howard University. Dr. Edgecombe and his family also lived on Legate Road about one block away. The number of blacks in Shepherd Park increased steadily over the years but the neighborhood was still very much an integrated one when we left for California eight years later in 1969.

By the time our fourth child was born on October 30, 1961 we were prepared for her arrival. She was delivered at Providence Hospital and we named her Paula Elaine, the "Paula" in honor of the late Reverend Silas Davis' twin brother Paul, Dorothy's favorite uncle who was childless. I think I felt more comfortable with Paula's arrival than with the first three children. Our financial condition was better than at any other time before. More time elapsed between this pregnancy and all the others. Anne Marie was already over four years old when Paula came along. But above all both Dorothy Ann and I agreed that with two boys and two girls our family was now complete. At age 31 and Dorothy at age 30 we were determined to bring our childbearing days finally to an end. A couple our age with four children was somewhat unusual. Many couples at that age were only beginning their families. That certainly was the case with my friend and fellow Labor Department lawyer, Jim Jones and his wife Joan, who had married a few years before. Although Jim was a few years older than I was, my children would wind up baby sitting for his kids when they came along a few years later.

In some respects having our children at an early age was a distinct advantage. We would still be young when they reached their teenaged years, a very difficult time for most parents. Being younger we were better positioned to understand teenaged behavior patterns and to respond from our own recent experience. We were still young enough to enjoy their friends when they came to visit. Most importantly we would still be in our productive years when the financial demands associated with sending them to college would be most pressing. When they were young having four children seemed like a lot, but as they matured and could begin to do more things for themselves, the size of our family did not seem large at all. I think our family was ideal and I never regretted having a single one of them.

*   *   *

My circle of friends and acquaintances expanded greatly as we became more involved with activities in the Washington community and as I advanced in rank at the department. Dorothy Ann was asked to join a social club called "The Merrymakers." The club consisted of 10 or 12 young professional women (mostly schoolteachers) nearly all of whom were married to young black professional men like me who worked for the government. Occasionally the Merrymakers would host a big party at a member's home and invite the husbands. Such gatherings gave us a chance not only to socialize, but also to size up how well the families were doing vis-à-vis each other from the standpoint of financial and professional success.

I became active in the graduate chapter of my fraternity, Kappa Alpha Psi, which met once a month at the house it maintained in northwest Washington. Before leaving Mayfair Mansions some of our friends with Arkansas connections formed a Friday night bridge club that met two or three times a month. We played highly competitive bridge for several years for one tenth of a cent per point. To come away from the evening winning fifty cents or a dollar meant you had a very good session.

I think the competitive bridge game may have led me to take up the game of poker shortly after we moved to Shepherd Park. Not long after our move, Eddie Williams and his wife Sally bought a house on Legate Road a few doors up the street. About that time the Twines leapfrogged the district and bought a house several miles north in the town of Wheaton in Montgomery County. The Macklins purchased a house over on Kansas Avenue N. W. Another lawyer friend of Ed Twine at the Justice Department, Bill Davis and his wife Glynnis, a schoolteacher, became part of our circle of friends also. The Davis' purchased a house on Locust Road a year or two after our arrival in the area. Floyd Keene, a dentist, and his wife Sylvia came to the neighborhood about that same time. Pretty soon we had the nucleus of a neighborhood poker game.

155

At first we played for the smallest stakes possible, literally for pennies. The inaugural group consisted of Ed Twine, Eddie Williams, Bill Davis, Buford Macklin and a neighbor from Mayfair Mansions, Doyle Carrington, an architect for the Veterans Administration. Basically we were all novices at the game and looked upon it primarily as entertainment. If you had any skill at all at most you might lose a dollar or two in the course of two or three hours. Occasionally the wives visited among themselves while the men played poker. Usually we got together no more often than once a month.

The occasional poker game was good therapy for me. I found the game very relaxing. I could shut out all the concerns I had on the job and concentrate totally on trying to figure out the weaknesses and strengths of my several opponents' games. While the rules of the game of poker are very simple, it is one of the most complex games of any I have ever played. In my view it is at least as difficult as chess, a game I also enjoy playing. The difficulty of the game lies in the interaction of trying to assess the psychology of multiple players, the influence of money on the behavior of different individuals, how the players differently assess and tolerate risk, and the players varying attitudes about winning and losing. The higher the stakes, the more important each of these aspects of the game becomes.

At some point in each of the last forty years, I have played poker with Ed Twine and Eddie Williams. In all that time I have not yet completely figured out their games and I think they probably will say the same thing about mine. I am convinced, however, that luck is a real factor in the game. Some players actually are luckier than others and tend to win despite having less skill than others have. Unfortunately, I am not one of the lucky players. The stakes have escalated somewhat, but not too much, over the 40-plus-year period. We now play at most a $5.00 limit game, maximum three raises with a $50.00 takeout for each player at the start. Other players have joined the game. Some remain; some do not, either because of death or some other compelling reason. Over this span of time the following men have been or still are a part of "the game": Otto McClairen, Buford Macklin, George L. P. Weaver, C. Robert Kemp, Melvin Humphrey (all now deceased): Walter Carrington, Lisle Carter, Ed Sylvester, J. Worden Yancey, Calvin

Raullerson, Sam Ewing, James Harkless, C. Payne Lucas, Robert Hill, Harold Hilton, Pete Purcell, Lloyd Mitchell and Henry Tomes. Among this group are men of significant achievement in various fields of endeavor. But around the poker table we were all equals.

The leveling effect of a poker game was demonstrated for me in another context at a Solicitor's office managers meeting held at a small Virginia conference center in 1966. In attendance were the Solicitor Charles Donahue and his wife, the regional attorneys from around the country and several key headquarters lawyers. After dinner one evening as we socialized in the hospitality suite a nickel and dime poker game got started among some of the lawyers. The solicitor's wife joined in as well. At first I paid little attention, but later I noticed that whenever the Solicitor's wife was involved in a contested hand some of the lawyers would quickly fold and concede the pot to her. I did not understand the concept of "customer" poker so when I finally was in a showdown situation with the Solicitor's wife I called her bet and won the pot. The way I learned, one played to win no matter the rank or status of the opponent. I was accustomed to conceding a hand for only two reasons. Either I thought my hand was not good enough to win or I did not have enough money to call the bet. Some of the lawyers commented on how courageous they thought I was to call the Solicitor's wife's bet. I never even thought about not calling and did not view it as an act of courage by any means. It simply was a poker game to me, nothing else. Although he never said anything to me about it, I believe the Solicitor remembered the incident and admired the quality of my character my action at the poker table demonstrated. A year or two later he asked me to become his special assistant.

*   *   *

Throughout the period of the civil rights struggles in America the Labor Department always seemed to be the lead federal government agency in developing innovative ideas and approaches for solving problems of discrimination in the society. The concept of "affirmative action" was born there, and given life in the Office of Federal Contract Compliance that was first established during

157

the Kennedy/Johnson administration. That was the office set up to use the federal government's vast procurement powers as a tool to extend and enforce equal employment policies to companies that do business with the government.

Here again, the Solicitor set up a special unit of lawyers to provide legal counsel and other services to the Office of Federal Contract Compliance. To head this new unit the Solicitor chose James E. Jones, my good friend from Little Rock. "Jim" Jones thus became the first black in the office to reach the Assistant Solicitor rank. We all were extremely proud of his selection. Jim was well-suited for this job because of his innovative mind and courageous personality. He had a way of speaking his mind no matter how unpopular or controversial his views were.

Not long after he became Assistant Solicitor in charge of the new Division of Labor Relations and Civil Rights, Jim Jones challenged the Solicitor to begin practicing in that office what the Department of Labor had been preaching to private employers about "affirmative action." He convinced Solicitor Donahue that he should make a special effort to hire more black lawyers into the agency. He suggested that the most direct way to accomplish that objective would be to extend recruiting efforts to the law schools at black colleges and universities.

By 1965 the number of black lawyers in the office had increased significantly from the three the office had when I joined the staff nine years earlier. Frank Hollis closed his practice in Wilmington, Delaware, and came to the Solicitor's office in 1961. Thaddeus Van Ware, a young recent graduate of Howard University law school, joined the office about that same time. A more experienced black lawyer who had been active in Texas politics, Kenneth Holbert, came to the department shortly after the Kennedy/Johnson administration took office. There also were two black women lawyers in the office, Peggy Griffiths and a recent law graduate named Anna Catherine Johnson. Anna Johnson married a very prominent black congressman from Detroit by the name of Charles Diggs. She later became a federal judge in Michigan.

One other lawyer in the office I thought was black but was never quite sure. Sol Robinson had an Ivy League pedigree both undergraduate and law school, was married to an East Indian woman, and looked very much like he was of mixed parentage. He did not hang out too much with my crowd but I finally came to the conclusion he was a black man by American standards.

Charlie Donahue was a very interesting man. An Irish Catholic from Portland, Maine; a graduate of Princeton and Harvard Law School. He was general counsel of the Plumbers International Union when he was appointed Solicitor of Labor by President Kennedy in 1961. His taciturn demeanor and speech were typical of those from his native state but he had a wry sense of humor. He was fair-minded and seemed to want to do the right thing. However, he would never be mistaken for a flaming liberal, or a person with a great deal of passion about the cause of civil rights. He was smart, observant and he listened well.

When Jim presented his idea about recruiting at black law schools Donahue agreed it was a good idea but suggested that the recruiting be done by the agency's regional attorneys in closest proximity to the black law schools. The regional attorneys, of course, were all white. Jim told him that using the regional attorneys for the task was not the best approach. Instead, he asked why not use the black lawyers in the office for that job. Give them the authority they needed to make the commitments necessary to encumber vacant positions, subject to the candidate's ability to negotiate the normal hiring screens later on. Donahue agreed and Jim was turned loose to proceed with the project.

Jim Jones first contacted an acquaintance of his at the Howard University Law School, professor Jeanus Parks. Parks was chairman of the Howard University committee on placement. They discussed the project and our objective of tapping into black law schools as a resource for new recruits at the Labor Department. Parks put Jim in touch with Professor Harry Groves at Texas Southern University who had done some work on locating the whereabouts of black law students in law schools throughout the country. By February 1965 Jim had identified five predominately black law schools, not including Howard University in Washington, D. C., and had obtained data on their enrollment and other important information. These schools were as follows:

1. Florida A. & M. College, Tallahassee, FL (15 students)
2. North Carolina College, Durham, NC (23 students)

3. South Carolina College, Orangeburg, SC (12 students)
4. Southern University, Baton Rouge, LA (10 students)
5. Texas Southern University, Houston, TX (15 students)

Howard University law school had by far the largest enrollment of black law students in the country at the time, more than 150 students. All of these are 1963 numbers, the latest then available. All the schools were in the South. All had been established at various times when blacks were denied access to white state university legal education under the "separate but equal" doctrine that prevailed in the South until the *Brown* decision. It is interesting to note that ten years after *Brown* v. *Board of Education,* no white Southern state university law school had an enrollment of more than two black law students. Among all non-Southern law schools only eleven had an enrollment of five or more black students.

Jim Jones selected three of his colleagues to make the recruiting calls on these five law schools in the early spring of 1965. Frank Hollis who had family connections in Houston and had lived there part time while growing up was given the job of recruiting at Texas Southern. Thaddeus Van Ware, who had finished Virginia Union College, was chosen to visit the two Carolina schools. I was selected for the visits to Florida A. & M. College and Southern University. Our primary task, of course, was to identify any graduating seniors we believed met the standards of quality and ability necessary to success as a lawyer in the Solicitor's office. Jim Jones and the Solicitor were confident that our experience and judgment could be relied upon for making good decisions. The agency also hoped our visits would be the initial step in establishing mutually beneficial lasting relationships with the various schools for recruiting purposes.

While each of us was briefed as to what we were expected to do in our visits, I was not fully prepared for what I encountered when I arrived at the schools I visited. I met first with the law school dean, Thomas M. Jenkins, at Florida A. & M. University. He headed a faculty of six professors. At Southern my contact was Aguinaldo A. Lenoir, head of a faculty of seven. Each school was in a period of transition brought about by the societal changes taking place as a consequence of the civil rights movement. Florida A. &

M. is located in the same city as its much larger white counterpart, Florida State University, which had an established law school. There was a great deal of uncertainty as to whether the black law schools could or would survive once desegregation of Southern professional schools became the norm, as was widely expected in a very few years.

This atmosphere of uncertainty about survival was not conducive to efforts to establish a long-term recruiting relationship with the black law schools. We had not given enough thought to this issue when we undertook the recruiting effort. Most of the senior law students welcomed the opportunity to be considered for a legal position at the Department of Labor in Washington. However, I got the distinct impression that federal government service was not the preferred career choice for most of the students. At Florida A. & M. in particular students saw themselves returning to their hometowns eventually to make their contribution to securing the rights and improving the lives of black people where they lived.

I had mixed feelings about the negative attitude some students apparently had toward coming to work for the federal government. As a recruiter I very much wanted to succeed in finding new black legal talent for the Solicitor's office in places the department had not looked before. On the other hand, I found myself admiring the sense of commitment to the cause of civil rights that the students exhibited by their desire to be directly involved in the struggle for liberation that was swirling all about them. I was reminded of the compromise I had made just a few years earlier to take the "safe" option of a job in the government rather than the far riskier one of hanging out a shingle somewhere in the black community. I wondered to myself what might have happened to me if ten years earlier I had shown self-confidence and courage equal to that of this generation of black law students.

I was not able to persuade anyone at Florida A. & M. College to take a job in Washington. However, at Southern University we hit the jackpot when a very bright young man by the name of Thomas Todd accepted our offer of a job. Thomas Todd became a star employee in the Solicitor's office, remaining on the staff for several years before moving on to a very successful career teaching and practicing law in Chicago. Frank Hollis also was able to persuade a young man from Texas Southern University to join the office. The benefits of this initial recruiting effort among black law schools cannot be measured solely by the number of new hires from this source. I believe the greatest impact of the effort was its very positive effect on the morale of black staff members already employed throughout the department. It demonstrated that the lawyers in the agency at least were willing to apply to themselves the same affirmative action principles the department so vigorously advocated for private sector employers and unions.

7

Advancing in Rank as a
Government Lawyer

In early October 1967 I got a call from the Solicitor's confidential secretary Valeria Harris that Charlie Donahue wanted to see me right away. She could not tell me why he wanted to see me but told me to be there at two o'clock that same afternoon. I took the department shuttle from my office in Silver Spring to department headquarters shortly after lunch. During the forty minute trip I continued to ponder what the Solicitor might want to see me about but came up with no answer. Ms. Harris ushered me into the Solicitor's office a few moments after I arrived. Charlie, who was not one for a lot of small talk, asked me to sit down and got right to the point of the meeting. He told me he wanted me to become his special assistant. He said he expected to be out of the office more than usual through the next several months and he wanted an experienced lawyer with common sense as his right hand man. He said he had thought about it a lot the last few days and had decided I was the right person for the job. He pointed out that I had more than ten years experience in the office, serving in a variety of assignments and had done them all very well. He felt that I had the temperament necessary for working effectively with higher ranking people.

The special assistants job was at the Gs-15 level, the same grade I held at the time as Counsel for Interpretations and Opinions in the Division of Labor-Management Laws. I knew no promotion was involved if I took the new assignment, but I hoped that the position might be upgraded in a few months if my work turned out to be as Charlie expected.

Having observed for several years the special assistant's role in the Office of the Solicitor, I knew that the job was a lot more powerful than the one I had. Correspondence, legal opinions, orders and directives prepared for the Solicitor's signature by lawyers in all the divisions and submitted by the responsible Associate Solicitors were subject to the special assistant's independent scrutiny before actually being seen by the Solicitor himself. The special assistant performed special and confidential assignments relating to all phases of the work of the Solicitor, including the responsibility for operational matters throughout the office. He acts as legal advisor and technical expert on interpretative and other matters within the responsibility of the Office of the Solicitor. I liked the idea of taking on the responsibilities associated with the job, even if no additional pay was being offered immediately. I accepted the assignment with alacrity.

Only later did I realize the risks involved in moving into this new role as a confidential assistant to a presidential appointee. As a mere staff attorney civil service rules provided certain protections against arbitrary removal from my position. On the other hand, the special assistant was a schedule "C" job, which meant that if for any reason my boss left his job I too was exposed to being removed by his successor, who in all likelihood would want to bring in his own trusted assistant. This would be the case whether the Solicitor left because of a change in administration or for personal reasons.

Of course, I knew that the presidential election was coming up the next year and it probably was going to be hotly contested. There already were signs that President Johnson would be severely challenged in the democratic primaries because of growing dissatisfaction with his conduct of the Vietnam War. But in late 1967 I was not really concerned about a possible change of administration or that Charlie Donahue might leave his post. Instead, I had my sights set on having a fairly powerful job that could lead to a higher salary not too far down the road. Besides, the new job would bring me in contact with the Secretary and others at very high levels in government. There was no telling what such exposure might lead to for me.

I discovered not long after taking the special assistant job that Charlie Donahue had been asked to head up the Johnson reelection effort in the state of Maine. Doing that job for the President in the Solicitor's native state probably would require him to be out of the office often. I think that is what the solicitor was referring to when he said in our initial conversation about my taking the job that he planned to be out of the office an unusual amount of time in the next few months.

I started work at the new position in late October 1967. I shared an office right next door to the Solicitor's very impressive corner office suite on the fourth floor of the Labor Department building. In the office with me were Jeanne Trexler, the Solicitor's management assistant, and Adella Wilkinson, a secretary. A connecting door provided access to the Solicitor's private office without going through the reception room and his gatekeepers. The view from my window overlooked the Washington Monument grounds. Mrs. Trexler was a very attractive middle-aged white woman with dark brown hair. She spoke with a clipped accent and dressed quite conservatively. I think she was from upstate New York. Ms. Wilkinson was a strikingly tall and shapely young black woman probably not much more than twenty years old. Her dress was just the opposite of that of Mrs. Trexler. Her dresses were short and very revealing and she seemed not in the least self-conscious about the effect her rather provocative attire inevitably had on men in the office. She had an outgoing, effervescent personality one would always remember once having met her. Although Ms. Wilkinson was truly an ornament for the office, her secretarial skills were excellent as well, a combination not found too often.

I had met Valeria Harris soon after she came to the front office in 1961 when Charlie Donahue took over the Office of the Solicitor. We often had taken the same bus to our homes in northeast Washington after work. She too was a very attractive black woman with an engaging smile and pleasant manner. But one should not be misled by Ms. Harris' pleasant demeanor because she was one tough cookie and had the reputation for being the best secretary of all among those of the department's top executives. (This assessment of Valeria's skills was confirmed a few years later when Walter Washington, the first elected mayor of the District of Columbia, selected her as his secretary.) I liked Valeria also because I thought she looked a lot like my wife. Deputy Solicitor Edward Friedman's secretary Jolene Miller also sat in the reception room with Valeria Harris. Jolene was a younger white woman who had come to Washington from Pennsylvania a few years earlier. Jolene's appearance and gait showed what appeared to be slight residual effects of either an accident or some type of illness at an early age. Nevertheless, she was a pretty girl whose skills and personality made her well suited for the work as secretary to a high level government executive.

My work as special assistant removed any doubt I might have had as to the central role the Department of Labor had in domestic policy formation in the Johnson Administration. Many of the ideas that were the basis for Johnson's "Great Society" initiatives for empowering the poor, extending full rights to blacks and other minorities, improving health care for the elderly, and dealing with labor-management conflicts came out of the Labor Department. The department also was in the middle of international trade issues because of its role in trying to mitigate the effects exports and imports could have on the well-being of American workers. The work was interesting and exciting. I never knew from one day to the next what new issues I might be involved in. One day it would be developing information to help department officials decide whether to intervene in a strike by public school teachers. Another project might be to assemble a task force of legal interns and junior lawyers to examine local anti-poverty agency rosters in cities where civil unrest had occurred to see if any employees were ineligible to continue receiving federal funds because of their involvement in such disorders. (Congress had inserted in the department's appropriations bill a provision forbidding the use of any manpower training or other departmental funds to pay any individual who had been convicted of participating in riots.) Taking this job was the best career move I made since coming to work for the government.

On March 31, 1968 President Johnson announced that he would neither seek nor accept the Democratic Party nomination for another term as President. The constant drumbeat of criticism of his conduct of the Vietnam War, and the strong showing of Eugene McCarthy and others in the early Democratic Party presidential primaries more or less forced him out of the race. Charlie Donahue was Lyndon Johnson's man so no matter whether the Democrats won or lost the general election in November, the Solicitor did not plan to stay around in the new administration. Therefore I would soon face a career decision of my own. Of course there was no urgent need for me to act at the time of the President's announcement. I could wait until the election outcome had been determined. But if I wanted to continue my legal career at the department there were some preliminary actions I needed to take before the end of the year.

*   *   *

In late March, 1968 Professor John Howard called from Pine Bluff, Arkansas, to say the Founder's Day Committee at Arkansas A. M. & N. College wanted me to be one of the speakers at the 95th Founder's Day celebration being planned for April 28, 1968. I was pleasantly surprised to get this invitation, especially from Professor Howard. He had been a fixture on the faculty of the college for many years and had brought the school many honors because of his renown as one of America's leading black artists. Ten years earlier during a visit to the campus to give an informal talk to Dr. Harding B. Young's accounting class he had mentioned possibly having me return to deliver the traditional sunrise message on Founders Day. I had hoped someday to have the opportunity to return for such a purpose. I was honored by the invitation and gladly accepted.

Founders Day at A. M. & N. College was always very special. Many alumni returned for the occasion just as they do for homecoming in the fall. My invitation was to be the speaker at the traditional memorial sunrise program, which literally is scheduled to begin at sunrise that Sunday morning. The featured speaker for the afternoon program that day was Dr. Hugh M. Gloster, president of Morehouse College in Atlanta, Georgia. Needless to say I was thrilled to be in the company of such a nationally-known educator and college administrator. The sunrise program is a solemn, religious type service, featuring performances of sacred music by the college choir, prayers by Dr. George Loder, a professor of education and also a minister, and introduction of the speaker by President Lawrence A. Davis, Sr. The service was held in the Caldwell Hall auditorium, which I had first seen nearly twenty-five years earlier when I came to the campus for the first time as a fourteen-year-old kid to participate in the statewide New Farmers of America public speaking contest.

167

Professor Howard told me that the theme for the 1968 Founder's Day celebration was: "Our challenge—comprehending the present student generation, and meeting their needs." Although Professor Howard said I was free to talk about a subject of my own choosing, I told him I was completely comfortable with the theme they had selected. I saw immediately how one might develop a speech around that theme, which incorporated ideas about students' central roles in the civil rights struggles of recent years.

I told the Solicitor about the invitation right away and indicated that I would be spending some of my time gathering materials and writing my speech. He had no problem with this. I chose to use the platform of Founders Day at my alma mater to challenge college administrators to understand that college students in the 1960s are a different breed than those of earlier eras; that they want to be involved more directly not only in matters affecting them as students, but also to have an impact on the larger societal issues that will affect their lives in later years. I thought that recent student protests at various colleges and universities around the nation provided excellent context for such a message in the spring of 1968.

I declined the school's offer to arrange for me to stay on campus. Both my family and Dorothy's family still lived in Pine Bluff in 1968 so I had plenty of options for lodging. I decided to spend most of my time with Dorothy's sister Jo Marva and her husband Jessie Rancifer. They had a nice house on Watson Boulevard just north of the campus. I always enjoyed being with them as Jessie and I had so much in common. We were in the same fraternity and had fun hanging out together. Jessie was from a prominent family that farmed land near McGee, a town fifty miles or so south of Pine Bluff. He and Jo Marva both graduated from A. M. & N. College in the early 1960s. Jo Marva was a public school teacher and Jessie taught at the college while pursuing his post-graduate degree in mathematics at the University of Arkansas. From the very beginning of my marriage to Dorothy Ann, Jo Marva and I were great friends. We could always count on her when we needed a babysitter for Rudy while we were still in college. Of all the Davis children, Jo Marva's personality was most like that of her father. She liked to tease and had the ability to mimic the voice and mannerisms of other people, including friends and family.

Perhaps the most difficult thing for me about delivering the Founders Day sunrise address was trying to make sure I got to the event on time that Sunday morning. April 28, 1968 happened to mark the beginning of daylight savings time and sunrise that day occurred at 5:12 A.M. That meant, of course, one less hour of sleep the night before. So Jessie and I had to end our Saturday night revelries somewhat earlier than usual in order for me to be in good shape for the task I had at Caldwell Hall auditorium the next morning.

The anxiety about speaking to an audience which included many of my former professors and concern about sleeping past the alarm and being late for the service led to a restless night. I made it to Caldwell Hall auditorium on time, but not in the best of shape. President Davis and other members of the Founder's Day committee greeted me warmly as we gathered for a few moments in the president's office before the service. My parents were going to be in the audience, along with a very good turnout of students, faculty members and staff. Frankly I was surprised at the number of people willing to get up that early on Sunday morning to attend a memorial service.

My talk seemed to go over quite well, especially with the students. I think my message also got through to the faculty and administrators, judging by the less than enthusiastic response of some at the breakfast at the student union building following the service. I had suggested in my talk that college administrators and faculty needed to listen more closely to what students had to say about changing the world they live in. Perhaps some of the more tradition minded among the faculty felt my talk bordered on encouraging rebellion among students. Reading the speech years later I could understand why some might interpret it that way. After all one must realize that during that period several colleges and universities had experienced student unrest and rebellion. The important thing is that President Davis clearly appreciated and welcomed what I had to say. Throughout his entire tenure as president, spanning nearly twenty-five years, he had been truly a student friendly administrator. His empathy for students no doubt can be attributed to the fact that he himself had come to the job of

169

college administrator directly from the ranks of the student body at A. M. & N. College.

*   *   *

Despite the shocking news of the night before that Martin Luther King had been shot to death in Memphis, I got up and went to work as usual on Friday, April 5. Jim Jones picked me up in his Volkswagen in front of my house at 8 o'clock A.M. As I got into the car we just looked at each other without saying a word for several moments. Finally he drove off toward Georgia Avenue via Kalmia Road. By the time we reached the point where Piney Branch Road turns into 13th Street one way going south, neither of us had gotten much beyond saying "What a shame: what happens next." We were literally still in a state of shock, trying to comprehend what the killing of Dr. King would mean on several different levels. We both had seen the King magic as a charismatic leader work to inspire a crowd at the march on Washington a few years earlier. Was there anyone who could replace him in that regard? Did it mean the end of King's dream of a society where blacks and whites could live together on the basis of equality, but with respect and understanding for the differences between them? Did the killing mean that J. Edgar Hoover had finally won? What if it turns out that it was Hoover who ordered the killing? What would be the reaction of the masses of black people? Of white people in general?

Jim and I, of course, had been following very closely the evolution of King's ideas and the shift in his focus to more global issues. He had begun to question President Johnson's Vietnam War policies; he had taken his campaign to northern urban centers like Chicago, attempting to address housing, employment and economic justice issues; he was in the midst of planning another massive demonstration in Washington aimed at mobilizing "poor" people and pressuring the federal government to do more to eliminate poverty in the nation. These were issues that ranged far beyond traditional concepts of "civil rights" and obvious discriminatory practices against blacks in the South. I said to Jim that these recent moves by King threatened certain powerful interests in the society—the military/industrial complex that Eisenhower had spoken about and the powerful financial and business

170

institutions that had always opposed the idea of wealth redistribution or anyone asserting a "right" to a job or a living wage. It was my opinion then that King was killed because he was a charismatic black man who ventured too far off the civil rights reservation. Just as we knew of King's power to inspire people to action, so did Wall Street and mainstream political leaders of both parties. I believed that the president and congressional leaders as well were fearful of King's ability to cause a serious disruption in the established order if poor and dispossessed whites as well as blacks began to respond to his message.

Everything looked normal when I arrived at my office shortly before nine o'clock A.M. but that was only a facade. There was a palpable tension, a sense of an impending explosion of emotion as people tried to go about their business as if this were just another day at the office. The feeling I was experiencing that Friday morning was what I imagine most white Americans felt the day after President Kennedy was shot in November 1963. The tragedy had occurred, there was nothing you could do about it, but you knew that the consequences were likely to be enormous for you personally, the nation and perhaps the world. In the Kennedy assassination though I remembered that some people in the office that day broke down and cried. Others seemed to seek out colleagues to talk about the tragedy and what it meant for the future. On that April morning in my office, however, no one except other black people seemed to want to talk to me about the King killing and its meaning. My white colleagues averted their eyes when we passed in the hall. I believe many of them felt the same sense of loss that I felt but were not certain how or whether to express it to me. Was it appropriate for a white colleague to offer his condolence? Or would such an expression reflect a feeling that they regarded King's death as a loss for black people only?

Before noon we began receiving reports of civil disturbances in black neighborhoods in scattered cities around the country. Not long thereafter from fourth floor windows at the rear of the Labor Department building one could see plumes of smoke rising above rooftops north of the city beyond the downtown area. Obviously, something was going on in the city along the 14th Street corridor, apparently in reaction to news of the King killing. At that time there had been no definitive news as to who shot Dr. King and cer-

171

tainly no news of the authorities arresting anyone in connection with the shooting. This led to rampant speculation and rumors, which in turn probably incited some people to act out in frustration, striking the most convenient targets in black neighborhoods.

Word came down from the Assistant Secretary for Administration that employees would be free to leave work early. Obviously there was growing concern about safety for personnel traveling through the city on their way home from work. Jim Jones and I decided to take advantage of this opportunity to leave the office early as our normal route home would take us directly through the heart of the city up 13th Street. We decided it would be prudent to take a more circuitous route that day. We left the building and drove east on Constitution Avenue, not turning north until we reached North Capitol Street over near Capitol Hill and Union Station. As we drove north past the rear of Howard University and the hospital center complex we saw military convoys approaching the city from the direction we were traveling. There were dozens of army trucks with canvas covered cargo space containing armed soldiers and other military equipment, headed toward the capitol and other government buildings.

We made it home without incident, but news reports indicated that some areas in the city were besieged by rioters breaking into, looting and setting fire to stores and small businesses. Appeals by the mayor for citizens to remain indoors and calm only added to my own anxiety about what was going to happen next. By five o'clock that afternoon everyone in my family was home. Our neighborhood was quiet. While we were several miles from the center of town I did not feel entirely secure. Georgia Avenue, which was lined with many small shops and businesses all the way to Silver Spring, Maryland, was only two blocks away.

Before nightfall Edgar Twine called from his home in Wheaton, a predominately white neighborhood in Montgomery County some eight or ten miles north of the city. He was very concerned about being out there surrounded by whites. I told him to bring Lillian, Eddie, Jr., and Debbie to my house where we could ride out this gathering storm together. Dorothy Ann had baked some chicken and made a fruit salad for dinner and said there was enough for our friends to share if they came over. I then called Eddie Williams' house and talked to his wife Sally. They too

172

wanted someone to talk to about what was going on. I told her that the Twines were on their way over and invited her family to join us as well.

The Twines arrived at our house in a very excited mood. Edgar said "Did you know there was an army roadblock being set up at the district line just a few blocks from here, but they let us through." It turned out that similar checkpoints were being set up at every major entry point into Washington from the Maryland suburbs. Soldiers were closely inspecting all vehicles entering the city. City authorities announced on the radio and TV networks that service stations would be allowed to dispense gasoline only directly into a vehicle's tank—and fuel could not be sold or purchased in any type of containers. The national guard had been called out to assist the local police in trying to restore order in the central city. The White House, the Capitol and other major government buildings were ringed by military units, some with armored vehicles and machine guns in strategic locations.

After dinner the eight kids in the house scattered, some to the basement and others upstairs, leaving the adults alone around the dining room table to discuss the events of the last twenty-four hours. Eddie Williams, who was employed at a rather important job at the State Department, probably had the most experience in politics of all those present. He had been trained as a journalist, had worked at a black newspaper in Atlanta after college and had been an assistant to Senator Humphrey. Edgar Twine, somewhat younger than Eddie and I, was doing well as a lawyer in the Civil Division at the Department of Justice, having recently been assigned to a very high profile case that required him to travel to Europe to take depositions.

The discussion turned first to the question of who really was responsible for the King killing. It was my view that a conspiracy existed, probably involving persons at high levels in the federal government. Given the general knowledge of FBI Director Hoover's intense hatred for King, it was easy for me to conclude that the job likely was done at Hoover's behest, if not by the FBI directly. Sally and Twine tended to agree with me on this. Williams was not convinced this was the case. He pointed out that King had a lot of other enemies, some within the civil rights movement itself. He recalled some of the bickering that went on among the

173

civil rights leaders in planning the 1963 march on Washington. Not everyone was pleased with how King operated and some were jealous of all the acclaim and honors that had come to him personally. The honors King received came as a result of the hard work, sacrifice and dedication of many little known individuals in the struggle, as well as his own efforts.

Williams, who had grown up in Memphis, also observed that there had been some disagreement about participation of certain groups in the protests going on in Memphis at the time of King's assassination. The killing could have been done by some disgruntled person who felt slighted in some way by a decision made in connection with the garbage workers protest.

I knew from my own experience that tempers could run pretty hot over policy issues in a mass protest effort. Some individuals on the frontlines of the struggle were not as committed as King obviously was to maintaining a totally nonviolent posture in all events. Some felt it was inappropriate to expose black women and young children to brutal police dogs, fire hoses and billy clubs as in the Selma march a few years earlier. I remember expressing these views at an emergency meeting of the D.C. NAACP branch following the Selma march in 1965. I had to acknowledge that Williams had a point when he said there may have been others who wanted to see King removed from his position of leadership. But I still could not believe that anyone associated with any of the civil rights groups would want to see King killed.

Everyone around the table agreed, however, that while the loss of King was a serious blow, the movement toward the goal of full citizenship rights for black Americans would continue. Both political parties seemed committed to that goal and the vast majority of the American people believed that our cause was a just one. The biggest danger we had to guard against was having the various civil rights organizations turn against each other in a struggle for ascendancy. We could not afford to have the NAACP, the Urban League, the Southern Christian Leadership Conference, the Student Non-violent Coordinating Committee, or the Congress of Racial Equality at each other's throats. All these groups were different. Each had certain strengths and weaknesses. But we felt they all served important functions in the overall struggle and all were necessary if we are to reach the goal.

After watching the eleven o'clock news, Lillian, Sally and Dorothy Ann went upstairs to oversee getting the younger children in bed. The Twines had decided to spend the night rather than drive back to Wheaton. Edgar, Eddie and I decided to play a few hands of poker while continuing to listen to news reports on the radio about the rioting that still was going on in parts of the city. We continued playing until nearly daybreak when someone suggested we should drive into the city to see firsthand exactly what was taking place.

By that time everyone else in the house had fallen asleep. We got in Williams' car and drove down Georgia Avenue towards town. We saw nothing out of the ordinary until we approached the intersection at Missouri Avenue. That intersection was controlled by several armed soldiers who ordered our car to stop. There was no other traffic on the street at that time. Two solders approached the car, one from either side. The one on the driver's side inquired as to where we were headed. Williams told him we had been watching and listening to the news all night and wanted to see for ourselves whether what we had heard about the rioting was actually true. They requested to see our drivers licenses, which confirmed that two of us lived in northwest Washington. We were told that we would not be allowed to proceed further south along Georgia Avenue as that area was closed to sightseers. In the distance we could hear the sirens of police and other emergency vehicles. We also could see smoke and the light of fires on the horizon south and west of where we were.

*　*　*

The presidential election campaign of 1968 was the most eventful of any I had experienced as a federal government employee. It was the fourth election I had endured since coming to government service. In only one of the previous three had the election resulted in a change in party control of the government. That was in 1960 when John Kennedy defeated the Republican candidate, Richard Nixon. In each of the previous elections, however, the position I held was not at a high enough level for me to be seriously concerned that my job might be in jeopardy, depending on the outcome of the election. Things were different for me in 1968.

175

The job I had usually turned over with a change in administration. While I knew that I was vulnerable this time around, I did not feel compelled to take any political actions that might help return the Democrats to power in the White House. Of course, as a civil service employee subject to the Hatch Act limitations, my available options for political involvement were very few. So throughout the 1968 election season I took the stance of an interested observer, a position similar to that of an avid baseball fan who roots for the home team. I intended to vote for the Democratic nominee and fervently hoped that candidate would win, but I was determined to wait until the election was over before deciding what my next career move would be.

It seems that everything that could go wrong did go wrong for the Democrats in the months leading up to the 1968 election. Perhaps their strongest potential candidate was assassinated before the primaries were over. The Democratic convention was marred by massive civil disturbances in Chicago. The protests were handled very badly by the police and Mayor Daley, who was one of the most well-known political leaders in the Democratic party. The candidate that emerged victorious from the convention, Vice President Humphrey, was linked inextricably to the Vietnam War policies that caused the incumbent President to decide not to seek reelection.

The Republicans too nominated a flawed candidate, one who had lost the election eight years earlier, and done very little in the intervening years to improve his image as a leader. However, he had the distinct advantage of portraying himself as a change agent. That probably gave him the edge he needed to win the election on November 6.

By mid-morning on November 7th, 1968 it was clear that Richard Nixon had been elected President of the United States. I was disappointed that Hubert Humphrey lost. I now had to face that reality and take the steps I had been postponing about securing my own future. But first I wanted to find someone who felt the way I did about the Humphrey loss to have a few drinks with at a long lunch hour. My good friend Bob Guttman, the Deputy Associate Solicitor under Harold Nystrom and a good Democrat, also was very despondent about the outcome of the election. He, Jim Jones and I left the office a little after noon and walked to a small French restaurant on Pennsylvania Avenue not far from the White House.

We took turns ordering drinks for each other while we talked about the election and how close Humphrey had come to pulling it out in the last few days of the campaign. I was the only one among the three of us who had a schedule "C" job and thus would have to find something else to do when the new administration came in after January 20, 1969. Although Guttman and Jones held positions at a higher grade than mine, they both were classified as attorneys in the normal excepted service. Therefore, they were protected by civil service regulations from summary dismissal by a new administration. Nevertheless, we all had made our mark in government service under Democratic administrations, despite having been hired while Eisenhower was President. They too were not sure what changes the Nixon Administration would bring and were concerned whether they would continue to thrive as they had the last several years.

After about the second round of drinks Jim Jones said to me, "Mac, you really should not worry too much about having a job after January. All you have to do now is return to your old job in the Division of Labor-Management Laws. I'm sure George Avery, the associate solicitor over there whom you have worked with in the past, would be glad to have you back. You would suffer no reduction in pay or grade." Guttman chimed in saying that happens all the time. He cited several cases in the Solicitor's office where people had done that when Kennedy succeeded Eisenhower in 1961. And even when the Johnson people came in following Kennedy's assassination during the 1963/64 period. Finally I said, "I'm not sure I want to go back into the bureaucracy." I told them I had enjoyed being in the middle of policymaking at the highest level of the department the last year and was not sure I could easily revert to being an anonymous cog in the big wheel of government. "Maybe it's time for me to explore some other options for employment." After all for the past several years the Labor Department had been urging companies and other private institutions to hire "qualified" blacks in professional and managerial jobs. I thought there might be some company out there possibly interested in someone with my background and experience. Our lunch ended at about three o'clock that afternoon and the three of us made our way back to the office feeling no pain.

*   *   *

The United States Senate did not get around to confirming the new Solicitor of Labor until the end of March 1969. The new chief lawyer for the department was Laurence H. Silberman, a very bright man still in his early thirties. Mr. Silberman, whose friends called him "Larry," came into the office for the first time the first or second week of April. I was still at my post in the special assistant's office. My old boss Charlie Donahue had cleared out his office shortly before Christmas 1968, leaving Deputy Solicitor Friedmen in charge during the transition period. But the Deputy Solicitor was busy during most of that time trying to land another job for himself. When Friedman left to enter private practice in March, Harold Nystrom, the ranking civil service lawyer in the office, became acting solicitor until Silberman actually arrived. For a brief time in early 1969, I, in fact, operated without much direction from a responsible political official.

I knew very little about Larry Silberman, except that he had strong political ties in the state of Kentucky. The Republican governor Louie B. Nunn and the newly elected Republican senator from that state, Marlow W. Cook, both were friends and supporters of his. He was friendly, but very businesslike. At our first meeting he said he wanted me to stay where I was while he got a feel for the job of Solicitor of Labor. Obviously he had seen my file and knew that I came to work at the department years ago under a Republican administration. I told him that I would be glad to stay on for a while but that I was looking at options for employment in the private sector, rather than returning to the safety of a staff legal position elsewhere in the office. He said he appreciated my candor and understood my desire to try my hand at something else.

While he had access to the records of key people in the office, he would occasionally ask me what I thought about a particular lawyer in the office. I think he really wanted my opinion but I believe he also was trying to ascertain whether I was the kind of person he could trust as a confidential assistant. I explained to him that I had gotten to know many of the lawyers on a professional level over the twelve years of my tenure. But very few of them were personal friends. I named several lawyers who I thought were outstanding legal talents. I also pointed out that sometimes legal credentials can be misleading.

I could tell right away that Silberman was considered one of the bright young stars in the Republican Party and that he had political ambitions beyond the level of Solicitor of Labor. But clearly he wanted to do well in the Solicitor's job. I think he realized I could help him in this regard, given my knowledge and experience in the office. We worked well together such that when he brought his own assistant into the office about six weeks later he explained to him that I would remain on board indefinitely and the two of us would be working together as his assistants.

Meanwhile, less than a week after the 1968 election I decided to call a classmate from the Indiana University law school, Congressman Lee Hamilton. Lee Hamilton had been elected to congress in 1964 from the 9th congressional district in southeast Indiana. The two of us entered I. U. together in the fall of 1953 and graduated with that class in 1956. He invited me to have lunch with him on Capitol Hill. We met for lunch in the cafeteria at the Longworth House office building where we reminisced about law school and how our careers had progressed along different paths. After lunch he invited me to come to his office to meet his staff. Presently, I told Lee that I wanted to leave government service and take a job in the private sector. I asked if he could help through any of his contacts with people in the business world. He said he would try and we left it at that.

8

Making the Transition to the Private Sector

Early in May 1969, I got a call at my office from a person who identified himself as K. Richard Edsall, the assistant general counsel of Pacific Lighting Corporation of Los Angeles. Mr. Edsall told me he was in town on business and inquired whether I might be free to meet with him the next day for lunch in the Mens' Grill at the Madison Hotel. He said he wanted to discuss the possibility of my taking a position with his company. I had never heard of K. Richard Edsall or Pacific Lighting Corporation. But I told Edsall that I would indeed be interested in meeting him for that purpose. Before hanging up I asked how would I know who Mr. Edsall was when I came to the restaurant since we had not met before. He said, "Don't worry about that, I think I will recognize you when you arrive."

I took a taxi to the Madison Hotel for my meeting with Mr. Edsall. Although I had driven by the Madison Hotel numerous times I had never been inside the 15th Street building. The Madison is what some would call a boutique hotel that catered to a very limited, special clientele. Its public areas were ornately decorated with Persian rugs, antique furnishings, Austrian shades and heavy velvet drapes. It was what I imagined the finest hotels in Europe might look like inside, which was quite a contrast from the undistinguished appearance of the hotel building itself. The Mens' Grill was located to the right past the reception desk through the hotel lobby. It clearly was designed as a small retreat where men could gather during the day or after work for drinks and cigars, and to watch sporting events on television without being worried about boisterous language and the presence of women.

Edsall was seated alone at a table facing the entrance. We made eye contact immediately so I knew he was the man I was to meet. I walked directly over to him, extended my hand and said, "I'm Rufus McKinney. You must be Mr. Edsall." He recognized me because he was expecting to see a black man and I was the only one of my race in the whole place. He called the waiter over and said, "I'll have another scotch mist. What would you like?" At that stage in my life my favorite drink was bourbon whisky, Jack Daniels if someone else was buying, but the less expensive Virginia Gentleman brand if I was buying. So I ordered a Jack Daniels and water.

Edsall was a very gregarious sort of person, not very tall, of medium build and a severely receding hairline. He looked a great deal like the senator from South Dakota, George McGovern. I figured he was in his early to mid forties. Edsall proceeded to tell me about his company. Pacific Lighting Corporation was a public utility holding company based in Los Angeles. It had two wholly-owned subsidiaries—Southern Counties Gas and Southern California Gas Company. Each utility operated in an area of the southern half of the state of California. Pacific Lighting Service Company also was part of the system. The law department was part of that company, which provided various other services to the parent and operating companies. He told me that the two operating utilities taken together constituted the largest natural gas distribution utility system in the United States, serving in excess of four million customers and a population of over ten million people. The company's distribution operations were regulated by the California Public Utilities Commission. But the interstate natural gas pipelines that supplied the utilities were subject to regulation by the Federal Power Commission here in Washington. He told me that he came to Washington frequently to participate in various cases at the Federal Power Commission. The company was interested in having me join their law department in Los Angeles.

Edsall then asked me to tell him about who I was, but it was fairly obvious to me that he already knew everything about me that had been included in the résumé I sent to Congressman Lee Hamilton following our conversation in November of the year before. He did not tell me how he came to find out about me and my interest in finding a private sector position and I did not ask. I did tell him about my large family and about some of the volunteer work I had done for the NAACP over the past several years. After a very good lunch Edsall said he would give his boss John Ormasa, the general counsel, a report on our meeting as soon as he returned to Los Angeles. I should expect a call from Ormasa within a week or ten days.

I left the meeting feeling much relieved. It was very clear to me that the people at Pacific Lighting wanted me to come to work for them and that I would get an offer soon. Sure enough, in less than a week John Ormasa called me at the office to say that he and Edsall had talked and he wanted me to come to Los Angeles for a round of interviews with senior management of the company on July 11. The company sent a round-trip first class airline ticket and arranged for me to stay at the Hilton Hotel on Wilshire Boulevard near company headquarters.

I could hardly wait to get home to tell Dorothy Ann the good news, even though no definitive offer of a job had yet been made. I said the company would not spend that much money to have me fly to Los Angeles to personally meet the general counsel, president and chairman of the board if they did not intend to offer me a job. I was very thrilled at the prospect of going to California for the first time. But beyond that the knowledge that my government career was about to end and a new chapter in my life about to begin filled me with a sense of adventure and challenge.

Everybody in the family except our oldest son Rudy shared my feeling that a change would be good for us at this time. Rudy was seventeen years old and had just completed the junior year of high school. He was looking forward to his senior year at Coolidge High School where he expected to move up to become the starting halfback on the varsity football team that fall. His coaches had told him that his play the previous season showed great promise of his becoming more than an ordinary high school running back. Rudy also was in love with a cute girl cheerleader at Coolidge and could not bear the thought of leaving her behind, perhaps never to see her again.

The younger children had no problem with the idea of moving to California. It was a good time for Fred because he had just completed junior high and would be going to high school for the first time in September. Anne Marie, who was twelve years old, was scheduled to enter junior high that fall so the change would not be all that disruptive. And Paula, the seven-year-old baby girl, was about to enter third grade and would have no trouble adjusting to a change.

Jackson, Mississippi was the site for the sixtieth annual convention of the NAACP which took place June 29 through July 5, 1969. Throughout my more than ten years as an active member and officer of the D. C. branch I had never been very involved in the politics of the organization at any level beyond the local branch. When I learned that the 1969 annual convention would be in Jackson, the capital of the state with the most deeply rooted hostility toward black people, and perhaps the most intensely segregated society of all the Southern states, I successfully campaigned to be selected as a delegate from the D. C. branch. The NAACP convention always attracted thousands of black citizens from all over the nation. I wanted to see for myself whether the civil rights laws and other regulations that had been instituted by federal authorities to guarantee to blacks equal access to hotels and other places of public accommodations could be made to work in a place like Jackson, Mississippi.

Betty Holton and Ed Hailes, two other delegates from the D. C. branch, met me at national airport on the morning of June 29 for the flight to Jackson, via New Orleans. We each were apprehensive about the trip, but were determined to be present for this history-making event. This was the first time the national NAACP convention had been held in the state of Mississippi. We were not sure what to expect when we arrived in Jackson. We knew, however, that it would be difficult to successfully put on such a large convention without some support and cooperation from local governmental authorities. The only building in the city with an auditorium large enough to hold the assembly of more than a thousand delegates probably would be the Jackson City Auditorium. We wondered what attitude the police and local political leaders would take towards such a large influx of people of color in this bastion of segregation. Would we be met with hostility when seeking service in restaurants and hotels? Would the visitors be treated with dignity and respect by the locals when seeking directions or information about the city?

We were pleasantly surprised on arriving at the Jackson Airport. There were large signs on display welcoming the delegates to

Jackson. Plenty of taxis driven by both blacks and whites awaited us outside for the drive into the city. The biggest hotel in town, the Heidelberg Hotel, served as convention headquarters. All the high officials and important guests of the convention stayed at this hotel in the center of town. My colleagues and I from the D. C. branch had reservations at a small motel not far from the downtown area called the Downtowner Motor Hotel. I think it is safe to say that convention delegates and visitors had taken every available hotel and motel room within ten miles of the center on Jackson for that week. The motel clerks were courteous as we registered and freely offered us advice as to the best places to eat nearby.

As I reflect on the events of that convention I must say that the local NAACP planning committee did an outstanding job in preparing the way and so did white political and civic leaders of Jackson. I do not recall a single incident of white/black confrontation or unbecoming conduct on the streets of Jackson during the week of the convention. In fact, the one incident that stands out in my mind was a positive one from the standpoint of interaction between the two races. It involved a white woman whose car broke down on a major through street and a black policeman who offered his help. The woman seemed to have no problem accepting the black officer's offer to be of assistance. And white passersby, while noticing what then was an unusual scene of a black man helping an attractive young white woman in distress, chose not to intervene in any way. No doubt, the city of Jackson by 1969 had made greater strides than most small Mississippi towns toward acceptance of the proposition that ordinary black persons are as entitled to being treated with respect as any law abiding white person. And one should not ignore the probability that part of the city's civility toward the many out-of-town visitors could be attributed to the fact of intense media coverage of the convention and a desire to avoid the unfavorable publicity that inevitably would accompany any other kind of behavior.

Participation as a delegate to the convention was a real eye opener for me. I got a close up view of the internal politics of the NAACP and a better understanding of where the levers of power were in the organization. As a mere member and activist at the local level I had assumed that the well-known national leaders like the Executive Director and Board Chairman were controlling powers within the organization. I discovered that this was not necessarily the case. The ostensible power associated with high office may not in fact be real power. I saw the overriding power of money—how large contributors, whether they be wealthy individuals, corporations or labor unions, can exercise immense influence, if not control, over important policy matters in the organization. In some instances individuals who represented the interest that is the source of financial support may occupy an official position in the organization. But often that person holds no such office or position. Being a delegate also gave me the opportunity to see the influence of the various regions and how some regions wielded considerably greater influence than others did. The D. C. branch is part of Region VII which includes branches in Maryland, Virginia and certain other southeastern states. Region VII is an area that is rich in individual NAACP members. And as such it is one of the more influential regions.

The 1969 convention took on a kind of celebratory atmosphere. The effects of the 1965 voting rights act had begun to take effect as evidenced by the election of black state and local officials in record numbers throughout the South. In fact, many delegates planned to remain in Mississippi a few extra days in order to witness the following week the installation of Charles Evers as the first black mayor of Fayette, Mississippi, a town just a few miles south and west of Jackson near the Mississippi River. Charles Evers, the NAACP field secretary for Mississippi, is the brother of Medgar Evers, who held the same job when he was gunned down from ambush in front of his home six years earlier by white supremacy advocates.

During the course of the convention Ed Hailes introduced me to Jack Young, president of the Jackson branch. Jack Young was a very prominent attorney in Jackson who had done work on behalf of the NAACP over the years. Hailes, Betty Holton and I were fortunate enough to be invited to a big Fourth of July party at Jack Young's home. We welcomed the chance to get away from the business of the convention and have some fun in the company of people from the local community. Jack Young had a nice house in town on a large lot that easily accommodated a good-sized crowd, picnic style. The thing I remember most vividly was that Jack roasted a goat over a fire outside for the occasion. There were plenty of drinks of both the alcoholic and non-alcoholic variety. About the latter Ed Hailes and I were curious because we knew that Jackson was in a "dry" county, meaning that liquor was not legally sold in package stores or by the drink in bars and restaurants. Despite this fact Jack Young's bar was well-stocked with all kinds of the best liquor. Eventually I got up the nerve to ask Jack how an upstanding member of the bar and pillar of the community was able to maintain such a fine bar in a dry town like Jackson. He proceeded to tell us that being in a dry town does not mean that liquor is not freely available to law-abiding citizens in Jackson. "All the liquor I need I buy from the sheriff of Hinds county," Young declared. "How can that be?" we asked. "Whenever I want a new supply I call the sheriff and put in my order. Then I take my car over and park it in the garage of the sheriff's office building in downtown Jackson. After that I go on about my business for the day. When I returned for my car that evening, the products would have been delivered into the trunk of my car. It's that simple," Jack said. "We've been doing business that way for as long as I can remember and everybody who is anybody in town is quite happy with the arrangement."

*   *   *

I left Dulles International Airport for my non-stop flight to Los Angeles at one P.M. on Thursday July 10. I arrived in Los Angeles that afternoon in plenty of time to get a good night's rest for my meetings the next morning with officials of the Pacific Lighting Companies. John Ormasa, the general counsel, had made arrangements for me to stay Thursday night at the Hilton Hotel at 930 Wilshire Boulevard, which was within an easy walk to the company offices at 720 West Eighth Street. On this my first trans-continental flight I discovered the meaning of "jet lag" when I awoke at my normal east coast time the next morning only to discover that it was four A.M. and still dark outside. Obviously my body had not made the adjustment to the three-hour time difference between Washington, D. C. and Los Angeles. I could not go back to sleep so I lay there in contemplative silence thinking of the interviews I had scheduled later that morning with people I had never met before. I also felt some anxiety about the major changes that would take place in my life and that of my family if the people I was about to meet formed a favorable opinion of me and decided to offer me a job in California.

I certainly would miss being close to Esther and her family and Lorenzo, a younger brother who had set up his practice in Washington after finishing the Howard University dental school in 1964. But I also had family in California. My sister Izora Prentice and her daughter Marsha lived in Inglewood not far from Los Angeles International Airport. Izora, an elementary school teacher in the Inglewood public schools, came to California from Cleveland, Ohio in the late 1950s. My youngest brother Ernest had settled in Los Angeles after leaving the Peace Corps and was enrolled in law school at the University of Southern California. Another sister, Ruth Dixon, lived with her husband Harold and their four children in the little Orange County town of Los Alamitos about 40 miles south of Los Angeles. An even larger contingent of my immediate family lived in the San Diego area. My brother George was pastor of a large church in the city of San Diego, and his assistants there were another brother Jessie and a sister Marvella Simmons. George had come to San Diego in 1960 shortly after receiving the master of arts degree from the Oberlin College School of Theology. George too had great success as a student at Arkansas A. M. & N. College, graduating in 1957. He was the founding pastor of Saint Stephen's Church of God in Christ in San Diego. So a move to California would simply mean reconnecting with a different set of my brothers and sisters.

The Pacific Lighting Companies occupied three buildings that took up the entire block of Flower Street between Eighth and Ninth Streets. Like all the buildings in this older part of the city, Pacific Lighting headquarters were all low rise buildings, none more than twelve stories high. Two of the buildings were of the same vintage, circa 1920. The third building was much more modern and of an entirely different design. It stood on the corner of Eighth and Flower Streets. This building was headquarters for Pacific Lighting Service Company where the law department was located. Access to the law department was through an entrance on Eighth Street.

I arrived for my interviews at about nine o'clock A.M. and was directed to general counsel John Ormasa's office on the 7th floor where I was greeted by his secretary, a flaming redhead, Colleen Dalglish. She promptly ushered me into Mr. Ormasa's private office. We exchanged pleasantries after introducing ourselves. I told him that my first cross-country trip was quite exciting for me. My plane's approach to the airport had given me a panoramic view of the Los Angeles basin and that was a most impressive sight to behold. And the ride from the airport gave me the chance to see much of what appears to be a beautiful city. John Ormasa was a man of average height who looked to be about fifty years old. He had a dark complexion and very distinct facial features, i.e. bushy eyebrows, heavy lips, a prominent nose and piercing dark eyes. I could not figure out at first what his ethnic background was. I later learned that his family was from the Basque area of Spain, although Ormasa was a native-born American citizen. He spoke rapidly with no accent that I could discern. His demeanor was most pleasant, but business-like. He proceeded to tell me more about the law department and to fill me in on the rest of the program for the day.

In addition to being general counsel Ormasa also was a vice president of Pacific Lighting Service Company. That company housed several other staff functions for both the parent holding company and the operating natural gas utilities. In 1969 the law department consisted of seven attorneys in addition to Edsall and Ormasa. These lawyers did all of the internal legal work for the company, including the regulatory work before the California Public Utilities Commission. The general counsel also managed the work of several outside lawyers and law firms that were involved in matters before certain federal agencies such, as the Securities and Exchange Commission, the Internal Revenue Service and the Federal Power Commission.

He told me that all lawyers in the department had to be fully qualified to practice law in the state of California. In other words, if I were to take a job at Pacific Lighting I would have to successfully pass the California bar examination. California was one of a few states that made no provision for lawyers from other states being admitted on the basis of reciprocity on motion of a member of the California bar. The one concession they did make for experienced attorneys moving into the state was to offer an attorney's bar examination. That examination was for one full day only, instead of the three-day examinations for law school graduates who are not members of the bar of any state.

Thirteen years had elapsed since I last took a bar examination. I did not relish the idea of going through that ordeal again so far removed in time from my law school days. But the thought never crossed my mind that I could not pass such an examination in California. While Ormasa did not say so, it was apparent to me that I would be the first black attorney in the department and the first black professional person brought into the company at a fairly high level.

I spent a little more than an hour talking with Ormasa about a variety of things, including my thoughts about the new Nixon regime in Washington. We talked about my various assignments at the Department of Labor. He explained that our next stop would be the office of his boss, Joe Rensch, executive vice president of Pacific Lighting Corporation, the parent holding company. We would be joined at lunch in the executive dining room by Harvey Proctor, another senior officer, and maybe Paul Miller, the chief executive officer of the company.

Joe Rensch's office was on the top floor of the building in a suite, that housed all the top executives of the company. These offices were furnished and decorated the way I thought an executive suite for senior officers of a Fortune 500 company should look. Everything in sight looked expensive. The carpets were custom woven; the walls clad in dark mahogany wood; the lighting indirect and subdued; the windows exquisitely dressed with drapes and molding; large works of original art strategically placed throughout. Sitting at several large desks scattered around the reception area the size of a small ballroom were the executive secretaries, each of them perfectly coiffed and dressed like models from a high fashion magazine. All of them were mature women, white, tall and slim. There was no buzz of office machines or ringing telephones. Everyone seemed to speak in measured, hushed tones.

Joseph R. Rensch was a Hollywood leading man type, tall with keen facial features, and a full head of steel grey hair. When Ormasa and I entered his office he came from behind this huge desk, greeted us and invited us to sit in comfortable upholstered chairs around an antique coffee table while he took a seat on a nearby sofa. Rensch told me he too was a lawyer, having joined

189

one of the operating utilities as an attorney some twelve years earlier. We talked about the colleges and law schools we had attended. Rensch had taken a mechanical engineering degree from Stanford University and a law degree from Golden Gate College.

Rensch was the first official of the company to ask about my long-term career goals. The question caught me by surprise. I had not really thought about how I should answer that question, although I realized immediately that I should have anticipated it. I told Rensch that I had had a fairly good career as a federal government lawyer and at age thirty-nine I was ready to try something different, a new challenge. Working as a lawyer for a large company in the private sector was something that now interested me and I wanted to find out whether I could also do well in that area. My goal was to find a situation that offered both a challenge and an opportunity to advance to the higher levels in the organization either as a lawyer or in management. I mentioned that some time earlier I harbored thoughts of going into business for myself as an entrepreneur. I had this idea of trying to convince General Motors, Ford, or Chrysler that they should separate warranty service of new cars from new car sales dealerships and franchise the service function independently. But I had not pursued the idea much beyond thinking about it.

Harvey Procter joined John Omasa and me for lunch in the executive dining room which was near the executive office suites. Proctor was a little older than the other officers I had met that day. He was a chain smoker with thinning red hair, tall and with an extremely heavy voice. It did not take me long to figure out that Proctor was the man who knew the most about the natural gas business from an operational point of view. He also was the most down-to-earth of all the executives and seemed easiest to talk to. I liked him right away. I told him I could get used to the kind of treatment I had received at Pacific Lighting so far that day. The executive dining room was headed by one of the finest chefs in Los Angeles and the food was at least the equal of that of any five-star restaurant in New York or Washington.

After lunch I returned with Ormasa to his office where he told me I could expect to hear from him again in a few days. My return flight to Washington was scheduled to leave LAX at about 4 P.M. I walked back to the Hilton, picked up my luggage and took a taxi to the airport. I thought it had been a very productive day for me.

*   *   *

Exactly one week after returning home from Los Angeles I received a call in my office from John Ormasa. He said he wanted me to come to work in the law department at Pacific Lighting Service Company. I thought the terms of the offer were quite generous. The salary offered would represent about a sixty percent raise in pay. The company would pay the expenses of my wife and me for a trip to Los Angeles to find a house. I was offered the use of a company car for commuting to and from work and we would be reimbursed fully for all out of pocket moving expenses, including first class airfare to Los Angeles for my family and me. I accepted the offer and told him that I could report for work on September 15, 1969.

When I got home that Friday evening I was in a mood to celebrate the impending changes in my life and that of my family. My spirits were dampened, however, when Dorothy Ann reminded me that there were a lot of things we had to do in order to make the move to California in time for me to start work there in mid-September, less than two months away. First, we had to find a buyer for our house. We needed the proceeds from the sale of the house in order to make the necessary down payment on a place in California. And we had to go house hunting in California right away if we expected to find something by the time we planned to move there. We needed to arrange for an adult person to take care of our children while we were in California house hunting. Finally, she reminded me that Rudy still was insisting that he wanted to remain behind in Washington to complete his final year at Coolidge High School. We needed to think of something that might change his mind about moving or make the move less traumatic for him.

Selling the house was not a problem. The agent found a buyer willing to pay twelve thousand dollars more than we paid for the house eight years earlier. Gail, Dorothy's youngest sister, now married to a nice young man named Richard Harrison, agreed to look after the children while we looked for a house in California. The

191

biggest problem was Rudy. The closer we got to the time for the move the more resistant he became to the idea of leaving Washington. While I may have mellowed some in my child rearing philosophy in recent years I still essentially believed in the old school approach, i.e., until the child became financially independent, parents had the final say in all decisions affecting them. However, I preferred not to impose my will if any way could be found to avoid doing so. But both Dorothy Ann and I agreed it would be a grave error for us to leave Rudy behind, even with a close relative. We wanted nothing but the best for our oldest child and we figured no one else could replace his natural parents in trying to insure that he turned out all right.

My wife and I spent the week of August 10, 1969 searching for a house suitable for our family that we could afford in the Los Angeles area. This was not an easy task. We wanted to locate in an area with good public schools and a fairly safe neighborhood. We hoped the schools would have multi-racial student bodies, but the primary concern was that the schools be engaged seriously in developing the minds of students and motivating them for high achievement. Unfortunately, we did not have a lot of time to make our decision.

A real estate agent the company had referred us to in Pasadena took us to several places in that area, including a fairly new development in South Pasadena. But we did not like the sterile atmosphere we found there. The agent finally told us about a house high up in the Altadena foothills that was being sold by its owner. We asked that she show us the house, even though the asking price was somewhat above the range we thought we could afford.

We liked the house the moment we set eyes on it. It seemed the right size for our family, four bedrooms, two and a half baths and about 3,300 square feet, all on one level. It was close to town but had a country feel about it; well landscaped, a separate two car garage, a large lot with lots of trees and well separated from nearby houses, some of which obviously were more expensive. The house next door had a swimming pool, a lighted tennis court, and a separate pool house and stood on about two acres. The rear of our house overlooked Rubio Canyon, the nearest houses in that direction about a mile away. The house was seventeen miles from downtown Los Angeles, not a long commute by California standards.

We would be in the Pasadena unified school district if we purchased the house. That district was involved in a highly controversial lawsuit over school integration and was in the process of closing several schools that had become surplus due to declining school age population in the district. John Muir High School, Eliot Junior High and Loma Alta Elementary were the public schools that served the area. We would have at least one child in each of these schools. We put in an offer to purchase the house before leaving Los Angeles to return to Washington. Even though the price was higher than we planned on I knew we would figure out some way to close the deal if our offer were accepted.

Meanwhile, Dorothy Ann and I decided that Rudy's opposition to the move might be softened somewhat if he could see the Los Angeles area for himself prior to the actual move. He agreed, and took a flight west to spend a few days with Aunt Izora in Inglewood and to visit one of Dorothy Ann's closest friends who had recently moved to California from Washington. While he was there we also arranged for him to meet the family of one of the big boosters for the John Muir football team, Hilda and Myers Howard. The Howards lived in Altadena not far from the house we hoped to buy. They had two sons, Wesley and Chester, who were very good athletes and members of the John Muir football team. The Howards very much wanted to have Rudy join the team because they had heard about his ability as a running back. The only problem was that Rudy would be coming into the program as a senior. Rudy knew that it would be difficult for him to break into the lineup against boys who had earned letters in previous years under Muir's coach.

Rudy returned from the West Coast trip still not convinced that California was the place for him. About that time I finally realized that what Rudy objected to most was leaving behind a girl he had become very fond of at Coolidge High School. Now both Dorothy Ann and I were more determined than ever to bring Rudy with us to California.

I was so caught up in my own life changing events in the summer of 1969 that I paid little attention to another momentous adventure that took place on July 20 of that year—the first manned landing on the moon. The U.S. astronauts' moon landing occurred about the same time I made the commitment to move to California and join the law department of Pacific Lighting Service Company. It was indeed a demonstration of America's technical prowess and the culmination of the long struggle to dominate the race to outer space with the Soviet Union. Maybe in the very long run the conquest of space will be important to the life of ordinary people. But I didn't think it had much practical significance for my generation, except in terms of adding a new, very expensive dimension to the arms race.

I gave Larry Silberman notice of my resignation as soon as I decided to take the job in California. I would end my tenure at the Department of Labor on September 5, 1969. It turned out that Jim Jones decided to leave the department at the same time to take a job as a labor law professor at the University of Wisconsin law school in Madison. The Solicitor's office decided to honor our services to the department at a joint going away reception at the end of August. The two of us had served under four Presidents (Eisenhower, Kennedy, Johnson and Nixon) and four Secretaries of Labor (James P. Mitchell, Arthur J. Goldberg, W. Willard Wirtz and George P. Shultz). More than one hundred members of the staff and some of their spouses attended the event held in the large conference room of the Labor Department building. It was a good way to close out my federal government career.

Dr. Michaels accepted our offer on the house in Altadena. That was a big relief, although it was problematic whether settlement could be completed before the end of September. At least we knew where we eventually would be living in California.

I never realized how attached I had become to the house at 1310 Locust Road in northwest Washington until my family and I gathered in the empty living room for one last time before leaving for California. I had not lived any place as long as I had lived in that house since I left Jonesboro, Arkansas, 20 years earlier. The place held a lot of fond memories for me. I watched our children, Rudy, Fred, Anne and Paula, grow up to become distinct, individual human beings in the Shepherd Park neighborhood. Attachments they formed with kids in the neighborhood have lasted until this day. Though the house has changed hands several times since 1969, deep down I still consider it "my house." Since moving back to Washington in 1972, I still go by the place whenever I'm in the neighborhood just to see whether it still looks the same or to assess whether I approve or disapprove of the changes that may have been made by the current owners. I think the children have similar feelings about the house and the neighborhood they grew up in.

9

Seeing America—Driving to California

Although Pacific Lighting Service Company offered to fly the family to Los Angeles, I decided to make the trip by automobile with the entire family. We had never driven cross country beyond the state of Arkansas. I thought this would be a good time for all of us to get a close-up view of what the country is like along the major East-West interstate highways that had replaced the legendary "Route 66" to California made famous in the song by Nat "King" Cole. We planned the drive carefully, arranging in advance every overnight stop along the way. We decided to patronize the Holiday Inn motel chain at each of our stops because we had had good experiences with Holiday Inns after the federal public accommodation law went into effect. That chain of motels seemed to welcome our business on our annual pilgrimages to Arkansas after 1965.

The moving company did not complete the job of packing and loading our things until late afternoon, Monday September 8th. That evening Earl Davy came by and took pictures of the family in the empty living room. We wanted to have these photos as a reminder because we had no intention of ever returning to the Washington area to live. The room was empty, except I remember we conveyed the living room drapes covering the French doors and the Austrian shades that Dorothy Ann and her mother had made shortly after we moved into the house in 1961. These provided a great backdrop for Earl Davy's parting pictures of the family. Friends and neighbors came by to say goodbye. I remember Frank and Jan Hollis along with their children, Aleta, Kevin, Sherry and Mona stopping by. In years past Frank Hollis had "held court" in that living room many times. Our place had been action central in the early 1960s for small parties put together at the behest of Neighbors, Inc. in an effort to establish dialogue between blacks and whites in Shepherd Park. Elliott Bovelle and his wife, our neighbors on Kalmia Road also came by that evening. Looking back on that evening I think I just did not want to let go of the experience of living in Washington. That is why we lingered so long after the movers had completed their work.

The kids spent their last night in Washington with friends, while Dorothy Ann and I stayed with Esther and Smitty. We planned to spend the first night on the road in Breezewood, Pennsylvania, considerably less than a full day's drive from Washington. So we took our time getting up the next morning, rounding up all the kids and loading the car for the initial leg of our trip west. We finally got on the road shortly after noon on Tuesday, September 9. The car I had at the time was a big Mercury four-door sedan that we had purchased new about a year before. It was real roomy inside. Dorothy Ann and Paula rode with me up front while Anne Marie sat between Fred and Rudy in the back seat.

There was very little conversation as we drove from Washington up 270 and on to Interstate 70 in the scenic Maryland countryside. At this early date in September the trees and other foliage along the road were still green and had not yet begun to show their fall colors, but as we drove further north and west towards Pennsylvania I noticed a distinct change in the temperature and humidity level. The air got drier and cooler as we reached the higher elevations in western Maryland and as the sun began to hang low in the western sky.

While I did not say much, I was thinking a great deal about the life I was leaving behind and what the future might hold for me in California. I had no doubt that we had made the right decision to leave government and try something new. Without question if everything went according to plan the family would be better off financially with my new job. But what if things did not go according to plan? While my salary at Pacific Lighting Service Company was not contingent upon my successfully passing the California bar, my job with them might be in jeopardy if I should fail the examination. I had not negotiated a formal contract with a term of years so my employment ultimately was an at will oral contract. I had not discussed at all with them what would happen if I failed the bar the first time around, as many applicants do. All John Ormasa had said to me during our discussions was that in the first few months of my employment there until my first opportunity to take the bar in the spring of 1970, I would be free to spend as much time as I thought I needed during the work day to study and prepare myself for the bar examination. The bottom line is that I was taking a very big risk, but I really did not look at it that way. Instead, I saw the move as a step forward from a career standpoint, with great upside potential. I soon dismissed the negative thoughts because at that point I believed I was capable of doing whatever I set my mind to accomplish.

We got to Breezewood before dark and checked in at the Holiday Inn not far from Interstate 70 West where it intersects with the Pennsylvania Turnpike. We took two adjacent rooms—one for the kids and one for Dorothy Ann and me. We established a routine that we would follow pretty much for the remainder of our trip. We would try to complete our day's driving before dark in time for the kids to take a swim in the motel pool. Everybody would then get cleaned up for dinner in the hotel dining room. Everyone had the opportunity for at least eight hours sleep. We would rise about six thirty A.M., have a full breakfast and get back on the road not later than eight o'clock A.M. My goal was to cover five to six hundred miles each day. I did not plan scheduled lunch stops, only snacks and soft drinks when we stopped for gas or restrooms every two hours or so. This type of schedule worked for me, but it did not always work for others in the car, especially Dorothy Ann and the girls. Our biggest disagreements on the trip were about the frequency of rest stops and the prospect of not being able to reach our next destination before dark that evening.

The second leg of our trip would take us from Breezewood, Pennsylvania, through the West Virginia panhandle, the heart of Ohio and Indiana and to our next overnight stop in Effingham, Illinois, just across the Indiana border. Except for western Pennsylvania, the scenery on this part of the trip was not remarkable. Fred, Anne and Paula, however came up with various "games" to help pass the time. One was trying to identify the make and model of cars we passed on the road. Another was the license plate game—identifying the state the car was registered in.

Rudy, however, had determined to remain silent and resentful throughout the trip. He would speak only when spoken to directly and rarely said anything more than yes or no. Fred became his spokesperson, since Rudy would not speak to me directly. Whenever Rudy wanted to tell me something he would communicate the message to Fred who would later relay it to me. Rudy's attitude about the move was a matter of great concern to both parents and tended to cast a pall over the entire trip. It bothered the other children less and less as the trip progressed.

The third leg of the trip from Effingham, Illinois, took us to a small town just west of Oklahoma City. The kids were excited about crossing the Mississippi River bridge at St. Louis. We also found the drive through southwest Missouri more interesting than most of what we had seen before. For the most part I resisted pressure from Dorothy Ann and the kids to stop at interesting sites along the way because I had a certain schedule I felt I had to keep if we were going to make it to Los Angeles on time. I kept reminding everybody that this was not a vacation trip, although I'm sure all the kids except Rudy were behaving as if it were.

When we left Oklahoma my next destination was Flagstaff, Arizona, making this the longest leg of the entire trip. We had considered making Albuquerque, New Mexico the target overnight stop but if we stopped there the final leg of the trip would have been over 800 miles. I did not want to arrive in Los Angeles totally exhausted from driving such a long distance. We arrived in Albuquerque at about the time we normally would complete our drive for the day. I decided to press on, however, while realizing that we still had more than 200 miles to go before reaching Flagstaff. While daylight lasted the beautiful New Mexico landscape was just enough to keep us distracted from the fatigue the whole family began to feel as we drove west toward our destination. By nightfall the kids had fallen asleep and it was difficult for me to stay awake as well, until I noticed lightning and what appeared to be a storm brewing in the distance to the southwest. It was a spectacular display of the wonders of nature as lightning flashed against the clouds and orange colored afterglow of the setting sun and western hills. It was well past ten P.M. when we finally found the Holiday Inn just west of Flagstaff. We decided to skip dinner and went straight to bed.

We had not anticipated having to go through an inspection by agricultural authorities at the California border. They asked whether we had any live plants in the car or any type of fruit. If we had such items they told us we would have to turn them over. Apparently they feared any such items brought into California might be infected in some way and could harm or destroy indigenous plants or produce. We passed inspection on both counts and were on our way. Before leaving the inspection station, however, the officer told us to make sure we had a full gas tank and extra water in the car before venturing too far into the California desert.

At first I thought the desert was ugly and not an interesting place, but as I began to observe it more closely I realized the desert too had a special kind of beauty. Coming as I did from the East Coast and the South where the landscape in summer was lush with trees and other plants full with green leaves and flowers, I just was not used to the ocher and brown colors that dominate the desert.

The approach to Los Angeles by car from the east in 1969 did not give one the feeling of coming into a great city like New York or Chicago. There were few if any very tall buildings on the horizon. Instead, you noticed the buildup in traffic and the fact of passing through a series of small towns along the freeway with increasing frequency. The closer we got to the city the enormity of the system of freeways that traversed the area became more and more evident. Fortunately, we drove into town late afternoon on Saturday so the roads were not totally saturated with workday rush hour traffic.

We decided to go by Izora's house first. There we would visit for a while and give everyone a chance to relax from the trip before going to the motel in Pasadena where we had made reservations to stay until our furniture arrived and we could move into the house we had agreed to buy in Altadena. We took the place in Pasadena also in order to make it convenient for the kids to get to the schools they would be attending in the Pasadena unified school system the following Monday morning. Izora greeted us warmly in her little pastel colored house on 82nd Street in Inglewood. Hers was what appeared to be the perfect house for her and her daughter Marsha, who was near Anne's age. Though the house was small it sat on a narrow but deep, well-landscaped yard with flowers in bloom all around. It had a separate garage and space for a small vegetable garden and potting shed next to the garage. While Izora had lived in the area for several years, she was not comfortable driving on the freeway. Therefore she avoided them. She was not very helpful in providing directions as to the best way to get from her house to our motel in Pasadena.

10

Signing On at the Gas Company—From Labor to Utility Law

The personnel manager at Pacific Lighting Service Company was Foster Hames, a very mild mannered and pleasant sort of guy. He was the person I had to see first when I arrived for work on Monday, September 15, 1969. Hames shepherded me through the process of induction and orientation into the company. I was photographed for my company identification badge and signed all the necessary papers for insurance, etc. Hames mentioned that at my level one of the perks was an annual complete physical examination by one of several private physicians the company had on retainer to provide this service to senior level professionals and managers. Before being hired, of course, I had to undergo a thorough physical examination in Washington by a doctor the company selected. I had not seen his report, and I assumed the examination revealed no disqualifying medical problems. Many years earlier, shortly after I came to Washington, I had established the practice of occasional physicals at Yater Clinic on Massachusetts Avenue near Dupont Circle. I knew I had what was then described as a mild case of "essential hypertension" or high blood pressure. Since there were no symptoms, and otherwise I seemed to be in good health, I never was asked to take any kind of medication for the condition. On my first visit to the company doctor, however, he strongly recommended that I begin taking daily a pill which he prescribed to control my high blood pressure. Every day of my life since that time I have taken medication for high blood pressure. I was shocked when the doctor told me the company must have really wanted me to come to work for them because normally they would not hire a person with the blood pressure readings shown on the report he had seen on my pre-employment physical examination.

Hames also explained the procedure for use of a company car for commuting to and from work. The company maintained a large fleet of cars at headquarters for this purpose. The cars were serviced and maintained at the company garage and those having commuter car privileges simply returned them each morning to the company parking lot near the garage. Having the car was a real valuable perk for me because it meant that Dorothy Ann could keep our family car during the day. She really needed a car for the important tasks of running the house and chauffeuring the kids back and forth from football practice and other afterschool events. While I kept the car overnight and on weekends at home, technically it was not supposed to be used by other members of my household for personal errands. This rule was more honored in the breach than in the observance. Any traffic tickets or other driving infractions were the commuter's own responsibility, however.

After an hour or so with Foster Hames I finally reported to John Ormasa's office. He told me that I would report to Dick Edsall. The two of them promptly took me around and introduced me to the other lawyers and department staff and showed me the office I would use. Another young law school graduate, John Zimmermann, joined the department the same time I did. He had just graduated from the University of Denver law school. All the lawyers on staff were very cordial, but two of them, Bob Salter and Bill Owens, were especially helpful during my period of becoming adjusted to practicing law in a corporate setting. They also became personal friends and our families eventually entertained each other at our homes. Owens came from a very prominent family and he apparently was rather wealthy. He lived in a spectacular house in the Hollywood Hills overlooking the city and was married to an interesting French woman. They maintained a home in Paris as well. Bob Salter, who appeared to be a little older than I, was married to a woman who had been an accomplished ice skater in her youth and still maintained some connections with the sport. They had a son a few years older than Rudy who was about to enter law school.

Soon after joining the company it became apparent to me that a significant expansion of the law department was in the works. In

202

less than one year at least four other attorneys were hired. Mario Roberti, the brother of a prominent member of the California legislature, came on board. A second black law school graduate was added to the staff. His name was Eddie Island, a native of Hot Springs, Arkansas. Island had an undergraduate degree from Fisk University and a law degree from Harvard University. He obviously was a very bright young man with all the confidence one would associate with a Harvard law degree. Frederick Peasley and John Friedmen also were hired within a few months after I started. As a mere staff attorney I was not privy to the long-term strategy behind the decision to so greatly expand the number of company lawyers. It later became clear that the entire Pacific Lighting family of companies was gearing up to deal with a major crisis in the natural gas business, and indeed in the energy business as a whole—a crisis in supply and rising energy prices.

My first several weeks at the company were spent on assignments that were designed to help me understand the natural gas business. I summarized articles appearing in various gas industry trade publications and other journals dealing with energy matters. These summaries would be circulated to the staff who presumably were too busy to read the full articles themselves. I read, summarized and distributed to lawyers and other managers, leading cases that had been decided recently by the Federal Power Commission and the courts.

Occasionally an assignment took me to San Francisco to monitor rate case proceedings of other utilities before the California Public Utilities Commission (C.P.U.C). My job was to file daily reports on these proceedings which Edsall would circulate to interested managers and executives in the company. The most interesting of these were cases involving Southern California Edison Company or Pacific Gas and Electric Company. Edison was our largest single natural gas customer. They purchased huge quantities of natural gas daily to fire their steam generators producing electricity to serve their markets in southern California. Pacific Gas and Electric Company (P. G. & E.), the largest investor-owned utility in the country headquartered in San Francisco, was perhaps our biggest rival in the state in terms of prestige and political influence. It also was the one utility in the state that activist consumer and environmental groups seemed to target most. Whenever P. G.

& E. had a rate case underway before the C.P.U.C. you could be sure that every significant consumer and environmental organization in California would intervene in the proceeding. Often they appeared in the case simply to disrupt or delay the process, figuring that the longer it took for the agency to reach a decision on a proposed rate increase, the better off consumers would be.

It was on one of these trips to San Francisco that I experienced my first earthquake. I had retired for the evening and was watching the evening news on television when the newscaster said, "Ladies and gentlemen I believe we are now having an earthquake." My room was on the tenth floor of the hotel. Immediately I noticed things moving about in the room and a swaying sensation as I lay in bed. I got up hurriedly, put on some clothes and shoes and ran down the ten flights of stairs to the hotel lobby. (Early on I had been instructed never to use the elevator during an earthquake.) When I arrived in the lobby everyone seemed to be going about their business quite normally as if nothing unusual had occurred. Of course, the quake was essentially over by the time I got downstairs to the lobby. Someone on staff told me there was nothing to worry about as this was a very minor tremor that caused no damage in the city. Apparently quakes of that size occurred fairly frequently in San Francisco and the natives were used to them. A little bit embarrassed, I took the elevator back to my room but did not have a very restful night.

While I adjusted fairly quickly to working in a corporate law environment I could not be completely comfortable in my new position until I had passed the California bar examination. My first opportunity to take the examination would not occur until March, 1970. As best I could I juggled my work assignments with reviewing my old law school notes in an attempt to recapture the mindset of preparing for law examinations. Beginning about the middle of October I tried to set aside about two hours during the workday for study. Unlike the Indiana bar experience thirteen years earlier I found it necessary this time to enroll in a bar review course. The course offered an intense two-month review of California law taught by a very distinguished faculty. The course boasted that its clients had a passing average nearly twice as high as that of bar examinees who had not taken their course. I felt I needed this insurance because the historic failure rate of California bar examinees was very high, in the forty to fifty percent range.

I enrolled in the California bar review course that began December 15, 1969 and ended February 14, 1970. The course met Monday through Friday from 6:30 to 9:30 P.M.. and for six full hours on Saturday. It was like having a second job. I was attracted to this particular course because I knew two members of the course faculty. John Bauman, a professor at the U.C.L.A. law school, had been one of my teachers at Indiana University. Gary Bellow, an associate professor at U. S. C., had been a deputy director of the United Planning Organization, a community action program in Washington, D. C. I had an encounter with Bellow at U.P.O. while working on behalf of the Washington branch of the NAACP in the early 1960s. Classes were held at a location very convenient to my office, the Rodger Young Center on West Washington Blvd. in Los Angeles. While I was enrolled in the bar review course I had little time for a social life or for relaxation with the family. I was driven to succeed in passing the bar on my first try.

Meanwhile, each of the children adjusted very well to their new schools. Rudy joined the John Muir High School football team and made a lasting impression when he ran 62 yards for a touchdown the first time he touched the ball in the second game of the season. From that point on he was a star of the team. The whole family found it exciting that John Muir's home games were all played in the famous Rose Bowl, which was only a short distance from the school. At the end of the football season Rudy was named the most valuable player on the team. I was as proud of him as he was of himself in making the difficult senior year transition to a new team.

Dorothy Ann decided to take an active role in the local League of Women Voters, an organization she had been very active in while we lived in Washington D. C.

Before leaving Washington Frank Hollis told me to make sure I got in touch with a lawyer friend of his as soon as I arrived in California. That friend was Robert Hall and his wife Frankie. They lived in the Crenshaw district in Los Angeles and had two children—David and Susan—about the same age as our two oldest children. Hollis was absolutely right when he said that the Halls were really "good" people. They accepted my family as if we had been life-long friends. Hall was a name partner in a law firm that included two other lawyers that we soon got to know well also—Dion Morrow and David Cunningham.

Bob Hall had a very successful law practice specializing in personal injury, real estate and family law. I greatly admired and perhaps envied the success Hall appeared to have in the private practice of law. I believe he had similar feeling about me and my work as a lawyer with a major California company. I learned a lot from Hall as we got to know each other over the years. From observing Bob I came to understand that it is possible to have a loving relationship with wife and family while at the same time maintaining a long-term caring and tender relationship with another woman in the same city. Several men in Hall's circle of friends appeared to subscribe to the notion that having a "woman" on the side was a badge of professional success in Los Angeles. Personally my conscience would never allow me to sustain any such dual arrangement for any length of time. In addition, I feared the possible consequences of such behavior to my marriage more than the fleeting pleasure to be derived from being unfaithful.

The notice from the secretary of the committee of bar examiners that I had passed the attorneys' bar examination came in the mail exactly six weeks after I had taken the exam. On May 12, 1970 I was certified to the California Supreme Court for admission to practice law and for membership in the state bar. I took the attorney's oath on May 26, 1970 before Judge Xenophon P. Lang of the municipal court, Los Angeles. This was the final step in the process of gaining all the credentials I needed for the right to practice law in the state of California. After that date my boss no longer had to think about whether an assignment he had in mind for me could be made without violating any laws relating to the unauthorized practice of law.

Immediately, the associate general counsel gave me the task of assisting him in trying before the C.P.U.C. the company's first general rate increase case in several years. I also took on the job of legal counsel to the marketing department of Southern California Gas Company. Another responsibility was working with our right of way people in obtaining and renewing local franchises, i.e., authorization from various municipal governments that enabled the companies to install and maintain its pipelines and other gas distribution facilities in public streets and rights of way in the communities we served.

The most significant of these assignments was that of helping to prepare and present a general rate increase case before the C.P.U.C. That state regulatory body has enormous power over the fortunes of any investor owned public utility company. All rates and terms and conditions of service the company offers to its customers must first be approved by the Commission. If company profits should exceed its authorized rate of return the Commission had the authority to order a reduction in rates or mandate refunds to customers. The Commission had the power to set conditions for terminating service to customers who may be delinquent in paying their bills.

Preparing and presenting a general rate case is an eighteen-month to two-year undertaking involving, in addition to the lawyers, a vast array of other professional disciplines within the company. It required the services of experts in finance, economics, accounting, statistics, engineering, sales, marketing, labor and insurance. The responsibility for overall direction of the effort rested with the vice president in charge of rates and earnings—the Regulatory Affairs Department. Everyone involved with the effort has an excellent chance of drawing the attention of the highest levels of company management because so much is riding on the outcome of the proceedings. If management thought your work contributed in a significant way to a successful outcome you surely would be rewarded financially. On the other hand, if things did not turn out so well your chances for advancement or even surviving were greatly reduced.

I found the work of developing and presenting a general rate case quite challenging, but different in many respects than anything I had experienced before as a lawyer. First, the testimony of every witness was written in advance in question and answer form, filed with the administrative law judge and served on opposing parties and interveners in the case weeks before the hearing actually began. When the hearing convened each witness would take the stand and swear that the filed written testimony was his own and submit himself to clarifying questions and cross examination. The volume of written materials that had to be prepared in advance was so staggering that it was not unusual to require the capacity of a van or pick-up truck to deliver the documents for our opening case.

While the lawyer's role is important, it clearly is not the most crucial one in developing and presenting the rate case. The company's policy witness who laid out the business reasons for seeking an increase in rates, the financial person whose testimony showed how capital costs had changed in the period since current rates were established, the rate design specialists who could demonstrate why rates should differ among customer classes or which customers were most responsible for incurrence of certain costs, the economists who might show why rates for certain classes of customers can best be justified on a cost of service basis while others should be predicated on value of service—all of these elements formed the heart of the case. My role as a lawyer during the "trial" principally was to coordinate these presentations, and at the end of the hearings prepare a brief that persuasively summarized the evidence which proves our case. Of course, the lawyer got the opportunity to show his legal skills most directly in the process of cross examining witnesses for the opposing parties and in protecting his own witness from answering objectionable questions while under cross examination.

Because everything about the case was so technical with lots of numbers and statistics, a lawyer not directly involved with the witness could easily lose focus and fall asleep during a hearing. The only drama or excitement during a rate case usually would occur when an appearance is made by some protest group or when the proceeding is opened up for participation by public witnesses. Otherwise, it is a very staid process with no surprises. Our largest industrial and steam plant customers invariably were represented by counsel who tended to view their role in the case as one of protecting their clients from rates that, in effect, provided a subsidy for residential and other low volume customers. On the other hand, we always maintained that rates to large industrial and steam plant customers, who by California law were required to switch to an alternate fuel in the event natural gas became unavailable or otherwise had to be interrupted, should reflect to some degree the value of our service to them. In this context "value" should take into account not only the price they would have to pay for an alternate fuel, but also the environmental advantages of

208

clean burning natural gas as a fuel. Rates to such large users based strictly on cost of service principles would yield rates that were much too low and place an excessive burden on residential customers. Trying to resolve this type of conflict is where the Commission performed its most important function as a regulatory agency in protecting the public interest.

Perhaps the most interesting case I had at the C.P.U.C. was one involving an attempt by the company to redesign residential rates in such a way as to minimize the dramatic swings in revenue that occurred with seasonal variations in mean temperatures. Space heating is one of the most significant loads on a natural gas utility system and that load is very temperature sensitive. The concept of "degree days" is very important in planning for supplies and in balancing system loads for any natural gas utility. It is a measure of the extent to which a day's mean temperature falls below a reference point on the thermometer. In California that reference point is 65 degrees. The greater the number of degree days in a billing period, the greater the usage for space heating. The average residential customer's gas bill for the winter months ordinarily is more than double the bill for summer months. Our rates people came up with the idea of lowering rates in periods of highest usage and increasing them when usage was down.

Our management thought our "Weather Adjusted" rates proposal was a pro consumer measure. During the course of the hearing it became quite apparent that residential customers took exactly the opposite view, most of them claiming that the gas company was proposing to charge them more for using less gas. The public's slant on the idea got most of the media attention and the proposal became a public relations disaster for the company. An overflow crowd of angry customers descended on the hearing room every day while I presented the company's case for the proposal. I found out later that the company brought in extra undercover security because of concerns for the safety of its personnel involved in the case. While I think the Commission believed the proposal we made had some merit they could not bring themselves to a clear-cut decision to adopt it, given the intensity of public feeling in opposition.

The work of obtaining and renewing franchises brought me in closest touch with the heart and soul of the gas company—the people who worked in the local company offices and facilities in cities and towns throughout the system. The overwhelming majority of the company's 10,000 employees worked in jobs scattered all over the Southern California area. In fact, I discovered that the operating company had a highly decentralized management structure. At the time the company had thirteen geographical divisions each headed by a division manager. The division managers had a great deal of autonomy and operated within their respective areas much like an independent local gas company.

In terms of customers served and revenues generated the orange county division alone would rank among the ten largest natural gas utilities in the country. The same probably could be said for the Santa Barbara, Riverside, and San Bernardino divisions as well. The job of division manager was one of the most coveted positions in the company. Each division manager was the personification of the gas company in his area. They were encouraged and expected to be active in local civic affairs and leaders in the local business community. One of the perks associated with the job was a company sponsored membership in the most prestigious clubs in the area. Located in the smaller towns and cities were local managers who reported to the division manager. Their job on a smaller scale was much like that of the division manager.

Most gas company franchises had been obtained many years earlier as municipalities were formed, and conferred rights for the company to operate its facilities in public rights of way for fifteen- or twenty-year periods. Our right-of-way people would notify the law department well in advance of the scheduled expiration of a franchise so that the process of renewal could be initiated. Given the vast extent of the gas company's service territory—from the city of Visalia on the north to the San Diego and the Mexican border on the south and from the Arizona border on the east to the Pacific Coast on the west—our franchises numbered several hundred.

The process involved filing an application for renewal with appropriate local governmental authorities, paying the necessary fees and shepherding the request through various reviewing officials, such as the city attorney, city engineer or city manager. Usually the final step is gaining approval from the city council. Our people at the local level always were critically important in this process because part of their job was knowing the key governmental officials and establishing cordial relationships with people in the community.

Because our local people did such an outstanding job of preparing the way, in over 99 percent of the cases renewing a local franchise was a very routine matter. But it was necessary for the company lawyer to appear in person at the council meeting when the matter of approving renewal of the franchise had been placed on the council agenda. In most small cities and towns the council met in the evening. Driving from downtown Los Angeles at the end of the work day to some small town forty miles away to attend a council meeting is not the most pleasant duty I had.

Sometimes we were successful in having the council clerk place the matter among items on the "unanimous consent" portion of the calendar at the start of the meeting so that I could leave as soon as those items were disposed of. Every effort was made to resolve any issues local officials might have well in advance so that there would be no need for questions or discussion during the course of the council session itself. But some city councils followed a practice of taking up the "consent" items at the end of the session. In that case I had to sit quietly in the audience through the entire session until it ended, sometimes very late at night. It was not unusual for me to get home from one of these council meetings well past midnight.

I never will forget the occasion I had to renew our franchise in the city of Placentia, a small town in the heart of Orange County. Orange County in the early 1970s was perhaps the most politically conservative jurisdiction in the state of California. There were few Democrats and even fewer blacks, although the number of people of Mexican descent was growing quite rapidly. When I arrived at city hall in late afternoon to attend the council meeting scheduled for acting on our franchise renewal application scores of people were milling about outside the building and in the halls around council chambers. I parked my car and walked through the crowd. Having come directly from work naturally I was dressed in a business suit and carried a briefcase. I could hear murmurs in the crowd as I passed through but thought little about it until I noticed that I was the only person of color in the whole area. Quickly I made my way to the council clerk's office and inquired as to what was going on with all those people outside who seemed to be in a very foul mood. He told me that the main item on the council agenda that evening was a proposal having to do with construction of a new low-income housing project in the city and that many local residents were strongly opposed to the idea. Apparently, some federal housing agency advocated the proposal and the people were there to demonstrate the strength of their opposition.

Clearly, the good citizens of Placentia were fearful that putting a low-income housing project in their town would attract the wrong kind of people—people who were poor, probably non-white, prone to violence. They probably mistook me for a federal official from Washington coming into their town to try to impose some form of integrated public housing for undesirable elements of the population on them. Only then did I realize why the crowd seemed so hostile to my presence. The clerk and I agreed that it would be best to move the franchise matter to the top of the agenda so that I could exit the area as quickly as possible. I was relieved when the council president concurred and I was able to get in my car and head back home to Altadena.

In this discussion I have used the term "gas company" several times. I should point out that in 1969 there were two gas utilities in the Pacific Lighting System—Southern California Gas Company and Southern Counties Gas Company. As a newcomer and part of the affiliate that provided legal services to both operating companies I tended to think of these utilities as a single unit. They both were in the same business—delivering natural gas services to customers in the Southern California area. But the two companies were quite distinct, each having its own full set of officers and employees and each operating in different geographic areas within the system's service territory. Socal traditionally served highly urbanized areas while Southern Counties' service area was more rural in character.

The two companies also had very distinct cultures and were highly competitive as they sought the favor and approval of the highest levels of management in the parent holding company. I had trouble at first understanding some of the differences that existed in their approaches to business decisions and practices. Often I had to be reminded that I was dealing with a "Counties" rather than a "Socal" person. Fortunately for me about a year after I

212

came aboard the two operating companies merged and became simply Southern California Gas Company. However, for many years thereafter some of the old loyalties lingered. Some employees continued to refer to themselves as a "Counties" or "Socal" person.

11

Joining the Altadena Community

I have always believed one should become a part of the life of the community where one lives. Doing so is essential to making that place your "home." Establishing a relationship with a local church in the Pasadena area was one step we considered important in making this our home. For the past thirteen years we had been affiliated with the Presbyterian Church. I liked that church's polity and structure very much and saw no reason to change. So we joined Westminster Presbyterian Church in downtown Pasadena soon after we settled in our house on Via Maderas Drive in Altadena. Westminster had a large, predominately white congregation with many programs and activities a young family like ours could find attractive in an ideal world, but the Pasadena area was not an ideal world in the early 1970s. After a short while I realized that racial integration of a mainline Protestant church is as complicated and difficult as racial integration of the public schools.

I discovered, however, that the principal impediment to personally achieving a level of comfort at Westminster was my own attitude about being a tiny minority in a sea of white faces at church on Sunday. I never had a problem with being a distinct minority in any other context—in government, business or social situations. In fact, being the "fly in the ointment" had been the norm for me since law school. On Sunday, at church, the norm for me always had been to be in the presence of a black congregation. I guess I needed that once a week immersion in the rituals and rhythms of a black church to recharge my soul, to enable me to meet the inevitable challenges I would face in the world of work that I had chosen. I felt, and I know my teenaged children felt, sort of out of place at Westminster, not because the people there were hostile or unwelcoming: they were not.

The feeling I had about Westminster might be attributed to the fact that it was such a large congregation. We had never been members of a large church before. We remained members but no one in the family could generate much enthusiasm for going to Westminster Presbyterian Church on Sunday. Rudy and Fred preferred to attend the black Baptist church in town where most of their friends attended, but I could not adjust to the style of worship there. My dilemma led to a serious erosion in my church attendance commitment which lasted for several years. I am sure that this experience helps to explain why even today, thirty years later, my family and I travel some fifteen miles across the city to attend Church of the Redeemer, Presbyterian, a black congregation with less than 200 members in northeast Washington. We pass by no less than a half dozen much grander "integrated" Presbyterian churches on the way to Redeemer each Sunday.

With all four of our children enrolled in schools in the Pasadena Unified School District, Dorothy Ann and I had little choice but to become involved with P.T.A. and other school-related activities. The Boosters Club at John Muir High School was very active and full of strong supporters of its athletic programs. I had not been in Altadena six months when I was approached by several long-time residents who asked me to run for the school board. I told them I thought it would be unseemly for me to run for public office so soon after having moved into the community. So I declined the offer. Later on I did serve on a citizens' task force that had been appointed by the school board and the superintendent to deal with plant utilization and districting. The district at that time was experiencing contraction in the school age population, necessitating closure of some schools and adjusting the boundaries of some attendance zones.

*   *   *

Largely because of Dorothy Ann's outgoing personality we met several new friends in the Pasadena/Altadena community. We spent a lot of time with Hilda and Myers Howard and their family. I discovered that the daughter of one of my college professors and her husband—Sylvia and Vernon Jones—lived in the area and we established contact with them right away. Sylvia was the daughter

215

of Oliver E. Jackson, professor of modern foreign languages at Arkansas A. M. & N. College, who taught the course in French I took in undergraduate school. Sylvia too was a foreign language teacher working in the Pasadena school system. Her husband Vernon was a scientist employed at the Jet Propulsion Laboratory (J. P. L.) located near Pasadena.

Sylvia and Vernon had just purchased one of the grand old mansions on Altadena Drive not far from Lake Avenue. They purchased it knowing that it needed a lot of work in order to restore it to its former glory. That was to be their long-term project. The house was of stucco construction with a red clay tile roof and ten-or twelve-foot ceilings. It had about 6,000 square feet of living space, sat on about an acre of land and had a large swimming pool in back. We enjoyed being consulted by Sylvia and Vernon as they undertook the job of decorating and restoring their home.

Another couple that became a part of our circle of friends in the area was Jim and Jean King. Jim too was a scientific type—a mathematician I believe—who was associated both with J. P. L. and Cal Tech. I understand that he was involved with highly classified work for a Defense Department agency. Jim had been one of the youngest men ever to graduate from Morehouse College in Atlanta several years earlier. Jean, like Dorothy, was very outgoing. She was a "serious" bridge player and we enjoyed getting together with them from time to time to play bridge.

We met Dr. J. B. Singleton, a dentist, and his wife Shirley through their nephew Eddie Island when he joined Pacific Lighting in 1970. J. B. had a very successful dental practice in the area. Shirley was a stunningly beautiful woman who taught in the public school system. They had settled in the Pasadena area after J. B. graduated from Fisk University and the Meharry Dental School in Nashville, Tennessee.

Another very interesting family we met was Mr. and Mrs. Raymond Jones. Ray Jones was in the real estate and construction business in Lawndale, a town near Los Angeles International Airport. His wife was very active in Republican politics and not just in California. They were quite well off and spent a lot of money buying "toys" for their young preteenaged son. Of course there were others in the community like Rush Miller we enjoyed meeting and socializing with as well. After my bar examination ordeal we occasionally got together for a friendly game of poker with Rush, J.B. and Vernon and some of their friends.

Meanwhile, our good friend Edgar Twine was offered a position in the general counsel's office of the Atlantic Richfield Oil Company (ARCO) in Los Angeles. He took the job and he and his family moved to Los Angeles in the spring of 1970. They decided to buy a very nice house in Ladera Heights, an area near the central city of Los Angeles. We regretted that they would not be living very close to us so that their children, Debbie and Eddie, Jr., could get together frequently with our kids during the week. But having them in the Los Angeles area was a blessing nevertheless because the families could exchange visits on weekends.

The Twines too had befriended Bob and Frankie Hall. Our families would meet at the Hall's house often on Sunday afternoon for impromptu parties. It was at one of these occasions that I first met "Zinnie" Lang, the municipal court judge before whom I took the oath of admission to the California bar. On a similar occasion I also met Hall's law partners David Cunningham and Dion Morrow and their wives. Another lawyer by the name of Charles Scarlett was also a close friend of the Halls. All three of them would later accept appointments to become superior court judges in Los Angeles County.

At the time I thought it strange that these men who appeared to be highly successful in their private law practices would take a local judgeship at the salaries then being paid for such positions. Of course, it is possible they were motivated by factors other than money. They might have felt their legal talents could be put to better use from the bench in the effort to achieve a more just society. The latter view is more in line with my belief that the position of "judge" stands at the apex of the legal profession. It is an honor to which most lawyers should aspire; one that should crown a successful legal career. Being made a judge should be a reward for sustained, outstanding contributions to the legal profession.

While a young lawyer may be extremely talented, it takes time and experience to acquire the wisdom that is necessary for being a judge. Therefore I think it is a mistake for a governor or the president to appoint any person to the position of judge who has not had extensive experience in life or some aspect of the legal profession.

Fathers sometimes live vicariously through the athletic exploits of their young sons. I confess to having done this to some extent through my sons Rudy and Fred. They both turned out to be superior athletes in two sports—football and track. At John Muir High School's annual athletic banquet at the end of the 1969-70 school year Rudy received top honors in football and track. He was ranked among the two or three best high school sprinters in the entire Southern California area at the close of the track season. My chest swelled with pride every time they called his name to come up and accept another honor at the awards banquet.

No doubt Rudy's accomplishments on the athletic fields inspired Fred because in his final two years of high school Fred equaled or exceeded Rudy's records for honors in the two sports they concentrated on. Whereas Rudy was a running back and sprinter, Fred excelled as a defensive back in football and a middle distance runner in track. Fred never achieved Rudy's size or speed, yet I think he was the tougher of the two. He had to be tough because his weight never exceeded one hundred and fifty-five pounds and the position he played required him to bring down much bigger players in open field tackles.

Neither of the boys were large enough to attract attention from U.C.L.A., U.S.C., and other top Division I football schools. We had decided that Rudy should attend Occidental College in any event and were not all that anxious for him to continue pursuit of athletic excellence beyond high school. We had greater things in mind for him. Yet Rudy made the Occidental football team as a walk on and was their starting running back for the better part of the two years he remained on the team. Rudy went on to graduate from Occidental College with his class in 1974. Fred enrolled at U.C.L.A. when he finished high school in 1972. He did not go out for an intercollegiate sport there, being content with intramural sports activities. Fred too compiled an excellent academic record at U.C.L.A. and graduated with his class in 1976.

12

The Brewing Natural Gas Crisis

By 1971 the more astute executives in the natural gas industry already realized that a price and supply crisis was brewing in that business. The senior officers of the Pacific Lighting Companies were in the vanguard of industry leaders who warned against eliminating the tax and other incentives designed to stimulate greater exploration and development of energy resources. They also were among those calling for changes in federal natural gas pricing policies that might help stem the growing deficit in the flow of natural gas into the regulated interstate market. Each year producers were finding it more and more attractive to sell their gas to the unregulated intrastate markets in producing states rather than to interstate pipelines at federally set prices. Natural gas distribution companies like ours relied largely upon interstate natural gas pipelines for the huge volume of natural gas required to serve their local retail markets.

These developments were accompanied by a shift in public attitudes about sales promotion practices of natural gas utility companies. If gas supplies were not abundantly available or in any way uncertain, many people questioned whether companies should be allowed to continue sales promotion programs. Also, greater national attention was being focused on environmental issues. Natural gas was recognized as perhaps the most environmentally benign of all the fossil fuels. Pressure began to build for the adoption of conservation policies and reserving natural gas for the highest priority uses.

A long-term planning horizon is essential in the natural gas business. So our management began to look at various "what if" scenarios, including what other options we had if we could no longer acquire from traditional sources the supplies we needed to meet gas demands in our market area. Company management realized that federal authorities in Washington would become increasingly important players in determining how some of these issues would be resolved in the years ahead. They also perceived that some changes may be required in our own approaches in dealing with some of these issues.

Marketing had been one of Southern California Gas Company's greatest strengths. The company had achieved unprecedented market saturation in fueling the four principal residential appliances—over 90 percent for water heating and clothes drying and over 80 percent for space heating and cooking. When I joined the company it had just launched major marketing efforts for gas air conditioning, decorative gas outdoor lights, and natural gas powered automobiles. Within a year or two the company had greatly reduced if not abandoned the gas lights and air conditioning marketing initiatives. Our advertising and marketing emphasis instead became one of promoting conservation and more efficient use of the commodity. The ubiquitous billboard ad featuring the likeness of the company chairman sold gas conservation and efficiency all over the Los Angeles area.

Early in 1972 senior management of the company began to consider what it might do to strengthen its presence in Washington and enhance its ability to work effectively in that arena. Over the years several consultants and law firms did work for the company in Washington. But like many other gas distribution utilities, the company relied heavily on its trade association, the American Gas Association (A.G.A.), to carry its message in Washington. As the nation's largest natural gas distribution company we had considerable influence in A.G.A. Socal managers and executives were quite active on all the important committees and policymaking bodies of the association. But a trade association has very severe limitations, not the least of which is the fact that some of its important members may have conflicting interests. And in those instances the trade association tends not to be the best vehicle for representing the interest of any of those members. Furthermore, trade associations tend to find the lowest common denominator or consensus positions on controversial issues which often do not adequately address the concerns of its larger members.

In early May 1972 I was called to a meeting in Joe Rensch's office. Several other senior officers of the company were there when I arrived, including Socal board chairman Harvey Proctor and John Ormasa. Rensch told me that the company had decided to upgrade its presence in Washington, D. C. and wanted me to move back there to head up its new office in the nation's capital. He said I had been selected for the job because of my extensive experience in government and my familiarity with the way Washington works. They mentioned several people in Washington the company had been using as consultants. These included Edward Falck, Will Jennings, David Richmond, William Harkaway and Edward Weinberg. They wanted to have someone on the scene who could help coordinate and manage the consultants' activities on behalf of the company. Also they saw the need to have a person there who could involve himself directly in industry and trade group activities on behalf of the company. Finally they mentioned the need for someone to monitor federal regulatory agencies and executive departments.

At this point in the meeting no one had mentioned Congress or anything relating to legislation. I thought this was strange and asked what about keeping track of activities on Capitol Hill. I distinctly remember Harvey Proctor saying in response that of course part of the job was to maintain awareness of what happens in Congress insofar as their activities may affect the company, but we are not asking you to become a lobbyist. I think Proctor felt compelled to make that disclaimer because he thought I might be offended, since lobbying probably in his mind was less than an honorable profession. He did not know that I had no such misgivings about lobbying.

I did not let on at the meeting that I was thrilled at the prospect of moving back to Washington while still working for such a fine company. Personally, I had not adjusted well to California living in the two and a half years I had been there. I never got the sense of my presence in Southern California as being permanent or long-term. Maybe it was the temperate climate, but I always had the feeling of being on vacation while I was there. There seemed to me to be something sacrilegious about going to the beach or having a cook-out on Christmas Day.

I told Rensch and the others that I was honored to be asked to take the assignment, especially after they told me I would be promoted to the rank of assistant vice president and special counsel. However, I said I wanted to talk to my family about it before giving my final answer.

I had no doubt about taking the job in Washington, but making the move would mean we would not be nearby for Rudy and Fred while they were in college. Rudy was completing his second year at Occidental College and Fred was scheduled to begin his freshman year at U.C.L.A. in the fall of 1972. However, I did not think it a bad idea for the boys to be left largely on their own at this stage in their life. Dorothy Ann agreed. The next day I accepted the Washington assignment and began making plans to make another cross-country move.

The company decided I would continue reporting to Dick Edsall in my new job in Washington. Edsall was an officer of Pacific Lighting, while the office I was to take over in Washington was billed as a Southern California Gas Company office. My new job made me an employee of that company as I was put on their payroll. Yet no officer of Socal had any apparent line responsibility for the Washington office. Although this seemed like an odd organizational arrangement I did not think too much about it at first. There were more important things to be taken care of at this point.

Edsall decided that the first thing to be done was for the two of us to take a trip back to Washington together. As the company's principal federal regulatory attorney, Edsall had traveled to Washington frequently to represent us in cases we had at the Federal Power Commission. He was the logical person for the job of introducing me to our various Washington consultants and law firms. These contacts surely had a vital interest in how my entry on the Washington scene might impact their situations.

Edsall and I agreed to meet at LAX early Monday morning the 5th of June 1972 for the flight to Washington, D. C. Edsall said it was his policy to arrive at the airport about two hours before scheduled departure time and asked me to meet him in the Admirals Club, a special lounge for American Airlines passengers. This lounge operates as a private membership club with access being restricted to members who pay annual membership fees and their traveling companions. The doors to the club remain locked so one gains entry by pressing a buzzer and someone inside has to release the lock. I presented myself at the front desk where several attractive female attendants checked me in so that when flight time arrived I could go directly to the boarding area where first class passengers are the first to board.

I saw immediately why Edsall would want to arrive at the airport two hours before flight time. The Admirals Club had all the amenities one could wish for while waiting for a flight. There were no crowds, only a few well-dressed men in business suits. Several plush chairs and couches in intimate conversational arrangements around beautiful cocktail tables were scattered throughout what looked like a huge living room. On one side was a fully stocked bar attended by a man in some kind of uniform. Bar drinks were not free but they were inexpensive. On the opposite side of the room from the bar was a stand where one could serve himself coffee or tea and fresh pastries. These items were free. There were racks with all the latest magazines and newspapers—the *New York Times*, the *Washington Post*, the *Wall Street Journal*, and even some international newspapers. I later learned that all the major airlines maintained similar clubs at the busiest airports around the country.

I soon spotted Edsall seated at the bar having a drink. Our flight was scheduled to leave for Washington at nine o'clock that morning. It must have been close to eight A.M. when I met Edsall. He was just finishing his first Bloody Mary when I sat down and said to him, "What a way to start the day." I was thinking about the plush surroundings, but he replied, "You're right. Whenever I fly I have to fortify myself well in advance because flying for me is not a pleasant thing to do." Here is a man who has to fly to Washington at least a dozen times a year on business for the company and he is telling me he is deathly afraid of flying? Yes! Edsall this hard-nosed lawyer hates to fly and says he has to have two or three stiff drinks beforehand whenever he boards an airplane.

We were among the first to board. The plane was one of the large Boeing aircrafts and the first class section was outfitted six seats across in sets of two in the center and two on each side. The entire first class section had only twenty-four seats. On the morning of our flight there were a total of eight passengers in the first class section. They were served by two full-time stewardesses who offered us a choice of coffee or other beverages before departure. As Edsall and I settled in our seats, he on the aisle and I next to the window, I could see the color in his face turn ashen and his hands tighten their grip on the armrests of his seat just as the plane began to taxi into position for takeoff. I tried to ease some of the tension by engaging him in conversation but it was clear that nothing could relieve his fear but the sound of the captain's voice saying he was turning off the fasten your seatbelt sign and passengers were free to move about the cabin. In those days the no smoking sign also went off almost immediately after the plane was airborne. In the few flights I had made before June 1972 I also had anxiety on both takeoff and landings but nothing near what I saw in Edsall's face that day. I now understood why he needed a few drinks to get himself ready for a flight.

While I had been working for Edsall for over two years we did not become close friends until after I took the Washington assignment. We had worked quite well together on several rate cases before the California Public Utilities Commission but our relationship had been pretty much a professional one. I knew he was married to Pat, they had two girls, and they lived just north of where I lived in the town of La Canada. One of his daughters liked to ride horses and I believe they kept one for her near their place. On this flight to Washington we talked a lot about our personal lives. I learned that Edsall was born in Mississippi to rather well-to-do parents; that he had gone to a private boarding school in his youth in Mississippi. I would never have known Edsall was from Mississippi by the way he talked or any other aspect of his behavior. His speech pattern was nothing like that of a Southerner, let alone a Mississippi native. He told me that he had left Mississippi at an early age and had been in California for many years. I think he was a graduate of the USC law school. He had worked for another California utility company before joining the Pacific Lighting system law department some ten years earlier. Most of our conversation, however, was about the Washington office and the people I was to meet there on this trip.

We arrived at Washington's Dulles Airport in late afternoon and were met by Sylvester, a taxi driver who had a long standing agreement whereby he would pick our people up at the airport whenever they came to town and make himself available to fill any need they may have for local transportation while in Washington. Sylvester drove us to the Madison Hotel. On our way into town

224

Edsall gave Sylvester the schedule for our meetings during the week and asked him to be on call to take us to and from our appointments.

That evening Edsall and I had drinks in the Madison Hotel bar where we met a lawyer named Max Edwards. Edwards had been general counsel at the Department of the Interior in an earlier administration and was well-acquainted with Edsall and several other company executives. I'm not sure whether Edwards currently was on retainer, but he behaved as if he had been from time to time in the past. I assumed Edsall wanted us to meet. I got the impression that Edward's role with us had been more to help on political rather than legal matters that might come up. We had a very pleasant dinner that evening in the hotel dining room. I did more listening than talking, as Edsall and Edwards exchanged "war stories" about various battles the company had fought in Washington over the years. One thing Edsall said that evening I shall never forget. He said, "We are a first class company. Whenever our people travel we go first class. We always stay at the best hotels the city has to offer. We entertain first class as well. Rufus, when you are out with government officials or other business contacts, don't hesitate to pick up the tab when the bill is presented." It was very reassuring for me to hear this from the person who had approval authority over my expense account submissions.

Several years earlier while litigating the most important case it had been involved with in Washington—the Gulf Pacific Case—the company had taken space in the Madison office building next door to the Madison Hotel. It was a small office set up to give our lawyers and other headquarters personnel in town a place to gather at the end of the day for debriefing, communicating with the home office, and to prepare for the next day's work. A secretary on loan from the Miller & Chevalier law firm staffed the office at the Madison. That secretary was Shirle Stafford. The Miller & Chevalier firm also kept the books for the expenses associated with the Washington office and the company carried Shirle Stafford on its payroll. The assumption was that she would continue working for the company as my secretary once I moved to Washington.

The next morning we walked over to the office where I met Miss Stafford for the first time. Shirle was a bright, perky redhead who wore glasses that tended to slip down on her nose, requiring her to constantly push them up again during conversation. She was about five and a half feet tall with an attractive figure. I would guess she was about thirty years old and she spoke with a distinct Southern accent, maybe Texas. She obviously was very intelligent and had an extremely outgoing personality. I liked her right away. I could tell also that she and Edsall were good personal friends as well.

The first meeting scheduled that morning was with Edward Falck, an independent consultant who had been on company retainer in Washington since the late 1940s. Falck had come to Washington in the early days of the "New Deal" after graduating from Columbia University. He was a utility rates and systems specialist who had held a high level position at the Tennessee Valley Authority. Edsall told me Falck in his day was one of the brightest men he had ever met and that Falck had forgotten more about the utility business than we would ever know. Falck maintained an office at 1625 I Street N.W. Over the years Falck had established close personal ties with some of our most senior executives, especially with Joe Rensch. Falck and his wife Ruth would entertain gas company people at their large home right off Chevy Chase Circle. Extending this kind of hospitality endeared him to many key people in the company. Falck was kept on retainer for many years out of gratitude and respect for the valuable services he had rendered in the past.

At our first meeting Falck was cordial but wary. He was an older man, well past sixty years of age. He had insisted on meeting at our offices rather than his place on I Street. I got the impression that he believed my coming to Washington would eventually lead to the company ending the long-standing relationship it had with him. During our conversation I noticed he continually emphasized his personal friendship with Joe Rensch, and other senior officers of the company. He was too smart to treat me in a patronizing manner on this our first meeting. I got the impression, however, that Falck had trouble understanding why the company would choose someone like me to represent them in Washington. He knew that I was a lawyer and had worked in government before. I think he expected they would pick a man of more imposing physical stature, rather than this black man who was just barely five feet six inches tall. Falck was very perceptive in correctly con-

226

cluding that the unfettered access he previously had to our most senior people probably would diminish and that he would wind up reporting to me.

That Tuesday afternoon Edsall took me over to Arlington, Virginia where the American Gas Association had its headquarters. There we met first with George H. Lawrence, the A.G.A. vice president and director of government relations and services. Mr. Lawrence, whom everyone called "Bud," thoroughly briefed me on the structure and work of our principal industry trade association. Everybody we met at A.G.A. treated us as very important persons, befitting our status as executives of one of their largest member companies and a major financial contributor. Although it had not yet been publicly announced, Lawrence would become the new president of A.G.A. later in the year. We talked briefly about a gas industry luncheon group that Lawrence and his counterpart at the pipeline trade group (INGAA) initiated a few years ago, called "The Gas Men's Roundtable." This group meets monthly at the University Club in downtown Washington. It is comprised of industry and government executives and provides a forum for the discussion of issues of timely interest to the gas industry. Usually a guest speaker from Congress or some government agency is asked to address the group. Lawrence invited me to become active in the organization immediately and I promised to do so.

The next two days Edsall introduced me to attorneys at three law firms that the company did business with in Washington. William I. Harkaway was a partner at Belnap, McCarthy, Spencer, Sweeney & Harkaway. This was a small law firm whose offices were in the seventeen hundred block of Pennsylvania Avenue near the White House. Harkaway had been an attorney at the Federal Power Commission a few years earlier. It turns out I had known Harkaway many years ago when we both were young lawyers fresh out of law school in the Solicitor's office of the Department of Labor. Harkaway left the Solicitor's office about 1960 and joined the staff at the Federal Power Commission. Edsall occasionally used Harkaway to assist in matters we were interested in at the Federal Power Commission.

Edward Weinberg was a partner in the Washington offices of a California firm—Wyman, Bautzer, Rothman & Kuchel. Tom Kuchel, one of the name partners, had been a Republican Senator from California from 1953 until 1969. That firm had excellent connections in both political parties and had been retained by the gas company to help from time to time on various political matters in California and in Washington. Weinberg had a small, but well-appointed office on Connecticut Avenue.

The third law firm we visited was Miller & Chevalier where we met with David W. Richmond, one of the senior partners. The Miller & Chevalier firm specialized in federal tax matters, although they had other capabilities. David Richmond, who we worked with most closely, had been very instrumental in setting up our small office at the Madison Office Building. During our meeting with Richmond it was agreed that that firm would continue to perform certain administrative services for the Washington office.

Before leaving town to return to Los Angeles Friday afternoon, Edsall and I met another consultant, William C. Jennings, who was an expert on pipeline safety matters. Jennings took us over to the U.S. Department of Transportation where he introduced me to several key staff people at that department's Office of Pipeline Safety. That agency has governmental functions that are very important to any company in the natural gas transportation business. They set and enforce compliance with standards designed to assure public safety and environmental protection in the transportation of natural gas and other hazardous substances by pipeline. From an operational point of view, the regulatory work done by the Department of Transportation for the natural gas industry is at least as important as the economic regulation done at the Federal Power Commission.

My journey back to California gave me the chance to reflect on how much had changed in Washington since I last lived there nearly three years ago. I also began to wonder what life for me and my family would be like in this changed environment. Politically, of course, things were entirely different. Richard Nixon and Spiro Agnew were firmly ensconced in the White House and well underway in their bid for a second term. Nearly all the political pundits made them an overwhelming favorite for reelection in November. While Democrats remained in control of the Congress there was no question but that the nation's political agenda was being set by Nixon and the Republican party.

While the fighting in Vietnam continued, there were signs that the Nixon administration would soon figure out a way to end the conflict. The administration had already begun to remove many of our ground troops, which eased somewhat domestic protests and opposition to our continued prosecution of the war. The administration seemed to place new emphasis on domestic issues, such as controlling inflation, reducing unemployment, reforming the welfare system and most importantly, instituting a bold new concept called revenue sharing. Revenue sharing would be a system of returning a portion of federally collected tax revenues to state and local governments who could to a great extent determine for themselves how such monies should be spent.

Perhaps more than any other change on the domestic front was the enactment of the National Environmental Policy Act in 1969. That law and follow-on legislation established a whole new environmental ethic in this country. It would impact in a very substantial way programs and activities of government agencies and private parties as they undertook to carry out actions that might have an effect on the ecosystem. The National Environmental Policy Act introduced a new tool that could be used by a variety of interests in a number of ways to restrict the freedom to make and implement business decisions.

The city of Washington too had changed dramatically. The new subway system was being constructed and many of the streets in the downtown area were nearly impassable for both cars and pedestrians. Small local businesses along those streets were forced to relocate or go out of business. The trend among major businesses, foundations, public interest groups and trade associations toward establishing a "presence" in Washington accelerated. Washington, rather than New York City, Chicago and Philadelphia, more and more was becoming the focal point of business and other important institutions in the economy and the society. Nearly every major law firm in the country had established a branch office in Washington, and that branch in many cases soon became larger and more influential than the headquarters firm itself.

Fancy restaurants proliferated all over the downtown area to accommodate the greatly increased numbers of high income, expense account executives operating in the city. And not all of those executives were in the private sector. Government salaries too had escalated in the drive to make public service more attractive to the "best and brightest" available talent and to try to achieve parity with salaries being paid managers and executives in private companies. Real estate prices rose to match higher income levels. Houses in town that sold three years ago for $40,000 now sold for $140,000. This in itself was a shock to the system for one who just recently had owned such a house and was now in the market for another one in the area.

When I worked as a government lawyer and as a volunteer for the NAACP I saw myself as one of the "good" guys, always trying to right some wrong or as a protector or advocate for the underdog. The question in my mind was to what extent my perception of my role would change, now that my job in Washington clearly would be one of advancing the interests of a private company as those interests interfaced with government agencies and other institutions. Could I still count myself among the "good" guys in this new role? I soon came to the conclusion that representing a private company's interests and being a "good" guy were not mutually exclusive roles. It helped somewhat that the company I represented was an investor-owned public utility that provided essential services and products to everyone in the Southern California area. But even beyond this fact I had to remind myself that every human institution, including government, is fallible. Moreover, being an advocate for a private interest does not necessarily make one an adversary of government or an opponent of good public policy and just causes.

There was something else about Washington that had changed but I was not quite sure what it was at the time. I think it had to do with attitudes and philosophies of the people who had taken charge of the federal government since the Kennedy/Johnson era. It seemed to me that there had been a perceptible shift in tone of the dialogue going on among key leaders in the executive branch. I sensed there was less talk about using government institutions as instruments for achieving the greater good for society as a whole. The idealism behind such programs as the Peace Corps, the "war on poverty," and laws to achieve social justice was not much in evidence among the new executive leadership. Instead, the notion that government in the immediate past had intruded too much in the lives of people seemed to prevail; and that it was time to retrench. Also, electoral politics, increasingly it seems, had become more a fund-raising contest than a test of ideas, policy and approaches to solving problems in the society. These changes in the Washington climate were somewhat unsettling to me, but not so disturbing as to cause me to change my mind about returning as the gas company's man in the nation's capital.

13

Becoming a Lobbyist—
Breaking New Ground

My father died on August 4, 1972. He was 78 years old at the time of his death. His was the first death in my immediate family during my lifetime. He died after suffering a massive heart attack while attending a church service in Little Rock, Arkansas. I consider it a miracle that he died in Arkansas and not in California. Less than a year earlier he had suffered a similar attack while he and Momma were visiting their children in California. After several days in intensive care at Daniel Freeman Hospital in Los Angeles and a month or so of recuperation at Izora's house in Inglewood, he had recovered sufficiently for the family to grant his wish to return with Momma to their home in Pine Bluff. I believe my father simply refused to die in California, a place so far removed from Arkansas, and the place he adored so much.

I learned of Papa's death as we made final plans for moving back to Washington. I was scheduled to start work at the Washington office on Monday, August 14, 1972. The family decided to have Papa's funeral on Friday, August 11 in Pine Bluff. I arranged my travel so that I could spend several days with the family in Pine Bluff prior to Papa's funeral and leaving from there to take up my new duties in Washington. While this worked out fine for me it again resulted in leaving Dorothy Ann with the task of supervising the movers in packing up our things for shipment back to the east coast. Only part of the family members would make this return trip to Washington, however. Rudy would start his junior year at Occidental College and Fred would enroll in the freshman class at U.C.L.A. that fall. Dorothy and the two girls flew to Washington later on when the house we had rented back east became available.

Papa was very well known as a pastor and preacher in the

Church of God in Christ. He had traveled throughout Arkansas and in other parts on the country as well during his ministry. For over twenty years he held the position of superintendent of the Sunday School Department for the denomination in the state of Arkansas. The duties of this office in the church required him to attend four or five district meetings held in various locations in the state each year. He also had a prominent role to play at the church's annual state convention in Little Rock. These meetings of course were in addition to the National Sunday School Convention each summer and the annual convocation the entire denomination held in Memphis in November. He had been a mentor and friend for many young preachers who went on to much higher office in the denomination. Getting word of his death out to all his friends in the ministry was a considerable task and it took some time. It was for this reason that the funeral was not held until one week after his death.

The little church where he was pastor was far too small to hold the large number of people expected to attend Papa's funeral. So church leaders decided to hold the funeral at Trinity Temple Church of God in Christ, the largest sanctuary of the denomination in the city of Pine Bluff. Trinity Temple's pastor was Elder Dewitt Hill, a man who had attended Arkansas A. M. & N. College during the time I was there in the early 1950s. Our family had been close to the Hill family for many years. The presiding officer of the denomination in Arkansas, Bishop L. T. Walker, saw it as his duty to preach Papa's funeral. However, Papa's lifelong friend in ministry, Bishop I. G. Glover of New York made the trip to Arkansas to pay tribute to his memory. His presence for the sad occasion greatly lifted Momma's spirits.

Friday, August 11, was a sunny, very hot day. All my brothers and sisters had gathered for the occasion, including a half brother from Detroit, Michigan I had not known before. His name was Ishmael. I learned that Papa had fathered Ishmael when he was a very young man before he and Momma had met. Throughout my childhood I don't remember Papa ever saying one word about the fact that we had an older half-brother. I think all of my sisters knew about Ishmael but I do not recall them ever speaking about him in my presence. Ishmael's existence just was not talked about in the family as I grew up. He looked just like us so there was no

233

mistaking that he was part of the family. After Papa's funeral, however, Ishmael was just another member of the family, and was included in future family reunions along with his wife and children. But I personally had trouble accepting Ishmael as my brother. I was never quite sure why. I suppose it had something to do with the feeling I had that the family made a conscious effort to suppress information about him. It could not possibly be attributed to any concern about having a reduced share of Papa's estate. In the seventy-eight years of his life Papa accumulated no wealth at all, except for the house he and Momma lived in on Havis Street, which he acquired about ten years before his death. The McKinney family, like many others of that generation, had to collect contributions from surviving children to pay the expenses associated with putting Papa away in proper fashion.

As families usually do when they come together for funerals we talked a lot about the deceased and our memories of him—the material and non-material legacy. I have found that Papa's non-material legacy was infinitely more valuable than any amount of money, land or goods. He was a good and decent man who raised a large family and instilled in every one of his children a sense of pride in who they are as individuals. He inspired all of us to try to better ourselves by seeking knowledge and understanding, while at the same time believing in a power beyond ourselves calling us to do justice, love mercy and to walk humbly with our fellows. He taught me the greatest lesson I ever learned in life—that true wealth is not measured in money, but in qualities of the mind and spirit. Although we were deprived in many ways, I never knew poverty. Papa taught me that poverty is a state of mind, not a condition of being without money or things. For this reason I never looked at any man as being "better" or superior to me no matter what his position, status or material wealth. He taught me that one earns respect by the way he conducts his life and how he treats other people, especially those who may be less fortunate.

Another legacy Papa left me was his belief that a man has to work hard and be responsible for himself and his family. Being responsible meant supporting and taking care of his family. He believed as did his father that his wife's primary role was to look after the home and provide love and nurture to the children. He saw this as a full-time job, one that was indispensable for a successful family. There was no confusion in his mind about gender roles in the family. I don't think Papa believed Momma's role was less important than his was; they were just different roles.

Papa's was a traditional black funeral. It lasted a long time, with songs and speeches that seem designed to make relatives and close friends break down and cry. It is often said that relatives of the deceased that failed to cry openly at the funeral did not truly love that person. I do not believe that is true, but just to be on the safe side and to avoid unnecessary gossip, I shed a tear or two at Papa's funeral. The tradition also calls for a feast or wild party to take place after the funeral. We settled for a feast since none of our immediate family, except me, were wild party types. No alcohol, no wine, just lots of good food supplied by members of the church and friends.

Through all of this Momma held up very well. She was the one who faced the biggest adjustment in her life. She and Papa had been married fifty-five years. Fortunately, Izora and others among my sisters were able to remain in Pine Bluff with Momma for an extended period of time after the funeral to help her sort things out and get adjusted to life without Papa. Eventually, we arranged for Momma to move to San Diego where she could be near several of her children who lived in the area.

*   *   *

I checked into the Madison Hotel when I arrived in Washington Sunday evening after Papa's funeral. I planned to stay there until we moved into the house we had rented in Kensington. It was only a short walk through the hotel lobby to the office building next door where Socal's office was located. I wanted to be in the office early Monday morning to orient myself to my new surroundings. Shirle Stafford was already in the office when I arrived at 8:30 A.M. The office suite consisted of one private office, a good-sized reception area furnished with a secretarial desk, two reception chairs, a small couch, a coffee table and a couple of lamp tables, and a conference room with a large table and several filing cabinets.

Shirle had already made a pot of coffee. She told me that the office subscribed to the *Washington Post* and the *Wall Street Jour-*

nal and these newspapers were there on the coffee table already. After a while we sat opposite each other at the conference room table having a cup of coffee as we talked about ourselves and the working relationship that was about to begin. Shirle explained to me how the office bills got paid through the Miller & Chevalier law firm. We talked about our plans to acquire more space by moving the office in the fall to the Six Hundred Watergate Building over near the Kennedy Center.

Our headquarters administrative services people signed a contract for the Watergate office space when management decided to send me to Washington. We retained an interior decorator to help us design and furnish the new space. I told Shirle one of the first things I wanted to do was to meet with the interior decorator. I was anxious to know when we could reasonably expect the new space to be ready for occupancy. Shirle said she would call Mrs. Geraldine Wilson of Wilson Design Associates right away.

Just as I got up to go to my office Shirle said, "There is something I would like for you to know before you leave. I'm pregnant." That announcement hit me like a ton of bricks. I knew that Shirle was unmarried. My first thought was to ask her how far along she was in her pregnancy. I was thinking about how such information would be received back at headquarters. She said the baby was due early in 1973. She did not volunteer any information about who the father was and I did not ask. All I could think about at that moment was possible loose talk at headquarters about management sending this black man back to Washington and the first thing he did was to get the young, attractive white secretary pregnant. Although I knew I had nothing to do with Shirle's being pregnant, I was concerned about what some might think and how unfortunate the timing of this disclosure was for me. I soon realized, however, that there was nothing really I could do about that.

I knew nothing about Shirle's social life. I soon learned that she indeed was a very outgoing person who had many friends and associates. In the first weeks of our working together it became quite apparent that Shirle knew a number of very prominent people in Washington. Her associates included wealthy people in business, in law, the arts and entertainment. She seemed to know all the important people who were neighbors of ours in the Madison Office Building.

Through Shirle I met the head of Bristol-Myers Washington office, the man who managed Congressman Wilbur Mills' ill-fated bid to win the Democratic nomination for President, Ethyl Corporation's man in Washington, the head of the Washington Performing Arts Society, and men who were investors or silent partners in several well-known Washington restaurants. Shirle also was perhaps the most resourceful assistant I ever worked with, before or since. She had ability to track down information on most any subject, and this was before the advent of the Internet and computers. These talents, along with her high intelligence, made her a most valuable assistant to anyone in the role I had as a Washington representative.

In the early 1970s the job of a Washington representative was not that different from that of an ambassador of a foreign country in Washington. It was to be the eyes and ears of your principal, keeping them informed of things they should know about policies and decisions being made in Washington that may affect the business. Where possible, the representative should seek to help shape those policies or decisions in such a way as to benefit his company. Perhaps the most effective legal way to influence decisions is by providing policy makers with information that may lead them to make better and more informed decisions. This is called "lobbying," which some have called the second oldest profession. Lobbyists like lawyers essentially are advocates for their client's interests. Sometimes the lawyer wins the case and sometimes he loses. The same can be true of lobbyists, but most often for the lobbyist the lines between winning and losing are not so clear-cut. After the question of "whether" there are always questions of "how" or "when." Sometimes the lobbyist's most valuable work can occur during the follow-on stages in the process.

From the outset everyone in the company from the very top level on down, agreed to observe the highest ethical standards in everything we did in Washington. Unlike some, we determined not to try to let our money do the talking for us in Washington. Nor did we rely primarily on high level political connections to get our point of view across. We maintained the same representation in Washington no matter which party controlled the White House or which party held the majority in the House of Representatives or the United States Senate. I always tried to maintain an official posture such that no one could really know what my personal political preferences were.

Since the lobbyist's principal tool is information, or perhaps more precisely, knowledge about his company and the business it is in, it is essential to have and maintain close relationships with knowledgeable people within his own organization. These are the people he must rely on to supply him with accurate and reliable information. It would have been infinitely more difficult for me to do my job had I not spent nearly three years at headquarters and established mutually trusting relationships with people there.

My first order of business was to identify the best sources of timely information about what goes on in government, especially in those institutions and agencies having the most to do with the natural gas business in particular and the energy business in general. In 1972 there was no Department of Energy. The governmental functions important to our business were scattered among several different agencies in the executive branch. The Federal Power Commission, an independent agency, regulated pricing and interstate transportation of natural gas. The Department of Transportation housed the Office of Pipeline Safety, which had responsibilities related to safety standards for natural gas transportation facilities. The Department of the Interior had a number of energy-related responsibilities. Among these were leasing of federal lands and offshore areas for oil and gas exploration and development.

About a year earlier the Nixon administration had instituted measures to control inflation, setting up a Federal Price Commission, the Pay Board and the Cost of Living Council. These temporary agencies had certain powers over price and wage increases of businesses such as ours. At the time the Pacific Lighting Companies were planning several international projects to import natural gas in liquid form (LNG) from abroad. These projects required us to deal with several federal agencies not usually a part of the regular beat of energy utilities in Washington. These included the Commerce Department, the Maritime Administration, the Export-Import Bank and the State Department. Therefore, our interests in Washington were quite extensive and covered a very diverse set of federal agencies.

The Bureau of National Affairs (BNA), Congressional Quarterly and a number of other private publishing houses produced daily, weekly and monthly services that provided information about the activities of governmental agencies. These of course were in addition to information and reports put out by Congress itself and matters published in the *Federal Register* and *Code of Federal Regulations.* In addition to the *Washington Post,* the *Wall Street Journal* and the *New York Times* were delivered to the office and spending time perusing their pages was a daily chore. However, the best source of information was federal agency employees and managers themselves. Establishing and cultivating relationships with key people in government therefore became a high priority.

It was important also to become active with energy-related trade associations and other public interest groups involved with energy issues. The American Gas Association (A.G.A.), of course, included among its membership all of the major natural gas companies in the country. Socal was the largest member of A.G.A. and its executives and managers exercised leadership and influence in that organization. As the Washington representative of that company, naturally I was expected to carry on in that tradition. Other significant energy trade groups for me to contact included the Interstate Natural Gas Association of America (INGAA), the Trade Association of Interstate Pipeline Companies; the American Petroleum Institute (API), representing the major oil producers; Independent Petroleum Association of America (IPAA), representing smaller oil and gas producers; Associated Gas Distributors (AGD), whose membership to some extent overlapped that of A.G.A.

Over time I developed contacts with my counterpart representatives in other companies that maintained some presence in Washington. This included the persons representing the other major California gas and electric utility companies—Ralph Dewey of PG&E, Alan Nedry of Southern California Edison, and Ron Fuller of San Diego Gas & Electric Company.

Later on I came to realize how important it was also to know and become involved with organizations such as the Consumer Federation of America, Resources for the Future, the Joint Center for Political & Economic Studies and other public interest groups. Such groups often have enormous influence in Washington and can make the difference between success and failure in any lobbying project.

My plans called for moving into our new offices at the Watergate Six Hundred Building before the end of the year. By that time the name "Watergate" had become infamous, a subject on the front pages of nearly every newspaper in the country. Earlier in the year, on June 17, 1972 to be exact, some men had been arrested as they were in the process of burglarizing the offices of the Democratic National Committee in one of the buildings in the Watergate complex. At the time the rumor was that the burglars worked for an arm of the Republican National Committee called the "Committee to Reelect the President" (CREEP). This group operated under the direction of persons high up in the Nixon administration.

Over the course of the summer months the story just would not go away, despite repeated denials by spokespersons for President Nixon that the arrested men were not connected in any way to the White House or President Nixon's reelection effort. The idea that they might be seemed incredible at the time. President Nixon had sailed through the re-nomination process at the Republican convention and was the odds on favorite to defeat Senator George McGovern the nominee of the Democratic party in the general election in November. Very few individuals believed the people around President Nixon could be so stupid as to try to pull off a stunt like burglarizing Democratic party headquarters offices. One would be hard pressed to find anything the Republicans could possibly gain by such an act. However, as the summer wore on it became increasingly evident that there were indeed some links between the men who had been arrested and persons involved with the President's reelection campaign.

I had my first meeting with the interior decorator just before Labor Day 1972. The new space we had leased at Watergate 600 consisted of approximately 1,750 square feet, about double the space we were in at the Madison Office Building. The space was on the 9th floor overlooking New Hampshire Avenue. The space was being designed to accommodate a possible addition to my professional staff at some future date, but we had no present plans to do so soon.

The design and all office furnishings were state of the art, in keeping with the high standards set by the other tenants in the surrounding area. These included offices for several foreign governments such as Qatar, Saudi Arabia, Sweden and Yemen, and certain silk stocking law firms as well. There was no question that we would be in a first class neighborhood. But there was one problem that our administrative services people apparently failed to take into account when they contracted for the space. The Watergate 600 building is in a fairly isolated location, a good distance from the center of downtown where most other Washington offices are located. Perhaps more importantly, it was very difficult to hail a taxi on the street in that part of town. Furthermore, a taxi ride from the Watergate to downtown or to Capitol Hill incurred a two zone charge, making the trip much more costly than normal.

Nevertheless, there was a certain cachet attached to having an office in the "Watergate." This of course became even more so after the scandal of the burglary of Democratic Headquarters. All of my friends looked forward to the opportunity of visiting at my offices at the Watergate after we moved there in November 1972. But for me I missed the convenience of being in the middle of everything in downtown Washington.

Meanwhile, the abbreviated Rufus McKinney family settled into their rented home on Carriage Road in Kensington, Maryland. Dorothy Ann and I decided not to rush into buying another house when we did not find exactly what we wanted on the house hunting trip we took back east in July. On the very last day of that trip we found the place on Carriage Road that was up for rent. The house recently had been purchased by a State Department foreign service officer who was about to leave for a two-year foreign assignment. We signed a two-year lease, figuring we needed about that much time to examine all our housing options in the Washington area. Another factor too was that the house we owned in Altadena had not been sold when we came back East in August. The house in Kensington was nice but nothing special. It was right off Connecticut Avenue near the Beltway.

Our daughter Anne would enroll in Bethesda-Chevy Chase High School and Paula would be in a very good elementary school in the neighborhood. Here again, our choice of a place to live was largely dictated by our need to have access to good public schools. Throughout my life I have refused to pay for sending my children to private secondary schools, while paying taxes to support public schools that cannot or will not provide them a decent education. I have never been able to afford that luxury. Our children knew that their parents had promised to defray the costs of a four-year college education for each one of them when they graduated from high school. This meant that I faced the prospect of having at least one child in college from 1970 until 1984, a span of 14 years. Faced with that financial responsibility in the out years, public secondary schools was the only way to go for us, given our level of income.

The fall of 1972 was a good time for me. I took on the job of driving Anne Marie to BCC High School on my way to work each morning. This gave us a chance to talk and for her to tell me about things going on in a teenaged girl's life. I made it a practice to tune the car radio to the popular morning drive time station WMAL which featured Hardin and Weaver. I liked their style of irreverent banter about people and life in the nation's capitol. Anne could not understand why I chose to listen to Hardin and Weaver instead of one of the urban ethnic stations that played contemporary "black" music. She thought the smooth talking Donie Simpson or the cool jazz on WHUR was much more interesting.

I explained to her that part of my job in Washington was to be knowledgeable about what goes on in "official" Washington circles. That meant the embassy parties, charity events, and the activities of government and business officials and personalities. So listening to Hardin and Weaver on the way to work gave me a head start in learning about what was happening in the city that might be important for me to know. Anne was not impressed with this explanation but no longer insisted that I change the station.

Anne was thrilled to be back in the Washington area and to renew some of the friendships she had before going to California. In fact two of her best friends from our old neighborhood, Martha Ann and Jennifer Holbert also were in BCC High School. Anne was a very strong willed girl who wanted to do something in high school that would cause her parents to pay as much attention to her as we had to the athletic exploits of her two brothers when they were in high school. The outlet she chose was the BCC High School cheerleading squad. Throughout the football and basketball seasons Dorothy Ann and I had reason again to be in attendance at the games as often as possible.

*   *   *

An important aspect of the job of a Washington representative is entertaining people you hope to influence. The forms of entertaining are limited only by the budget allocated for this purpose and the imagination and creativity of the representative. This part of the job was all new to me. The only guideline I had was the conversation I had had with Dick Edsall earlier about ours being a first class company, ever ready to pick up the check when I was out with business associates and government officials. I decided to put some structure to my entertainment strategy by trying to figure out what entertainment venues might be most appealing to the contacts I wanted to cultivate.

Of course, there were many possibilities in the Washington area. Fine dining is one entertainment outlet that is appealing to many. In the early 1970s fancy restaurants had begun to proliferate throughout the downtown area. Being able to get a reservation at such places, especially on short notice, was a surefire way of impressing an important official. Being able to do that was a function both of your status and of how often and how much you tended to spend at the particular establishment. It was important, therefore, for the representative to become known to the principal gatekeepers at the fancy restaurants in town.

Some Washington representatives raised this process of becoming a well-known host to a high art. I learned from one of the best, a man named John O'Malley, who did not even live in the area but was known by nearly every maître d'hotel in Washington. John O'Malley was a contract lobbyist from Newport Beach, California. His principal client was an Australian airline but he also had a contract with Southern California Gas Company by which our senior management could call upon him for special, sensitive work from time to time either in California or in Washington.

Although I worked with O'Malley for over ten years he never told me the secret of how he came to be so well known in restaurant circles throughout the Washington area. However, I suspect it had something to do with judiciously spreading large tips around at holiday time in the various restaurants. It helped also that O'Malley was a gregarious and pleasant person who seemed never to meet a stranger. He greeted everyone as if they were bosom buddies such that even if in fact they were strangers the other person would be too embarrassed to admit it.

Becoming a well-known host at the better restaurants in town takes time. Eventually I would attain some success in this area, but my relatively quiet personality and ethnic identity may have limited what I could reasonably expect to do in this area.

By 1972 Washington was blessed with several theatres and other places where one could enjoy live entertainment. The recently completed Kennedy Center housed three first class performing arts spaces—the Eisenhower Theatre, the concert hall and the opera house. Each of these venues offered subscriptions for a variety of performances throughout the year, from the latest Broadway plays to concerts by world-renowned symphony orchestras. In addition, the National Theatre and the Arena Stage were still in business offering first-class legitimate theatre. A first-class Washington office operation certainly needed season tickets to at least one of these theatre outlets.

Within the first few months of my tenure in Washington representing Socal I took out a subscription to one of the series offered by the Washington Performing Arts Society (WPAS). WPAS, a performing arts presenting organization, was founded in the late 1950s by Patrick Hayes, a very personable man with a vision for elevating the level of exposure to a broad range of the performing arts in Washington. I figured having tickets readily available to concerts and other performances at the Kennedy Center would be an excellent way of entertaining government officials, business associates and visiting company personnel as well. Finally, season tickets to Washington Redskins football games are an essential part of the Washington representative's tool kit. In 1972 season tickets to Redskins games were next to impossible to obtain from official Redskins sources. All such tickets had been sold out ever since Coach Vince Lombardi began to restore the team to its former status as an NFL power several years earlier. Coach George Allen continued the Lombardi legacy and great things were expected of the team in the 1972 season.

Bill Grief of Bristol-Myers, our neighbor at the Madison Office Building, told me he planned to be in Europe for most of the football season and offered to sell me his four tickets for the 1972 season only. Without hesitation I took him up on the offer, even though I had to pay a stiff premium above the official price. But there hardly is any better way to make a lasting favorable impression on someone whose behavior you are trying to influence than by offering tickets to a Redskins game. Interest in the Redskins was especially high during 1972 because the team had a highly successful season, making it all the way to the Super Bowl against the unbeaten Miami Dolphins team.

During the last few months leading up to a Presidential election not a great deal of work gets done either on Capitol Hill or in the executive departments of government. At that time everybody is focused on the upcoming election. While the House and Senate usually return from their August vacation right after Labor Day, members of the House are all preoccupied with getting reelected and so is one third of the Senate. On the executive side, politics trumps policy and regular program operations as the men and women whose tenure at the agencies is contingent on the election outcome go into a holding pattern. Few important decisions get made during that time. This tends to be true whether of not the White House incumbent is an overwhelming favorite to be returned by the voters in November.

In the fall of 1972 President Nixon still was an odds on favorite for reelection, despite the nagging problems his campaign faced as a result of the Watergate burglary. His opponent, Senator George McGovern, was a fine and decent man but he was widely regarded as being too liberal and out of step with the prevailing political mood of the country. McGovern raised such radical issues as income guarantees and redistribution at a time when Nixon's policies were leading in the opposite direction. This pre-election lull in governmental activity provided just the right unhurried atmosphere for me to get adjusted to my new job, figure out who the players were at the agencies and other organizations important to us, and do the things associated with moving the office to the Watergate complex.

That the 1972 election turned out to be a landslide victory for the Nixon-Agnew ticket came as no surprise. But there was a lingering pall over the results because the press and the Democrats refused to let go of the Watergate burglary story. We moved into our new offices at the Watergate shortly after the election and began

245

making plans for a formal announcement of the arrival of South-ern California Gas Company in Washington.

Our senior management decided it would be most appropriate to mark the company's entry into the nation's capital by hosting a very nice reception in our new offices. The official hosts would be our most senior officers who would travel to Washington for the event. Those attending would include Joe Rensch, president of the parent holding company, the general counsel John Ormasa, Socal's chairman of the board Harvey Procter, along with the exec-utives in direct charge of the alternative gas supply projects that were being planned or already underway. Working with the pro-ject managers, I was primarily responsible for putting together the guest list. We especially wanted to have key Californians in the Nixon administration to be in attendance, as well as our contacts in the agencies, our friends in Congress (members and staff), and Washington representatives of other companies we might be work-ing with in various endeavors. We engaged the most prestigious catering firm in the area to serve the occasion and spared no ex-pense to make sure it was a first class event. We set the date for February 15, 1973, three weeks after the second inaugural of the Nixon-Agnew administration.

The 1973 inaugural of course was the first one occurring dur-ing my tenure as a Washington representative. As the leading nat-ural gas distribution company in the nation it was appropriate that we take some role in such a historic event. My boss agreed that Dorothy Ann and I should attend the largest inaugural ball that year which was held at the Kennedy Center. We did so in style, en-gaging a limousine for the evening. We joined with three couples we knew—Mr. & Mrs. Eddie Williams of the Joint Center for Politi-cal Studies, a black Republican colleague of theirs, Mr. Clarence Townes of Richmond, Virginia and his wife, and Reginald Gibson, a black tax lawyer with a Chicago company, and his wife.

With the ladies dressed in their fanciest ball gowns we were not prepared for what inaugural balls are really like. I had visions of an elegant ballroom with plenty of room for dancing and social-izing at comfortable tables sipping cocktails served by well-dressed waiters. Inaugural balls are nothing like that. In-stead, it's more like 3,000 people being jam packed into a room with a design capacity of 1,000, except they are all wearing fancy clothes. The concourse and hallways of the Kennedy Center served as the ballroom and every one of them was packed with so many people that it took nearly an hour to move from the entry doors to the main concourse fronting the three Kennedy Center performance venues. There were no tables or chairs in sight, just a sea of people pushing and shoving each other about. It was exciting nevertheless and I was thrilled to be there. I was also disappointed to discover that this was what inaugural balls are like in the modern era.

Our party had trouble staying together. We did spot a few familiar black faces in the crowd. The Nixon administration strongly supported the idea of black enterprise and believed that black businesses too should have a piece of the federal procurement pie. They were advocates of small and minority businesses partnering with larger majority firms and saw this as an avenue for improving the overall economic status of black Americans. So it was not surprising to see well-known black Republicans and businessmen like Ted Adams, Clarence Pendleton, Art Mczier, Art Fletcher, John Wilks, George Haley, A. J. Cooper and Sam Jackson in such a gathering. After milling about for a couple of hours my group had had enough and decided to return to the limousine.

Clarence Townes, who was well connected in certain Republican circles, suggested that we head for the invitation only private dinner sponsored by a Young Republicans Organization being held at the Sheraton Park Hotel. There was only one problem. No one in our party had an invitation to the dinner. Townes insisted he could get our entire party into the affair so we directed the driver to take us to the Sheraton Park Hotel. We all got out and approached the ballroom as if we belonged, with Townes leading the way. Townes said let me do all the talking and he proceeded to demand of the young persons controlling entry "Where is my table?" The young man looked at the distinguished looking group of black men and women with bewilderment. Townes said something to me, addressing me as "Mr. Ambassador" and Eddie Williams as "Mr. President." The young man obviously thought he was being confronted by some African head of state and his party and did not want to create an international incident over the minor matter of our not presenting tickets or an invitation. He said, "Just one moment, your excellency," and hurriedly went over and instructed hotel attendants to set up a table down front for our party.

We made a grand entry and nearly every head turned, curious to know who this very notable group of Africans were. We ended the evening in a very relaxed and pleasant place with an elegant meal to boot. If the hosts eventually found out our true identity, they never said a thing to any of us about it.

The Socal office opening reception was a big success. There was a good turnout of government officials, including the Indonesian desk officer at the State Department, the head of the Bureau of Natural Gas at the Federal Power Commission, key staff members from the offices of both California senators, Alan Cranston and John Tunney, as well as a few members of Congress. All the top officers of the American Gas Association were there, as were the heads of the Pipeline Trade Association and other energy trade groups, along with quite a few of my counterpart Washington representatives of companies and organizations concerned about energy policy matters.

This was my first experience seeing many of our senior officers at a purely social event. It was reassuring for me to discover that presidents, chairmen and other big shots in the business world behave just like ordinary people after they have had a few drinks. They tend to lower the shields that surround them because of their exalted company positions. Thus, rank and file employees can see who they really are as people. For me personally it meant a lot to have the large group of our senior people here for the occasion. I think it sent the message to all who may have been skeptical that Rufus McKinney indeed was Socal's man in Washington. He is entitled to the respect that comes with holding such a position for a major company in Washington.

By far the most important agency Southern California Gas Company was concerned with in Washington in the fall of 1972 was the Federal Power Commission (FPC). Its chairman, John Nassikas, led the five-member independent bipartisan commission. The FPC had extensive regulatory authority over the two interstate natural gas pipeline companies that supplied nearly ninety percent of the natural gas we sold to customers. These two pipelines—El Paso Natural Gas Company and Transwestern Pipeline Company—continually had cases before the Federal Power Commission involving rates and terms and conditions for their service to us. We always participated in those cases in order to protect our own financial interests. Our involvement also was necessary to try to ensure that our customers were not put at a disadvantage vis-a-vis other customers of the pipelines.

However, another concern we had was the increasing difficulty our pipeline suppliers were having in contracting with producers for new supplies to serve our market. El Paso and Transwestern were in competition with purchasers who could offer market prices as contrasted with the regulated price set by the Federal Power Commission. Producers claimed that the prices interstate pipelines were permitted to pay for natural gas were not high enough to make it attractive for them to allocate the resources needed to explore and develop new reserves dedicated to that market.

Gas distribution companies like ours faced a serious dilemma. On the one hand we wanted to keep prices we paid our pipeline suppliers as low as possible in order not to unduly inflate the costs that had to be covered in rates we charged our retail customers. On the other hand we wanted to ensure that adequate gas reserves were developed to maintain the ability of pipelines to meet our long-term gas supply needs. Therefore, we supported policies that allowed producer prices for newly discovered natural gas to rise. The theory was that producers thus would have a sufficient incentive for new exploration and development. But consumers would be protected against precipitous increases in the price of "old" gas that had been discovered and developed previously. We wanted the FPC to continue strict controls on the price of "old" gas.

The FPC's authority to set prices for producer sales to interstate pipeline companies had been a highly controversial political issue for many years. In the 1940s the U.S. Supreme Court, in a rather tortured interpretation of language in the Natural Gas Act, had decided that the FPC could legally assert jurisdiction over wellhead prices of natural gas sold to interstate pipelines. Natural gas producers never really accepted that decision as correct. Over all the years since, the producers tried without success to persuade Congress to overturn that Supreme Court interpretation.

As gas supplies for the interstate market diminished under

the FPC's price control regime the agency attempted various stratagems to alleviate the problem. They tried "vintage" pricing, i.e. allowing higher prices for more recently discovered gas. The result was an extremely complex system of pricing that only lawyers and experts could fully understand. Trying to solve the problem through the regulatory process was not satisfactory to any of the stakeholders. Large industrial users were most vulnerable because service to them could be curtailed when supplies were not adequate to meet both their needs and those of higher priority residential and commercial users.

Agitation for a legislative solution continued throughout the 1960s and the early 1970s, led primarily by producer interests in Washington. Arrayed against the producers were various consumer groups who argued that removing producer price controls would result in windfall profits for producers and exorbitant natural gas prices to consumers. But as the natural gas supply situation in the interstate market worsened in the early 1970s it became increasingly apparent that Congress had to do something to alleviate the problem.

Socal decided upon a very aggressive strategy to try to insure its ability to continue to meet the demands of its customers and carry out its public service obligations as a natural gas utility. The company and its senior officers believed they had a legal and moral obligation to do everything within their power to take care of the natural gas demands of the people it had undertaken to serve.

First, it took a position in favor of limited decontrol of certain producer prices. Politically, this was a risky posture to take for a company fully subject to regulation by a California state agency. Many in the public viewed this as an anti-consumer posture for a local utility company. Higher prices paid to producers translated to higher gas costs to Socal and eventually higher rates for our customers. Second, the company initiated several projects to acquire gas supplies from non-conventional alternative sources. Among these were: 1) a proposal to build a coal gasification plant in New Mexico to convert coal, which was plentiful, into synthetic gas which could be substituted for natural gas: 2) a proposal to import gas in liquefied form from Indonesia: 3) a proposal to liquefy natural gas produced in Alaska and ship it by cryogenic tanker to a special terminal to be built near Santa Barbara and 4) join with several other companies in a proposal to build a natural gas pipeline from gas fields in northern Alaska through Canada to the lower forty-eight states.

All of these proposals had two things in common—they all were very costly and they all required some form of support or approval from the federal government. My assignment to Washington was made with the idea that having a representative on the ground in the federal city might facilitate the effort to gain that support and help the company achieve its overall gas supply objectives.

In order to make the coal gasification project viable we needed to persuade Congress to authorize federal agencies to guarantee the loans we had to incur in financing the project. The Indonesia LNG project would involve building several cryogenic tankers at a cost of more than 500 million dollars each. For these we needed support from the maritime administration programs that provided subsidies for ship construction costs and financing guarantees or other help from the Export-Import Bank. In addition, the State Department had to be kept abreast of developments in our dealings with Pertamina and Indonesian government authorities. Of course, we had to seek certificates of public convenience and necessity from the Federal Power Commission for the transportation and other facilities that would be built to implement the Alaska LNG and the coal gasification projects.

The Washington office's role in Federal Power Commission matters primarily was to provide support for the teams of lawyers, rate design specialists, economists and other experts from company headquarters who had direct responsibility for participating in FPC proceedings. Providing that support involved a number of things. Among them was keeping abreast of general regulatory policy developments at the agency, keeping track of appointments both of new members and key staff people. We monitored the orders, hearing schedules and other releases issued daily by the agency. Our role was to be a communications link between the agency and headquarters managers. Occasionally, it became necessary for me to cover a particular FPC hearing when the assigned lawyer in the case had a conflict. More often, however, I arranged meetings with agency staff persons to brief them on factual information about the company and its planned activities that might be important for them to know. Perhaps the least attractive duty I had in the early days was actually delivering and filing documents with the clerk in cases we were involved in at the agency.

It did not take me long to realize that I alone could not do a proper job of covering all the issues and concerns Socal had in Washington. After a few months in the role as the company's assistant vice president and special counsel (my formal title) in Washington it became apparent that headquarters managers in many parts of the company felt free to request my help on matters they had that might involve some federal agency or Washington based organization. Our people in charge of the coal gasification project wanted to be kept informed of developments on strip mining legislation as it made its way through Congress. The coal we had contracted for in New Mexico to supply that project was to be extracted by strip mining methods. Our risk management people were deeply concerned about bills in Congress dealing with no fault insurance, which could affect our posture as a self-insurer. Our regulatory affairs people were interested not only in what went on at the FPC, but also with regulations issued by the temporary wage and price control authorities established by President Nixon to help control inflation. The Securities and Exchange Commission staff had challenged our parent company's exemption under the Public Utility Holding Company Act. So our most senior officers needed someone to keep a close eye on the comings and goings of key staff people there and on any appointments of new commissioners.

I do not want to give the impression that I had primary responsibility for such a broad range of issues on behalf of the company in Washington. Most definitely I did not! Every one of our projects had a highly competent team of executives and managers at headquarters charged with the responsibility of managing each of these activities.

It was not unusual to have a headquarters person detailed to the Washington office for weeks at a time to help achieve a particular lobbying objective. Too, there were the retained lawyers and consultants at our disposal on these matters as well. My role was to know the right people to contact and to facilitate the process in every way possible. It was a very heady and important role, though

252

not a highly structured one that I thoroughly enjoyed. In fact, I came to believe mine was one of the best jobs in the company. I carried out the job as best I could as the single company manager permanently assigned to Washington for nearly four years. It was not until 1976 that we added other professionals to my staff on a full-time basis.

*　　*　　*

It is next to impossible to keep a normal work schedule while representing a major company in Washington. Often the day begins with a breakfast meeting downtown at 7:30 A.M. with one of the many trade associations. Such groups like to get the day started early so as to interfere as little as possible with the lobbyist's regular activities. More often than not you have to put in at least an appearance at some reception on Capitol Hill after six o'clock P.M. The "good" lobbyist normally also will have one or two dinner engagements every week. So the typical workday is about fourteen hours. For the representative of a California company the schedule can be even more complex because one has to factor in the three-hour time differential between the East and West coasts. If the Washington representative takes lunch at noon, that is about the time his colleagues in California are arriving at their offices. When he returns from his business lunch around 1:30 or 2:00 P.M., there is about a one-hour window for cross-country communications before West Coast contacts take their lunch hour. Assuming a one-hour lunch for our West Coast friends, the Washington representative has two additional hours at most to be in contact with his California offices before beginning his nightly round of receptions and dinners. Keeping such a schedule for any length of time can put a tremendous strain on a marriage and make it difficult to maintain harmonious relationships with adolescent children in the family.

I liked the work but gradually it dawned on me that my legal skills were less and less an important part of the job. I continued reporting to Dick Edsall in the law department until 1974 and maintained my status as a member of the California bar. However, more and more I saw myself as part of the Socal management team rather than as a lawyer providing legal services to that team. The transition was made complete in May 1975 when I was elected to the office of Vice President of Southern California Gas Company and put in charge of national public affairs. I had personal misgivings about leaving the legal staff and officially becoming part of the Socal management team. I did not discuss those misgivings with anyone, not even my wife. During the first few years it seemed odd when I found myself saying in some meeting that an idea or a proposed action needed to be checked out by our lawyers. I was not accustomed to being in that position. Because of my background there were few challenges when I suggested that the lawyers should take a look at something we were about to do.

*   *   *

The second Nixon administration had no honeymoon period. They found it increasingly difficult to avoid almost daily front page stories about Watergate. But soon a new issue emerged centered around Vice President Agnew and his conduct in office as governor of the state of Maryland prior to his election as Vice President. Vice President Agnew had become a lightning rod for criticism because of his acerbic characterizations of Democratic leaders and liberal politicians who opposed the Nixon agenda. The unrelenting probes into Agnew's performance as Maryland governor eventually led to the disclosure of his taking money from supporters for personal use without reporting it as income. Early in 1973 he resigned as Vice President after pleading "no contest" to federal charges of income tax evasion.

Agnew's resignation seemed to embolden the Democrats even more to believe they could bring down President Nixon as well. Eventually a special prosecutor was appointed to examine the Watergate break-in allegations. Throughout most of 1973 and into early 1974 I firmly believed there was no way Nixon could be forced to abandon the presidency. To me there just was not enough there to rise to the level of a crime committed by the President of the United States.

Ed Sylvester, a friend and poker playing buddy, maintained from the beginning that Nixon could be ousted because of his actions related to Watergate. When Ed would say that at our games I dismissed his comments as wishful thinking. I had known Ed as a strong Democrat from our years of working together at the Department of Labor during the Kennedy/Johnson years. During the 1960s Sylvester was director of the Labor Department Office of Federal Contract Compliance. I had great respect for Ed Sylvester's political astuteness, which almost equaled his ability to win at the poker table. But I thought this time he was wrong and told him so many times in 1973. Ed Sylvester, who went on to become staff director of the House District of Columbia Committee, obviously had much better connections in the Democratic party than I did and knew what he was talking about.

The Nixon administration's preoccupation with Watergate made it difficult for them to focus enough on the number one problem the nation faced at that time—the growing crisis of the supply and price of energy. Most observers believed the energy problem had supplanted inflation as the number one issue on the nation's domestic agenda. For a number of years the level of our dependence on foreign sources of crude oil had been increasing. Some experts believed our increased dependence on oil imports was dangerous from a national security standpoint.

Through most of the 1950s and 1960s it was cheaper to import oil from Middle East sources than to produce it domestically. Oil lifting costs in the Middle East were only a fraction of what they were in the United States. Potential profit margins on imports thus were greater than on U.S. production. This remained true until political leaders in Middle Eastern oil producing countries wrested control of oil reserves from the American and European multinational oil companies and began asserting their own political control over the vast oil resources lying beneath their lands. The cartel Middle Eastern countries created—the Organization of Petroleum Exporting Countries (OPEC)—adopted policies to extract higher prices from oil consuming nations.

No single federal government agency or official had clear responsibility for dealing with the energy issues until the department of energy was created in 1978. The Nixon administration took the first steps toward organizing the government to better handle energy issues in 1973. It established a new position on the White House staff called the Energy Policy Office, giving that office responsibility for bringing some focus to the government's efforts to deal with the energy problem. Initially a former Colorado governor, John Love, was appointed to that position. He later was succeeded by Charles DiBona. Although the head of the White House Energy Policy Office quickly became known as the energy "czar," his real authority was quite limited. He had no legislative mandate to take over functions and decision-making powers that by law were lodged elsewhere in the government. Therefore the office was not equal to the task of centralizing control over federal energy policy.

Congress later intervened and created the Federal Energy Administration (FEA) and the Energy Research and Development Administration (ERDA). These new agencies were to take the lead in implementing "project independence," the administration's plan to lower the level of the nation's dependence on oil imports. The FEA took over certain energy programs and functions that had been at the Interior Department and other agencies. Also, it was to become the main instrument for developing and advancing policies best designed to respond to the energy problems confronting the nation. ERDA was responsible for leading efforts to develop new alternative and non-conventional energy resources. Socal supported the creation of these new agencies and believed they eventually could be helpful in our alternative gas supply efforts.

These were very exciting times to be in Washington representing a major energy company. The Senate committee chaired by Senator Jackson (D. Wa.), and its counterpart committee on the house side led by John Dingell, seemed to take turns nearly every month holding hearings inquiring into the causes and effects of the nation's energy problems. Federal Power Commission Chairman John Nassikas spent much of his time during this period either testifying or preparing to give testimony before one of these committees. He was the federal official called on most often to explain why natural gas prices to consumers were rising so rapidly and why supplies to the interstate market were declining.

Democrat congressional leaders and administration officials obviously distrusted each other. Neither side could agree on what should be done to alleviate the energy crisis. And both Democrats and Republicans frequently castigated oil industry officials when they appeared at congressional hearings believing they were manipulating or withholding supplies in order to drive oil and gas prices even higher. The congressional hearings soon took on a circus like atmosphere with standing room only crowds. Lobbyists, reporters and other interested observers spilled outside the hearing rooms into the halls waiting to get in to see the action. Good seats inside the hearing room became so difficult to obtain that senior lobbyists at some firms sent a secretary or clerk hours before the hearing was scheduled to start just to hold a seat for his later arrival to monitor the hearing.

Representing a major California company gave me some advantages when it came to dealing with Congress. It enabled me to approach fully ten percent of the members of the House of Representatives on the basis of a constituent relationship. Throughout the 1970s California boasted of having the largest congressional delegation—43 congressional districts. That number increased by two in the decade of the 1980s. Being a constituent rivals being a generous campaign contributor as a basis for preferred access to an elected official. With such a large congressional delegation California was bound to be represented on every committee that was important to Socal gas company. More often than not at least one Californian from each political party had a key committee assignment. This was true for the Ways and Means, Interstate and Foreign Commerce (later Energy and Commerce), Science and Technology, Appropriations, Public Works and Transportation and Interior and Insular Affairs Committees.

My first priority on Capitol Hill throughout my tenure here was to cultivate relationships with the staffs and members from California, especially those from districts in the southern half of the state. I considered it a duty to let those members know Socal's position on the important energy policy issues and how our company, its employees and customers were likely to be affected by policies being contemplated by federal authorities. If we did a good job of covering the California delegation, we will have accomplished a great deal in communicating whatever message we needed to deliver in Congress.

*　　*　　*

Dorothy Ann and I decided that during each school year we would pay for two trips home for Rudy and Fred—one for the Christmas holidays and one at the end of the school year. Beyond that they were free to travel wherever the money they earned would take them. Fortunately for me I got the chance to see them on my frequent trips to company headquarters in Los Angeles.

Both the boys did well in school academically and each graduated on time. Rudy finished Occidental College in June 1974 and Fred graduated U.C.L.A. two years later. It was a financial struggle as neither of them received any kind of scholarship. For the most part they stayed out of serious trouble while in school but we did have some anxious moments. Rudy especially was a source of concern because he tended to be somewhat rebellious, and prone to being influenced by the people around him.

The early 1970s was a period of great unrest among young people everywhere, especially on college campuses. I was particularly concerned when Fred called to tell me about he and one of his friends being stopped by the police in Westwood near the U.C.L.A. campus. They were questioned about an alleged robbery that occurred in the area. He of course knew nothing about a robbery and felt quite strongly that they had been stopped simply because they were young black men walking in a white neighborhood. He was very upset to be targeted in that way and was concerned that the police were really trying to convey the message that young black male students should not stray off the U.C.L.A. campus, certainly not after dark.

Fred saw it as an attempt at intimidation designed to circumscribe the freedom and behavior of black students. I took the opportunity to try to give Fred a lesson about his real status in that community and the vulnerability of innocent young black men to completely uncalled for acts of extreme violence at the hands of the Los Angeles police. I told Fred it was my view that the Los Angeles police were a law enforcement agency that was subject to little if any control from civilian government authorities. They were largely a law unto themselves and were confident they would not be held accountable to anyone except themselves for their actions, particularly against blacks and other minorities. I told Fred I understood fully how he felt about the incident, but advised him that the worst thing he could do in such a situation was to lose his cool and take a confrontational posture with the police. I tried to impress upon him that many young black men had been gunned down in cold blood by the police in similar situations. If he had to do something I suggested he write a very dispassionate letter to the police chief expressing how he felt to be targeted that way by the police. Years later Fred thanked me for that advice.

14

Hiring the Staff to Do the Job

Toward the end of 1975 John Abram gave his approval to the idea of adding other professionals to my staff in Washington. First I wanted to hire someone with knowledge and experience in dealing with federal executive departments and agencies. I envisioned an individual who knew his way around at places like the policy formation offices at the White House and all the executive departments and independent agencies that would be critical to the success of our LNG import projects. The second person I wished to hire would be assigned to Capitol Hill to work primarily on legislative issues important to what Socal and its various affiliates wanted to accomplish in Washington. Third, I contemplated bringing in a regulatory affairs specialist whose primary beat would be the Federal Power Commission. Finally, I felt I needed an office manager type who could take over the administrative functions that had been performed for us by the Miller and Chevalier law firm.

Implementing this plan would require considerably more office space than we had. So I approached the Watergate Six Hundred management about the availability of additional space at that location when our lease was to expire at the end of 1976. They told me that a contiguous space to meet our requirements would not be available there, but they may be able to find additional space on another floor of the building. John Abram and I agreed that having scattered offices would not be satisfactory. Therefore, early in 1976 we began looking for suitable office space in other buildings in downtown Washington. But I felt that our need for additional staff was so great that if the right persons surfaced we could bring one or two of them on board even while we searched for more adequate office space to accommodate them. Therefore my recruitment efforts intensified to find someone to help carry the ever expanding loads being place upon the Washington office.

As soon as the word got out that Socal planned to increase its Washington office staff I was flooded with inquiries and expressions of interest about the job. Several factors no doubt contributed to the tremendous interest. Foremost among them was Socal's reputation as a solid company and industry leader. The company stood at the apex of all the natural gas distribution companies in the country. Nearly every person in Washington familiar with the energy business readily acknowledged this. People wanted to work for a company they figured would be around for the long haul.

Also, by that time it was apparent to a lot of people in Washington that Socal was involved in cutting edge issues in the energy area. We were into synthetic fuels, LNG imports, natural gas pricing reforms and alternate fuels for automobiles. For the foreseeable future these were the issues that would be on the national energy agenda. Working for Socal in Washington certainly would put one in the thick of the debate and perhaps a role in resolving some of the nation's energy problems.

1976 was an election year and the Democrats were odds on favorites to win the presidency that November because of the damage done to the Republican party by the Watergate scandal and President Nixon's subsequent resignation. Many mid- to high-level bureaucrats in the Nixon/Ford administration were looking for a place to land, safe from the expected housecleaning that usually accompanies a change in administration.

The persons we planned to hire would come into the company at a fairly high salary level by Socal standards. We called such positions that reported directly to a vice president either "manager" or "manager of" a particular function. The relevant vice president and his immediate superior as well usually were involved in the hiring decision. Of course, I did the initial screening of all the applicants. Those I thought worthy of consideration I would personally interview. Those I thought my boss John Abram should look at, I passed their résumés on to him and we would talk. Abram and I went through this process with more than a half dozen applicants during the first half of 1976. The candidates that emerged from this process who also wanted to join the company were two outstanding young men with excellent qualifications.

James A. Rooney was selected for the executive agencies liaison job. Rooney was a 1966 graduate of Georgetown University who after his service in the navy had worked in sales at Mead Corporation and Xerox in Washington. Upon his nomination by Mead he was selected for the presidential executive interchange program at the U.S. Department of Commerce. He joined Socal from his position at the Council on International Economic Policy at the White House. His experience as a senior staff member at the Council on International Economic Policy dealing with energy imports, LNG and the international energy agency, was ideal for the job we envisioned for Rooney.

Thomas E. Biery was chosen for the congressional liaison job. Biery was a 1969 graduate in petroleum engineering from the University of Oklahoma. He had worked in various engineering jobs for Standard Oil of California. Since 1974 until he joined Socal in October 1976 Biery had worked as legislative assistant for energy in the office of Senator Dewey F. Bartlet (R. Okla.). Both Abram and I thought this combination of practical experience with an energy company and work on Capitol Hill with a senator from an energy producing state made Biery well-suited for the congressional lobbying job.

First on the agenda for each of the new hires was a trip to Los Angeles for an intense orientation to the gas company and meetings with our key headquarters people. I set up a schedule for this orientation which took at least one full week.

In the meantime we took out a five-year lease on brand new space in an office building that had just been completed at 1150 Connecticut Avenue in the heart of downtown Washington. The new location gave us ample office space for the new managers as well as room to accommodate our frequent headquarters visitors. We moved into our new quarters during the week of the Jimmy Carter inaugural in January 1977.

The addition of Rooney and Biery to the staff gave me greater freedom to devote time and effort to reaching out to public interest groups, think tanks, and other influential groups and individuals in Washington to help them understand why we were undertaking these massive gas supply projects. Our premise was that if they knew the full ramifications of gas supply shortages—the impacts on a gas dependent economy like that of California—we stood a better chance of enlisting their support and achieving the objectives we had in Washington. Rooney and Biery were well qualified and capable of doing their jobs with the agencies and Congress on the particulars of our agenda. I was especially pleased with Rooney's enthusiasm and initiative. He had excellent contacts at the Department of Commerce and at all the agencies that are involved with international energy matters. These contacts were extremely valuable to us in the Arctic Gas Pipeline proposal in which we were partners, and the Pac-Indonesia LNG project.

The one regret that I had about hiring Rooney and Biery was that I knew they would not remain with me very long. They were both young and ambitious men on their way to much greater heights in their careers. Biery was the first to leave after being in the job for about one year. He decided that he could not put his heart and soul into his work for a regulated utility that required advocacy of policies that he perceived to be at odds with his fundamental free market philosophy. This commitment to free market principles was instilled in him at the University of Oklahoma engineering school and during his years at Chevron. The time he spent on Senator Bartlett's staff, a conservative Republican, strengthened his belief in free market principles. I think Tom was troubled most by Socal's positions on the issue of decontrol of wellhead prices for natural gas and its view that development of synthetic fuels required federal financial support. I respected Tom's honesty in acknowledging his internal conflicts and wished him well when he left to take a job with one of the oil and gas producer trade associations.

Rooney adjusted well to his role in the Washington office and remained with us for about three years. He left in 1980 to take a high level job in Boston with a company in the business of developing low head hydro-electric projects and building a system to import Canadian gas and electricity to the New England states.

When Jimmy Carter took office in January 1977 the nation was in the deepest throes of the energy crisis. Oil imports were at an all time high and world oil prices were rapidly escalating. The prevailing public perception was that we were running out of natural gas and that there was a need to husband this clean burning fuel for so-called high priority uses only. It was becoming more and more difficult to gain approval for any major energy production facilities, such as power plants, because of objections on environmental grounds. Congress and the executive branch were in virtual stalemate over energy policy. The oil price controls President Nixon had imposed as an anti-inflation measure several years earlier were still in effect, despite the strong objections of all the producers and many others as well. The administrative measures that had been taken by the Federal Power Commission in an effort to alleviate the problem of declining availability of natural gas for the interstate market had not been effective. In addition, the winter of 1977 was unusually severe along the eastern seaboard and several natural gas systems experienced outages that led to plant shutdowns and weather related unemployment.

Faced with all of these problems President Carter was compelled to take some kind of dramatic action. In a televised speech from the Oval Office, dressed in a sweater instead of the usual business suit, Carter declared that the nation faced in the energy crisis what was the moral equivalent of war. He called on citizens to do everything within their power to conserve energy.

One of his first actions was to appoint a blue ribbon panel to come up with recommendations for the government to deal with our energy problems. He created also a special task force among his closest advisors and charged them to develop specific proposals both for new legislation and executive action.

The actions being taken or contemplated by the new administration led me to recommend that I set up a meeting between senior Socal officials and one of the principal energy policy planners on the White House staff. I thought it would be desirable for us to have such a meeting as early in the planning process as possible, and before any plans had taken their final shape.

President Carter had brought with him people from Georgia and elsewhere whom we did not know. Several of the President's advisors had little if any known association with any aspect of the energy business. Carter himself was largely a stranger to Washington and its ways as were most of the people close to him. I felt we had an obligation to approach the Carter team and to try and brief them about the concerns we had as a major energy provider in the largest state in the country. My boss John Abram agreed this was a good idea and told me to set up such a meeting and that he or chairman Harvey Proctor and perhaps Bill Wood of our Pac-Indonesia Project would travel to Washington to attend.

I arranged the meeting for Thursday February 17, 1977 for myself, Bill Wood and Harvey Proctor with Al Alm, Carter's White House staff member who was coordinating the development of the administration's energy policy plans. The meeting was held in the old executive office building right next door to the White House. At that time White House security was not nearly as strict as it became later on. All we had to do was give them our social security number and have a picture ID when we showed up for the meeting. Since the meeting took place less than a month after Carter and his team were installed in office, everyone on staff was still getting settled into their new quarters. So there were signs of some disarray in the staff operation. Nevertheless, Mr. Alm welcomed us cordially. Pat Garner and his staff at Socal headquarters had prepared a short briefing paper which described the company, the activities it was pursuing in the gas supply area, and why they were so critically important to the economy of the area we served.

It became apparent very early in the meeting that Alm was primarily interested in receiving whatever information we had to offer about our company and our views on the issues we considered important to our business. He was not forthcoming about his own ideas or the policies the task force was exploring at the time. Nor was he free even to tell us who the members of that group were.

I got the distinct impression that Alm knew very little if anything about the nature of the natural gas industry. We had to constantly remind him of the difference between natural gas and the gas he was familiar with that is pumped into your automobile at service stations from an underground tank. He had trouble understanding how natural gas is priced and measured—in cubic feet, therms and BTUS—not gallons. It was not evident that he knew anything about how gas is produced and the systems that exist to deliver it to markets. We explained the difference between the primary fuels and electric power; how fuel prices, storage costs, etc., affect the choice of fuels in some industrial applications. In short, we wound up giving Alm what amounted to an elementary energy course.

As soon as we left the building we each was astonished at what we had just been through and asked the same question: you mean to tell me that this guy is in charge of coordinating and developing national energy policy plans for the President of the United States? How can it be that a person with so little knowledge of the subject can be elevated to such a position in this day and age! The experience reflected what initially at least was a fundamental flaw in President Carter's approach to the energy problem. His team did not trust anyone who came from or had actual experience in the energy business. His primary sources for advice and counsel came from academics and what I would call skeptics who believed that people in the oil or gas business could not be trusted to act in the public interest.

It was pretty clear that their basic approach to solving the energy problem was from the demand side of the equation. Thus, the emphasis would be on actions to reduce energy consumption—imposing energy efficiency standards for autos and appliances, insuring that the price of oil and gas reflected all direct and indirect costs of production, eliminating all promotional rates for gas and electric utilities, establishing a hierarchy of uses for clean fuels, and repealing the oil depletion allowance and other tax incentives for oil and gas producers.

We came away from the meeting having heard very little that offered any hope that the Carter people might provide any help on our gas supply development efforts. The Washington office of the gas company indeed faced a significant challenge in the days ahead. It would not be easy to move forward on the company's Washington agenda in an administration that appeared to have serious reservations about many of the things we were trying to do.

*   *   *

While President Carter's task force was putting together a national energy plan, Congress was moving ahead on creating a new cabinet level department, consolidating in one place the major federal energy functions. The Department of Energy Organization Act became effective October 1, 1977. The new department absorbed the Energy Research and Development Administration, the Federal Energy Administration, the Federal Power Commission

266

and the various power marketing functions previously housed in the Department of the Interior. Creation of DOE was the logical final step in the process that had begun during the Nixon administration to bring some order to the management of federal energy functions.

The gas company supported the idea of establishing the DOE, but had some misgivings about the people likely to be appointed to fill the 17 policy level positions there. Some of these concerns were relieved when the president named James R. Schlesinger as his first Secretary of Energy. Schlesinger, a noted Harvard economist, had considerable experience in Washington. He served in the Nixon administration as an assistant director of the Bureau of the Budget, as chairman of the Atomic Energy Commission and as director of the Central Intelligence Agency.

*   *   *

While interviewing people to replace Tom Biery as our congressional liaison person I had a most interesting experience. I really wanted to hire a woman for this job. I had several reasons, one of them being a desire to improve the profile of an all-male professional staff. I had also come to believe women lobbyists had some advantages over male lobbyists in terms of gaining access to congressional principals. A certain element of male chauvinism perhaps contributed to this attitude on my part. Nevertheless, I was determined to find a woman for the vacant position if possible.

One of the persons being considered for the job was a young black woman with excellent credentials. She was a recent graduate of the Harvard law school and had spent several years as a legislative assistant to Senator Edward Brooke, a black Republican senator from Massachusetts. The salary I was prepared to offer was considerably above what she currently was earning. Yet she turned the offer down for a most revealing reason, after we had spent more than an hour in my office talking about the job and the opportunities it may open up for her.

She finally told me that she did not think she could work for any profit making business. She thought there was something fundamentally wrong with the idea of "profit." Despite her degrees from Radcliffe College and the Harvard Law School, she equated making a profit with exploitation and seemed to think there was something inherently evil about it. She told me she wanted to spend her entire career either in government or in some form of public service employment.

I shall never forget that interview. I have asked myself many times since whether the attitude that job candidate had about profit might explain to some degree the limited success blacks have had in business in this country. Is there something in black culture in America that would foster such anti-capitalist notions? The candidate was from the South, having been born in North Carolina. I presumed she had some experiences with being black in the South that were not too different than my own, although she was quite a bit younger than I. But most of the blacks I knew from the South were "strivers"—people trying to make a success of themselves in a world we knew was controlled by whites. But the notion of "integration"—of blacks having a chance to achieve success in mainstream businesses and other "white" institutions was still relatively new, even in 1977.

15

Confronting a Personal Family Crisis

I made two or three trips a year back to headquarters during the first couple of years of my tenure as Socal's Washington representative. The frequency of such trips increased significantly later on as the Washington office was integrated more into the management structure of the company. It was while I was in Los Angeles for a headquarters visit in 1975 that I got a very distressing call from my good friend Buford Macklin. He said, "Rufus, you better get back to Washington right away! My wife (Cathy) just told me that Dorothy Ann is moving out of the house." At first I did not think Buford was serious and told him to stop joking about a thing like that. He insisted that this was no joke. "If you don't believe me, talk to Ed Twine. I just spoke with Twine to find out how to reach you in Los Angeles. I told him all about the situation. He will confirm everything I've told you." As soon as my phone conversation with Buford ended I called Twine. He confirmed what Buford had said to me and added that Dorothy apparently moved out of the house the day before.

I still could not believe what I had heard from two sources was true. Even though Dorothy Ann and I had not been getting along well the last several weeks, I had no idea that she was seriously contemplating calling an end to our twenty-four-year marriage. And surely she would not move out of the house while I was away on a scheduled headquarters visit without at least calling to tell me about it. I was devastated not only by the news of her leaving but also by the way I found out about it. I had no choice but to cancel my unfulfilled appointments in Los Angeles and return to Washington immediately. I told no one at the company why I had to suddenly return to Washington, except to say that an urgent personal emergency had come up.

During the five-hour plane trip back east I thought a lot about the things I had done in the last few years of our marriage that might help explain why Dorothy Ann moved out and the way it was done. I tried to recall things she had said or done in recent months and conversations we had that might provide some clue that she wanted to be rid of me. As in most marriages ours had its ups and downs. Through most of the summer of 1975 Dorothy Ann and I had not been getting along well, but there had not been any cataclysmic events that I could recall. Anne, our eldest daughter, graduated from high school in May and Dorothy Ann and I may have disagreed on the size of party we should host for her graduation.

I had been concerned somewhat about the time Dorothy Ann was spending at the Saturday lectures at the Congregational Church on 13th Street conducted by a professor at the Howard Divinity School. Apparently she had been introduced to the lecture program by Buford Macklin's wife Cathy. The Macklins' marriage had gone on the rocks early in the year. I feared that the breakup had something to do with doctrines being espoused by the leader of the lecture series. I had heard that the lecturer, a kind of a mystic, had extraordinary powers over women who were at that certain stage in life.

I thought I had been a good, but not a perfect, husband. One thing Dorothy Ann always told me was that I was a good "provider." I was never sure what inference she wanted me to draw from what she left unsaid. Nevertheless, there were great times in our marriage that I fondly recalled as my plane approached Dulles International Airport that autumn afternoon. The best vacation we ever had was just two years ago when we spent a full week in August at the Buccaneer Beach Hotel in St. Croix, U.S. Virgin Islands. Her mother, Mrs. Colclough, came up from Pine Bluff to look after the kids while we were away. Our villa at the hotel was right on the beach. We spent the late afternoon hours watching the sunset from our front porch and every evening we fell asleep to the sounds of ocean waves splashing against the shore. During the day we wandered to secluded coves and places along the beach where we behaved again like young lovers. We drank the delicious island drinks made with the sweet local Cruzan rum. We visited with friends who lived on the island. The husband managed the Hess oil refinery there. His wife was active with Dorothy Ann in the League of Women Voters. They were kind enough to take us up in the Hess company small plane for a bird's-eye view of St. Croix and the neighboring islands of St. Thomas and St. John. It was indeed an ideal vacation that I shall never forget.

Fortunately, I always drove my own car to the airport so that I would not have to bother anyone to come and pick me up when I returned. In the mid-1970s the long-term daily parking fee was cheaper than round trip cab fare to Dulles. I quickly gathered my bags, took the parking lot shuttle to my car and began the lonely ride through the Virginia countryside to the Beltway, across the Potomac to Connecticut Avenue and to our house in Chevy Chase, Maryland. I arrived home about six thirty in the evening—with plenty of daylight left at that time of year.

I was not sure what to expect when I entered the house. I had been told that Dorothy Ann had taken with her all the furniture and furnishings she wanted when she moved out. Apparently she did not want very much because it seemed that most of our furniture was still there. She left the Drexel dining table, taking only four of the eight dining chairs, leaving both armchairs! From the living room she had taken the Henredon credenza, one of two lounge chairs, an etagere and some artwork, but had left the large sofa we had bought in California. She took the girls' bedroom furniture but left the boys' bedroom beds. I was not surprised to find that she left the entire bedroom furniture we had shared. She never forgave me for buying that furniture for our Mayfair Mansions apartment before she arrived from Bloomington to join me after my graduation from law school in 1956. I was also surprised to find the black spinet piano still there and the old television set. From the family room she took the cane bottomed period sofa and chair, but left the stereo set, taking only the large custom-built University speaker we acquired when we lived in Mayfair.

The fact that so much of our furniture remained in the house gave me reason for hope that Dorothy Ann's leaving was only temporary. I thought to myself, maybe she intended just to send me a strong message that some changes had to take place in our marriage or it would indeed be over. If this assessment of the situation was correct I had little doubt of my ability to persuade her to return home eventually. So my spirits were lifted somewhat.

271

After the walk through of the house that now seemed devoid of life I proceeded to try to locate where my family had gone. A couple of calls was all it took to discover where they were living—a high-rise apartment building on New Hampshire Avenue in nearby Maryland. I called and asked to come over so that we could talk this situation over. She agreed and I got in my car and rushed over there. I knew exactly where it was because I had been there many times before. It was where Frank and Jan Hollis had moved after they left their place in Shepherd Park. My thirteen-year-old daughter Paula greeted me warmly when I entered Dorothy's new apartment. Anne was out at the time. I was greatly surprised to find that Carl Davis, Dorothy's only brother was there with her. Apparently he had come all the way from California where he lived then to be with his big sister in her time of crisis. Everyone was cool and completely under control. The three of us sat down and I proceeded to ask Dorothy Ann if she was all right and she said yes. I then said, "When do you plan to come home?" She answered, "Mac, I've made my decision and I intend to stay here." I knew right away that then was not the right time or circumstance to pursue the question of when she would come home. But I did say how disappointed and hurt I was that she had left and told her she was welcome to come home whenever she changed her mind. After getting another big hug from Paula I left.

*   *   *

All of this was happening during one of the most intensely stressful periods of my professional life. The promotion to vice president shifted my reporting relationship within the company. I would no longer report to Dick Edsall in the law department. Instead, I began reporting to John Abram, a Socal senior vice president. Abram was put in charge of Socal's consolidated governmental affairs functions, including federal, state and local governmental contacts.

I knew John Abram well from my law department assignment years earlier as counsel to the regulatory affairs department, which Abram then headed as vice president. About a year before Abram had hired as his executive assistant a bright young man named Pat Garner who had worked in Washington as an assistant

272

to Roy Ash, who held a high-level position at the White House. I had met Garner before and sensed that he viewed his assignment as the person in charge of program planning for the new governmental affairs department placed him in position to supervise my activities in the federal area. I was determined not to allow that to happen. I saw his role as being one of staff support for the Washington lobbying function, for which I had complete responsibility.

I had been elected president of the Gas Men's Roundtable for the year 1975 which meant significant additional responsibilities as well as being projected on to the larger stage of energy politics in Washington. The Gas Men's Roundtable (the name was changed to "The Natural Gas Roundtable" after women began to take a leadership role in the organization in the late 1970s) was a monthly forum where leaders of all three segments of the natural gas industry came together with federal regulators and members of the energy press to hear from energy policy makers and to exchange ideas on current issues in the industry. Bud Lawrence, president of the American Gas Association, and Jerry McGrath, head of the pipeline trade association INGAA, served the organization respectively as permanent secretary and treasurer. Other officers were elected annually, with the office of president rotating among representatives of the three industry segments.

As president of the organization my job was to plan for and preside at the monthly meetings and help secure appropriate speakers for these occasions. It had been the tradition to obtain as speakers ranking and leading members of Congress that are actively involved with energy industry issues: also, policy level officials in the administration and the regulatory agencies and occasionally a leading energy industry figure. The meetings were always held at the prestigious University Club on 16th Street next door to the Russian Embassy.

I believe I was the first black person to become a member of the Gas Men's Roundtable; I certainly was the first person of my race to head such a prestigious energy industry group in Washington. I was determined to demonstrate to everyone that a black person could provide capable, effective leadership to such an organization. By every measure I had a successful term as president. Fortunately, natural gas policy was the hottest energy issue in Washington in 1975. Under my leadership the Roundtable was able to attract as speakers that year many, if not most, of the leading congressional figures who were involved in the unsuccessful effort to pass a natural gas bill that year, including Senator John Tunney (D. Ca.), Congressman John Dingell (D. Mich.) and a fairly new congressman from Texas, Bob Kruger.

Another priority issue on Socal's Washington agenda in 1975 was to try and convince Congress to authorize some form of support for synthetic fuels development and our Wesco coal gasification project in New Mexico. Socal and its partners in the Wesco project, Texas Eastern and Utah International, were in the forefront of this effort. Along with others we succeeded in placing provisions for loan guarantees in the ERDA authorization bill. That bill passed the House and Senate and was enacted into law. This was our most successful lobbying accomplishment of the year.

However, we were not as successful in our effort that year to have money actually appropriated for such purposes or in convincing Congress to pass a comprehensive synthetic fuels program. A majority in the Senate favored such a program but the effort twice was thwarted in the house—in 1975 and 1976, each time by a very thin margin.

The work we did developing support for synthetic fuels eventually paid off, however, during the Carter administration. In 1980 Congress enacted the Energy Security Act, which authorized $20 billion in spending to support a crash program to produce clean synthetic fuels. That act created a synthetic fuels corporation to manage the effort, headed by a seven-member board. But the grand program never really got off the ground, being plagued by allegations of mismanagement from the outset and later becoming the victim of the changes in policy direction that accompanied the installation of the Reagan administration in 1981.

The coalition that was formed around the synthetic fuels issue worked very effectively together. It included Bill Grant of Utah International, Jerry Verkler of Texas Eastern, myself and Ed Irwin of Socal, and a couple of independent consultants with strong ties to the Texas congressman, "Tiger" Teague, who was in charge of the bill in the House. Ed Irwin, a very savvy Socal manager, was detailed to the Wesco project and was assigned for extended periods to the Washington office to work with me on securing federal support for synthetic fuels development. Ed was a most interesting character, who could charm the rings off a bride's finger. I was so impressed with his people skills that I decided that at my first opportunity I would make him a permanent part of the Washington office staff.

Of course getting the ERDA authorization bill passed with loan guarantee authority included was only the first hurdle for the Wesco team. It was highly unlikely that federal authorities would offer financial help for more than one coal gasification project in the country. Wesco was one of two major proposals being considered for certification by the Federal Power Commission at the time. Our competitor was the Great Plains coal gasification project to be built in South Dakota. That project was being sponsored by a group of Michigan companies led by Art Seder and American Natural Gas Company.

While Wesco was further along in the process of gaining approval at the FPC, it was by no means clear that we would eventually get the nod over Great Plains in the contest for federal financial help. From a political point of view they well may have had the advantage because they were constituents of one of the most powerful energy policy makers on Capitol Hill—Congressman John Dingell. In a crunch I had no doubt that Dingell would use his influence to tip the scales in favor of Great Plains in any contest between the two projects for federal financial assistance. No one in the California congressional delegation had comparable clout or the inclination to come to our aid in such a contest.

We also reached a critical stage in the process of gaining approval for our Pac-Indonesia LNG import project during 1975. We filed at the Federal Power Commission our application for a certificate of public convenience and necessity to authorize construction of a LNG terminal facility near Santa Barbara. We correctly anticipated there would be intense opposition to this proposal from the environmental community and many others as well because of safety concerns. The proposed terminal facility was in an active earthquake zone and was thought to impinge also on ancient Indian burial grounds in the area.

We had our hands full trying to convince policy makers in Washington that a LNG terminal could be built and operated safely in such an area. Natural gas is converted to a liquid form by greatly reducing its temperature. The process of doing that also compresses the volume by several orders of magnitude such that it can be transported economically by tanker. The mere attempt to describe the activities that would be taking place at a LNG terminal was enough to scare the average person. The LNG would arrive at the terminal in very large cryogenic tankers and offloaded into specially designed vessels and reconverted to gaseous form for introduction into the natural gas distribution system.

One of our biggest challenges was to develop position papers and other presentations that might allay public fears about the safety of these processes. As part of this effort the Washington office took responsibility for setting up briefings for members and staff where we would bring in our technical experts and executives to explain and answer questions. We also arranged tours so that public officials and others could come to California to observe close up the preparations that were being made to bring this project on line.

That summer Indonesian President Suharto was scheduled to meet with President Ford at Camp David. We viewed this visit as an opportunity for us to bring our proposal to import Indonesian gas to President Ford's attention. We worked very hard with our friends at the State Department and secured their commitment to include our Indonesian LNG project in their briefing of the President for his talks with President Suharto.

My involvement with all these issues in 1975 probably contributed to my failure to pay proper attention to the signs that my marriage was in serious trouble. I made the fatal mistake of assuming that the success I was having in my work would endear me more with my wife and family. Unfortunately, marriages don't work that way. I now realize that success at work does not translate to success in your personal relationships with wife and family. I also found out that the longevity of the marriage confers no immunity; marriages of any length of time can fail if not cultivated and nurtured every day. Dorothy Ann and I had been married nearly twenty-five years. I mistakenly thought our marriage could not fail because we had so much invested in it, including four children three of whom had nearly reached adulthood. It was months before I finally accepted the reality that Dorothy Ann and I would never reconcile and that our marriage was indeed over.

16

A New Challenge—Learning to Play Golf

The year 1975 marked the beginning of another passion that has pervaded my life since that time—the game of golf. Actually I had been introduced to the game twice before, each time by a neighbor. The first time was in the late 1950s by Doyle Carrington, a next door neighbor in Mayfair. Carrington had just moved to Washington with his wife Jo Ann from San Antonio, Texas, to take a job at the Veterans Administration as an architect. One summer afternoon Doyle asked me to take a ride with him in his red convertible to the driving range at East Potomac Park. After watching him hit a few balls Doyle asked me to try it. Hitting the golf ball looked very simple to me. I had played a little baseball as a boy in Jonesboro. I figured since I could hit a moving baseball with a bat it could not be that difficult to hit a golf ball while it was motionless on the ground with a golf club.

I stepped up and took a mighty swing, made contact but never saw where the ball went. That is, until someone several yards down the line of players to my right yelled "fore" and players began to duck. I did not realize what was wrong as Doyle quickly came up and began apologizing to the other hitters. I had hit a big slice, the ball going off almost parallel to the line of players just missing the players at the end of the line to my right. I was extremely embarrassed, to say nothing of nearly having to defend myself in a fight with the angry golfer who was nearly hit by my errant shot. Carrington never asked me to hit golf balls with him again, although he played often up at the nearby Langston Golf Course.

My second experience at golf occurred in 1970 when our neighbor across the street in Altadena, California, also an avid golfer, was looking for a playing partner. He thought a person of my status should enjoy the game. He played regularly at the Pasadena Municipal Golf Course at Brookside Park near the Rose Bowl. However, this time I declined the invitation to go to the golf course and instead decided to first buy a few golf balls, a putter and one or two clubs so that I could practice in my own back yard. I tried this for a short while but soon came to the conclusion that golf was a pointless, uninteresting game. Why would grown men spend hours in a field hitting and chasing after a little white ball and then hitting it again when they found it?

In the early summer of 1975 I was persuaded by my friends Ed Twine and Buford Macklin to start playing golf as we sat around a poker table in the basement of my home in Chevy Chase, Maryland. A few months earlier Buford, who had been playing for some time, had helped Ed Twine get started in the game. And Ed, a very competitive person who was looking for someone he thought he could beat, insisted I should try the game. A week or so later my family and I were at an afternoon cookout at Frank Hollis' house when I casually mentioned my plan to take up the game of golf. One of Hollis' neighbors, Dr. James Stanback, was there and said he too was a golfer. He told me right away that I should not buy any clubs at first because so many people invest large sums of money in equipment before they really know whether they will like the game or not. Stanback said he had dozens of golf clubs and other equipment in his garage and would gladly lend me all the equipment I needed to get started. If I did not wish to continue playing after I had tried it for a few months all I had to do was return the clubs and equipment. That way I would not be out of a lot of money unnecessarily.

That was indeed a great offer that I accepted immediately. We walked down the street to his garage and we assembled what he called a starter set with golf bag and all. It included a driver, 3-wood, 9,7, 5, 3 irons and a putter. He said these are all the clubs you need to learn the game. One piece of advice Stanback gave me I shall never forget. He said, "Rufus, don't go to a golf course right away and try to play this game. The best thing you should do is go to a professional teacher and take a few lessons. In any case, you should not even think of going on a course until you have spent several months at the driving range three or four times a week just hitting balls." I thought this was good advice because I was determined not to embarrass myself again as I had done the first time I tried to hit a golf ball.

For several weeks I left work and went directly to the driving range at East Potomac Park, or to a commercial driving range on Rockville Pike where White Flint Shopping Center is now located. And whenever I got the chance on weekends the driving range is where I would be. But one part of the advice Stanback gave me I did not follow; I failed to go to a golf professional where I might be taught the correct fundamentals of the game. Instead, I began reading golf magazine and other publications in an effort to teach myself how to play. I listened to my friends who played, some of whom barely hit the ball better than I did. When I finally started going to Falls Road Golf course or the nine hole course at Sligo Creek with friends, someone would say after an errant shot, "You've got to keep your head down; you looked up too quickly; you're standing too close to the ball; you're standing too far from the ball; or take the club back inside; sweep it off the tee; hit down on the ball." I was thoroughly confused, but I persisted.

The one friend I had who really knew how to play was Wilbert Shannon, a Kappa brother and long-time buddy. Shannon was a student of the game and had been playing for a long time. He carried a single digit handicap and was a member at Hobbits Glen Golf Club in Columbia, Maryland. He and his friend Joe Bruton usually were the first group off at Hobbits on Saturday and Sunday morning. The starter liked that because they played at a very fast pace so that following foursomes were never held up by the first group. He was a good informal teacher who was willing to play occasionally at some of the public courses I played where the green fees were more affordable. Shannon was not that interested in betting with his competitors and he would never take a wager with me. His philosophy was that golf is a game that the player can never master and is difficult enough in its own right. The player's challenge is always the same—trying to get the ball into the hole in as few strokes as possible.

With Shannon's help I was determined to develop my game to the point that I could consistently break a hundred strokes per round. Shannon told me that if you can consistently shoot in the mid to low nineties you can play golf with anyone, including the pros. Only then did I realize that more than ninety percent of all golfers never break ninety and much more than fifty percent never break a hundred.

I had other reasons to begin playing golf as well. After being promoted to vice president I was now in a select group of employees who were entitled to certain perquisites associated with the position. One of these was the privilege of attending every year what we called the executive group off-premises conference. This was an annual meeting which only officers of the company and their spouses attended. The conference invariably was held at a very nice resort or conference center either in Santa Barbara or the Palm Springs area. Sessions at this conference were always planned so as to allow ample time for golf in the afternoon.

I had always heard that much important business is conducted on the golf course so I wanted to be in position to take advantage of this if in fact those rumors were true. I knew that several of our senior officers played golf. Among the golfers were my boss John Abram, my former boss Dick Edsall, and Bob McIntyre, an officer I believed was destined to lead the company some day. Later I came to realize that the notion that a lot of serious company business gets done on the golf course is highly overrated. But it is true that one can learn a great deal about a person while playing golf with him. If one is disposed to being intemperate or quick to anger those traits will tend to come out on the golf course. One can also learn something about a person's honesty, trustworthiness, and how he deals with adversity or bad breaks by the way he behaves while playing golf.

My interest in the game was heightened also when I began dating a woman who played golf following the breakup of my marriage. Playing with Bette Treadwell created an additional incentive for me to improve my game, for I was not about to accept being bested in any athletic endeavor by a woman. I had been introduced to Bette, a native Californian, by Eddie Williams. She worked for the National League of Cities, one of the organizations I was attempting to cultivate as an ally on some of our national energy policy issues in Washington. Bette was a top assistant to the executive director of the league, Alan Beals, and knew many prominent local elected officials around the country. While my initial interest in Bette may have grown out of a work-related purpose, our relationship quickly developed into a more personal one which lasted for several years. She was a most interesting, independent and exciting woman. She came into my life at a critical time and helped me to survive an experience that did tremendous damage to my psyche.

My interest in the game of golf eventually led to my raising with my boss the question of a country club membership for me in Washington. Many of my colleagues who represented companies here as I did held country club memberships and considered such memberships important or even necessary to doing a proper job of entertaining their lobbying contacts. In keeping with my company's desire to be viewed as a first class organization and as a major player in our industry in Washington, I thought such a membership for me would be appropriate. Also it would be in line with the policy at headquarters of providing several company managers and executives having significant public contact responsibilities with country club memberships to help in carrying out those duties on behalf of the company.

I had no trouble convincing my boss at the time, Bob McIntyre, that I should have a country club membership. He told me to investigate the possibilities and let him know.

I soon discovered there were a number of very prestigious country clubs in the area. Nearly all the Washington representatives for major companies who held company sponsored memberships belonged to one of five or six clubs—Burning Tree, Congressional, Chevy Chase, Columbia, Bethesda, or Kenwood. When I began my research apparently not one of these clubs had a member who was black. My first challenge was to find out whether any one of them might be disposed to consider breaking the color barrier. I learned that the head of our industry trade association was a member of Congressional Country Club. When the question of my possibly becoming a member there was raised with him he graciously consented to look into it. Shortly thereafter he reported to me and to my boss that the club would be favorably disposed to receiving an application from me, if I could find the requisite number of sponsors among the club's members. That was not a very difficult task as I had become fairly well-known in the Washington representative community in the five or six years I had been here in that capacity. Several energy industry associates offered to sponsor my membership.

281

I submitted my application around the end of 1977. The club offered and I accepted a "summer" membership in 1979. A summer membership entitles the holder to use all clubhouse facilities but not the golf course. Its purpose is to give regular members the opportunity to observe the applicant for a period before any commitment is made to extend a full membership. About one year later in 1980 Congressional Country club accepted me as a full member and I have remained a member in good standing since that time. Another ten years passed before the second black person became a member of Congressional.

My membership in Congressional was accomplished without fanfare of any kind. As far as I know it received no publicity in the local press. I note, however, that at the time the state of Maryland had begun to bring pressure and threatened to withdraw certain tax advantages enjoyed by country clubs if it was determined that the club had a policy of excluding blacks, other minorities and women from membership.

17

Dual Allegiance Pressures and the Pioneer Black Manager

My elevation to officer rank in 1975 was for me personally a source of great satisfaction. The announcement of my promotion was reported in the *Los Angeles Times*, the *Wall Street Journal* and in the business section of the *Washington Post*. In addition, the news of my appointment was prominently carried in all the company's internal news organs, the bi-weekly *Gas News* and the weekly management newsletter. Many of my fellow black employees also took pride in knowing that for the first time a person from their ranks had made it to the upper management level.

I did not know about all the perks that came with the position; access to executive dining room privileges, eligibility for year end bonuses, the ability to commit company resources (up to a certain dollar amount) on your signature alone, being invited to participate in the annual executive off-premise conference in Palm Springs or Santa Barbara, eligibility for stock options. When my boss told me of my promotion he did not mention any of these perks; he only spoke of the new salary level. I found out about the perks only as the occasion arose for them to be accorded or exercised. My first bonus in January 1976, for example, came as a very pleasant surprise to me.

While I did rejoice in my good fortune of becoming an officer, I wanted the appointment to be more than a mere token of the company's commitment to equal opportunity for its black employees. I was concerned about being located 3,000 miles away and thus not easily accessible to rank and file employees. I would not run into my fellow black employees daily in office corridors and in the employee cafeteria. Opportunities for informal interaction with others about what life in the company was like for them were very limited. I believed (and hoped) that many in the ranks would find it easier to approach me about their problems and concerns on the job, the idea being I might be able to resolve some problems outside normal channels. I did not wish to become an ombudsman, but I did want to freely share my own experience and knowledge about what it takes to succeed in the corporate environment. I wanted to be a source of inspiration and hope for others in the company. Being at headquarters every day perhaps would have allowed me to do a better job in this regard.

Southern California Gas Company was a very large organization whose employees were scattered over a vast area of Southern California. In my very limited time at headquarters during the first years of my tenure I got to know only a small percentage of the total number of black employees. But I did know most of the other black employees who had reached mid-level management or the professional ranks. Several followed me as attorneys in the law department—Eddie Island, Loren Miller, Maxine Thomas.

As an officer I felt compelled to use whatever influence I had with senior management to move others among my black colleagues to higher level responsibilities. I knew from my earlier experience at the U.S. Labor Department how easy it was for talented blacks in the workforce to escape the notice of persons with authority to make decisions about promotions. While my first priority was successful execution of the duties I had in Washington, I also thought I had to do something to boost the fortunes of other deserving blacks in the company. I believed that doing my job well provided the best evidence that blacks could indeed handle higher level managerial responsibilities.

By their very nature investor-owned public utilities tend to be very conservative organizations. Certainly this was the case in the 1970s. Southern California Gas Company, like others in that business, did not seek the spotlight when it came to involvement in social issues. It wished neither to lead the pack on such matters as EEO nor to be the last to do the right thing. But the men I encountered at the top rungs of the company during the 1970s and early 1980s were all fair minded individuals who were sensitive to the need to improve the position in society of blacks and other disadvantaged minorities. The role I assumed with regard to the company's EEO posture was a completely informal one. Nevertheless,

I think my boss was pleased that I took it on. In fact he may have assumed I would do as much given his knowledge of my background in this area.

I am most proud of instituting a practice of periodic informal meetings with black employees of all levels during one or more of my headquarters visits each year. Sometimes only five or six of us would meet for dinner after the workday ended, share our experiences and discuss how our respective careers with the company might be enhanced. Other times arrangements would be made for a much larger group of black employees to meet at a hotel facility for dinner and a more formal program of networking and professional development discussions. Berlinda Fontenot-Jamerson and some of her colleagues in the personnel department had a key role in arranging these meetings.

One issue that frequently came up at these gatherings concerned promotion policies and how blacks in so many cases were passed over in favor of whites with lesser "qualifications." A great deal of passion usually was evidenced whenever this issue was discussed. I needed to choose my words carefully in responding to the concerns employees had about this problem. It was important to avoid saying anything that might be viewed as minimizing the seriousness of the problem or giving the impression that my own success in moving to a higher level was proof that the company would not condone discriminatory promotion practices.

I recalled what I had said years ago in a speech on equal employment opportunity at the naval security station on behalf of the NAACP. There I had stressed that EEO policies articulated at the highest levels sometimes could be distorted or misapplied by lower level supervisors. Judgments about who is most deserving of a promotion can be highly subjective and there is often room for disagreement about any choice that is made.

I pointed out that in a for profit business smart managers have a strong incentive to reward superior performers over those with more impressive paper credentials whose productivity is lower. The opposite often is true in the field of education and among certain other non-profit institutions where academic credentials seem to be a more important factor in promotion decisions. The high school or college teacher whose promotion comes automatically upon acquiring that advanced degree is a familiar example. It is important to understand that academic credentials are not a ticket to success in the world of business.

More often than not when we really got down to cases in the company, it turned out that the black employee believed having a college degree made him more "qualified" than a white without a degree, regardless of their relative performance ratings in jobs they had held before.

I tried to stress that while degrees and formal training are important indicia of potential, they are not proof of performance. In business doing a job well, productivity, and contributing to overall success of the unit are more important considerations in promotions. Often I expressed the view that a reorientation of thinking may be required and urged challengers to pay more attention to performance measures beyond training and credentials in positioning themselves for advancement in their organization.

The job of division manager probably was the most coveted one in the company, conferring a status that many believed to be superior to that of all but the most senior level officers. Division managers presided over all gas company operations in each of about twelve designated geographic areas. Several of the divisions were comparable in size to many natural gas distribution companies around the country. Art Spencer became the first black division manager soon after I became a vice president. A few years later Chance Williams and Billie Ware also achieved that high level in the company. I like to think my advice and influence with certain colleagues in senior management played some part in these division management appointments.

One of my most troubling experiences as a pioneer black in corporate management in the early years came from a source I did not expect, i.e., militant activists in the civil rights movement. I learned that some committed activists seriously questioned the choice I made to accept employment with a for profit company. Their thinking seemed to run along two lines. The first being that profit making businesses inherently exploit workers and the public for the benefit of a few owners of capital. Therefore business at best is unethical and selfish, if not evil. I call this the "anti-capitalist" or socialist model activist. The second line of reasoning holds that the first obligation of any member of an oppressed group is to use his talents directly in the liberation

286

struggle, especially those with leadership skills that are well suited to advancing the cause of liberation.

I was confronted with such attitudes in 1977 at a NAACP conference at the Mayflower Hotel. That organization had convened the conference to examine the ramifications of President Carter's energy policy proposals for American blacks. The NAACP board chairman, Margaret Bush Wilson, had asked me and several of my colleagues who worked for energy companies to serve as "resource" persons for the meeting.

The "resource" person's role, of course, was to provide technical assistance to organization officials and other activists present, answering questions about the Carter proposals and helping them to understand the issues involved. Serving with me as resource persons were Edgar Twine of ARCO, Bob Bates of Mobil Oil and Tom Hart of Westinghouse. A number of other well-known blacks were there as well, some who had held high office in previous Democratic administrations. One of these, Andrew Brimmer, had been a member of the Federal Reserve Board. Another, Hobart Taylor, had been among President Lyndon Johnson's black kitchen cabinet in the late 1960s.

During the course of the meeting I noticed from the tone of comments and questions from some in the audience growing hostility toward the "resource" persons. Instead of questions several in the audience began to attack us, accusing those who worked for energy companies of "selling out" to the enemy. "How can a nice young man like you work for a utility that terminates service to people who cannot pay their utility bills; or for an oil company that charges exorbitant prices for an essential commodity." These were the kinds of questions being asked of those serving as "resource" persons at the meeting.

After a while I had had enough of that kind of abuse. I asked the moderator if I may be permitted to address the group, and he consented. I proceeded to tell the audience of my background and of my credentials in the civil rights struggle over the years. I then asked rhetorically, "What was the civil rights struggle all about if it were not about opening opportunities for young black men and women in fields of endeavor that previously had been closed to them?" I told the audience in no uncertain terms that I make no apologies for the position I held with a major natural gas utility.

Having prepared myself though education and hard work, I proudly took advantage of the opportunity to break new ground, to open new doors, to set an example for young men and women who will follow, and hopefully exceed my own achievements in the business world. Then I sat down. For a moment there was complete silence. And then there was wild and sustained applause as the entire audience reflected on the statement I had just made. I interpreted that applause as an affirmation of what I already knew: that my work for a profit making company in no way compromised my commitment to the cause of civil rights. The National Association for the Advancement of Colored People had not lost sight of its ultimate goal of opening new opportunities and helping to propel ever increasing numbers of its constituency into the mainstream of American economic life.

18

Restoring Order in My Personal
Life—Marrying Again

I knew I had found the woman I wanted to spend the rest of my life with in the fall of 1979 when Glendonia Boutte met me in Las Vegas, bringing with her a sweet potato pie she had baked. The pie was still warm when I met her plane from Los Angeles. She said she wanted to do something special to mark the occasion. My friend Ed Twine had introduced me to Glendonia, called "Donie" but only by her very best friends, almost two years earlier during one of my frequent trips to Los Angeles. Twine had spoken to me several times before about this very attractive woman who had become one of his and his wife Lillian's best friends. He told me that she had recently divorced an unkind husband and that she seemed to be a very nice girl.

I called Donie in March of 1978 at her office at Crocker Bank in downtown Los Angeles and asked if we might have dinner that same evening. She declined the dinner invitation but said she would be pleased to meet me for lunch the next day at a restaurant near her office. I decided that lunch was probably all she would agree to, since we had not actually seen each other. All she knew about me was that I was one of the Twine's friends of long standing. Of course she had a right to be somewhat wary of me since she apparently knew Edgar Twine very well. Any friend of Twine's, she probably thought, is likely to have some of his bad habits when it comes to dealing with women. So the safest thing for her to do was to meet me at a very public place in the daytime, under the pressure of having to return to work if the conversation happened not to go well.

She chose a little restaurant right off Wilshire Boulevard about a block from her office. I do not recall the restaurant's name but I remember it being quite crowded and not well lit. We recognized each other in the lobby immediately; I had told her I would be wearing a light tan colored suit. I had no trouble picking her out. There weren't any other black women and few of any other description in the place. But that is not why I knew who she was when she entered the building. She was strikingly beautiful and all eyes turned to get a glance at this perfectly proportioned woman, about a size ten, in a cream colored soft silk dress. Twine had done an excellent job of describing how Donie looked; about five feet five in height, light brown skin complexion, perfectly fixed black hair, a fine body and shapely big legs. We were shown to a booth right away. She declined the offer to have a cocktail. I ordered a bourbon and water.

We proceeded to tell each other about ourselves. I told her I had been married for a long time, had been separated since 1975 and was just recently divorced. She already knew who I worked for and that I made frequent trips to Los Angeles from Washington, D. C. I described my children, their ages and what they were now doing. She told me she was from Indianapolis, but had lived in Los Angeles for about ten years. She too had gone to undergraduate school at Indiana University, but sometime after my law school days there. I told her how pleased I was to meet another Hoosier. She told me a great deal about her family. Her father and mother both grew up in Indianapolis. She had three sisters and one brother, all of whom were married and also lived in Indianapolis. I was somewhat surprised when she took out her wallet and began showing me pictures of various members of her family, her young nieces and nephews along with their parents. I asked whether she too had children and she said no.

She was quite proud of the kind of work she did at Crocker Bank, one of the larger banks in California. It had to do with "cash management," something I told her I was not very good at since I had not been able to accumulate much cash over the period of my life. I meant this as a joke but it was true nevertheless. My confession about not being a wealthy man didn't seem to matter too much to Donie. It certainly did not turn her off completely and our conversation continued in a very normal fashion. Her lack of an obvious reaction pleased me tremendously.

We continued talking way past the usual lunch hour. I think

we both lost track of the time. The place was almost empty and the waiter made it a point to inquire every few minutes whether we wanted anything more as the time approached three o'clock. We walked together back to the imposing Crocker Bank building. As we parted I promised to call her about meeting again real soon.

Walking back to my Flower Street office I asked myself more than once, "Is this woman for real?" She did not seem to have the air of the typical Los Angeles black woman, at least the ones I had been exposed to. The conversation was not all about clothes, beauty shops, cars and being badly treated by old boyfriends. She was very intelligent and had a serious demeanor, despite her very good looks. Obviously she had an important professional job at the bank. I said to myself, "Rufus, I think you like this woman a lot."

There was no way I was going to get any work done when I got back to my office about three forty-five. I kept thinking about Donie. I did not want to appear to be too anxious so I waited nearly an hour before calling to tell her how much I had enjoyed our lunch and asking whether we might schedule dinner on my next trip to Los Angeles. I told her I was scheduled to be back in California for a conference in Santa Barbara in late April. Perhaps we could see each other again during that trip.

During the eighteen months or so that intervened since our first meeting until the time she joined me in Las Vegas I continued my relentless long-distance pursuit of Donie. At first it was a delicate balancing act between a relationship I had maintained for some time with a very caring woman in Washington and my new West Coast interest. Bettye Treadwell had been there for me at a very critical time in my life. I cared a lot for her but I never thought we might some day get married. She too had a good career, at the National League of Cities and was a serious professional person. However, I knew that she was a married woman who had been living apart from her husband for many years. In a sense her being married was a form of protection for both of us, since we could not legally get married even if one of us in a moment of passion desired to take that step. She never spoke about getting a divorce and I didn't press that subject since I had no intention of marrying Bettye. She was great fun to be with and I learned a lot from her about life and relationships. She had never had children and I did not think she was the "mothering" type. I could not see her in the

291

role of stepmother to Paula and Anne. At that stage I think they still had hopes that Dorothy and I would resume our married life together. So they kept their distance and never developed a personal relationship with Bettye.

On the other hand, from the very first moment I could envision getting married to Donie. There was something about her that led me to believe she could comfortably adjust to being around my children. That was very important to me. I felt compelled to maintain a home—some place where Anne and Paula, if not my two grown sons, could return to whenever they wanted. I never lost the desire to be their father, despite being deprived of the opportunity of living with them every day. Being a father went far beyond simply providing financial support—doing that did not satisfy the need I had to be involved in their life. In Donie I felt I had finally found a woman who might understand this aspect of who I am.

Now that I think back on it I cannot put my finger on any particular thing Donie said or did that caused me to believe she could be a good stepmother to my children. It certainly was not that I thought their natural mother was not doing an adequate job in that regard. Perhaps the fact that Donie lived a continent away and was not around all the time allowed me to freely imagine in her the ideal qualities of a mother. Perhaps it was instinct. In any event, my initial judgment of her was further confirmed as we got to know each other better.

Donie remained somewhat wary of me for several months after our first meeting. I invited her to meet me at the NAACP national convention in Portland, Oregon, at the end of June 1978. She politely declined the invitation, saying she had to care for her young niece Lisa from Indianapolis who was visiting for the summer. My offer to have both her and her niece come to Portland did not change her mind.

Later that summer the National Urban League met in Los Angeles. At my suggestion, Socal hosted a reception for league officials and other leaders from around the country attending the conference. Of course, I invited Lillian and Edgar Twine as my guests. My Washington friend Bettye attended this conference with me so I did not invite Donie. She heard about the reception and called me later to chide me about not being invited and telling me she learned the reason why. She told me she probably would have declined anyway because she and some of her friends were leaving that day for a short vacation in Las Vegas.

In September the Pacific Lighting financial executives invited me to come to their annual conference at Rancho Bernardo near San Diego. They wanted me to tell them all about how the Washington office was structured and give them some insights on the final stages of the debate over natural gas legislation, which was then before Congress. Rancho Bernardo is a very nice resort with beautiful golf and tennis facilities. The spouses of all the executives are invited to this conference as a special treat. And for the first time to my knowledge the unmarried executives were told they were free to bring their significant others as well. So I invited Donie to join me there as my special guest. She asked what kind of room accommodations would be made for her, expressing concern that it would be highly inappropriate for the two of us to occupy a single room together at such an event. I told her arrangements had been made for us to have separate rooms near each other in the hotel.

There was another problem as well. The conference ran from Wednesday until Saturday and there was a formal dinner on Thursday and Friday evenings. Donie said she could not take off from work the entire time. I wanted her to be there each evening for the dinners so I offered to have her fly in from Los Angeles on Thursday evening, fly her back to Los Angeles the next morning and have her return that evening for the weekend. Reluctantly she agreed to this arrangement. So for the first time I had a female companion attending one of these off premises conferences with me. Having her there was well worth the effort of getting her to and from the San Diego airport. I was especially proud of the way Donie got along with my business colleagues and their spouses. Meeting so many strangers in a totally unfamiliar environment could have been a little stressful for her. But we handled all the social occasions without incident.

I think the whole experience caused her to lower somewhat (but not totally remove) the defensive barriers she had erected because she was unsure of who Rufus McKinney really was. The conversation she had had earlier with her good friend Lillian Twine about me obviously did not completely allay her concerns. Years later Lillian told me about that conversation. She explained to Donie that we had met many years ago in Washington and our families had remained very close over all that time. She told Donie that as long as she had known me I had always been "a gentleman."

Because the work I was doing in Washington on natural gas legislation was so critical to our fortunes as a company during the 1978 through 1980 time period my boss insisted that I make a special effort to attend as many of the weekly executive group meetings at headquarters as possible. We had an understanding that it would not be feasible for me to make every such meeting, but he strongly urged that I attend at least once every month.

The short turn around trips to Los Angeles were not nearly as enjoyable as I had found them earlier in my tenure in Washington. So I always tried to tie them into some other company-related activity that might extend the time and give my internal body clock a chance to make the adjustment after a transcontinental flight. I also wanted to have a reason to be in town long enough to meet Donie for dinner. She was busy and so was I. Trying to get to know someone with the thought of developing a serious relationship is not easy to do if you are separated by 3,000 miles and can see each other only occasionally. Throughout the rest of 1978 and well into 1979 I saw Donie only once every month or so. But I wanted to get to know her better.

Meanwhile, life for my children continued developing quite normally. Paula and Anne became beautiful young ladies. Paula followed in Anne's footsteps and became a cheerleader for the Bethesda Chevy Chase High School football team. She went out for the girls track team as well in her junior and senior years before graduating in the spring of 1979. She went on to Spelman College, graduating in 1983. As promised, I bought Anne a car shortly after she graduated from high school in 1975. It was a Ford Pinto, not a very good car that seemed to break down often. She proceeded to pile up hundreds of dollars worth of parking tickets on the University of Maryland campus during her time there, before graduating in theatre arts in 1979.

She spent a few years exploring opportunities to become a singer before settling into a more mundane existence. She definitely had the talent to be an entertainer but she was not willing to make the necessary sacrifices. Learning from my experience in purchasing the car for Anne before she was ready for the responsibilities of ownership, I delayed giving Paula a car until her graduation from college. I bought her a Ford Escort soon after she went to work in San Diego. While the Escort was new, it had none of the bells and whistles, such as air conditioning, power steering and power brakes. It was truly just something to get around in. Paula never let me forget how I scrimped on the car I purchased for her. It was fun shopping for the car with her in San Diego. She was so anxious to get the car she agreed with everything I suggested in the way of saving money on the price of the vehicle. But she still had that car when she got married in 1989.

After graduating from U.C.L.A. in 1976 Fred decided to go to Yale University for graduate studies in economics. He did very well there, receiving the Ph.D. degree in economics. While at Yale he took an assignment for a year to serve on the staff of the Council of Economic Advisors to President Jimmy Carter. The two of us bachelors spent much of that year (1978) living together at my home on Pauline Drive. We were rarely at home at the same time as we kept such different schedules. Occasionally our paths would cross, but I tried not to have overnight guests when I knew Fred would be there.

Rufus, Jr. came to Washington about a year after graduating from Occidental College in 1974, but not before he and his high school sweetheart Vida Conliffe got married quietly without the approval of her parents or his. He seemed determined to follow in the footsteps of his father by marrying much too early. Eventually Rudy enrolled at the Howard University law school, receiving his law degree in 1980.

On one of my trips to California in 1979 Donie agreed to drive down to San Diego with me to meet Momma. Momma had a very nice ground floor two-bedroom unit in an assisted living complex right off Highway 94 in an area called Bay View Heights a few miles east of downtown San Diego. She had made a good adjustment to living in California. She was happy to be living near several of her children and their families who could look in on her every day, while she lived independently from each one of them. The real light of her life, George, Jr. was pastor of Saint Stephens Church of God in Christ located less than three miles from where she lived. Of course Momma was greatly loved by George's entire congregation of more than a thousand members and occupied a place of honor in the church. Sister Marvella lived nearby with her three daughters, Beverly, Brenda and Rosemary. Sister Ruth and her husband Harold lived in La Jolla just fifteen or twenty miles north. And my oldest brother Robert, who was not married was contemplating an offer Momma had made to him to leave Chicago and come live with her in San Diego.

I had none of the misgivings I had earlier when I took Bettye by to see Momma while we spent a weekend together playing golf at Torrey Pines. Bettye was what Momma would call a "fast" woman. She smoked, played golf, wore pants and liked to party. I think Momma sensed all of this, despite the fact that Bettye and I were on our best behavior during our visit. And Bettye seemed to like Momma a lot. But Momma sensed that Donie was different. She had a much softer personality and this pleased Momma very much.

Donie and I spent several hours talking with Momma—and Momma was a great talker. I never ceased to be amazed at the people and events from the distant past she would frequently recall. Usually she would say something like "Rufus you remember Sister Ophelia who came to visit us in Jonesboro in 1938?"; or she would talk about an incident that took place when she and Papa attended a district meeting in Marked Tree, Arkansas, some thirty years earlier. Or she might mention the name of a neighbor who lived in Jonesboro while I was a boy and say, "Don't you remember him?" Rarely would I know who she was speaking about. Sometimes I would just say yes I seem to vaguely remember, but I can't quite picture that person in my mind as clearly as you do. Once when Donie excused herself for a moment Momma said to me: "Rufus, I sure like Donie a whole lot more than that other woman you brought down here last year." I knew then that Donie had passed the ultimate test; if I could reel her in it would be all right with Momma. The rest was up to me.

From that point on I tried to see Donie every time I had occasion to be in California. I was successful in doing so most of the time. However, once or twice I made the mistake of calling her too late; like most single women she wanted to have advance notice and would not hesitate to decline a call for a date that came at the eleventh hour, whether or not she had something else to do. Since becoming a bachelor in 1975 I had become accustomed to calling my female friends in Washington at the last moment for weekend dates. Usually because I worked such irregular and long hours during the week I hardly had time to think about arranging for a companion for the weekend. Donie made it clear to me that she would not tolerate that kind of treatment.

In June, 1979 Donie decided to come to Washington on the return leg of a business trip to New York City. She planned to visit Shirley and Raymond Wood, friends from California who were now living in the Washington area. We had occasion to see each other twice during that visit; once when Raymond and Shirley had friends over at their house in Oxen Hill for a party in Donie's honor and again when I took her, Shirley and Raymond to dinner and a Mark Russell show at the Blue Room of the Shoreham Park Hotel.

Part of my regular beat as vice president for national public affairs for Socal was attending national conventions of the NAACP, the National Urban League, and similar civil rights and public interest groups. In 1979 the National Urban League met in Chicago in late July. League officials had asked me to lead an energy workshop panel discussion on national energy policy issues during the conference. Other panelists included the chairman of the Pennsylvania Public Service Commission, Wilson Goode, who later became the first black mayor of Philadelphia, and Linda Taliaferro, a Westinghouse lawyer who would later succeed Goode as the Pennsylvania PSC chairman. I thought Chicago would be a great place for Donie and me to meet and spend some time together. I asked her to join me there and she agreed, saying one of her good friends lived in Chicago. Her name was Eleanor Temple. Eleanor was a middle school principal in the city. Donie planned to come to Chicago several days in advance of my arrival so that she and Eleanor could visit since they had not seen each other for a while. I decided to fly to Chicago on Saturday, the day before the conference began. Donie and Eleanor agreed to meet my flight from Washington at O'Hare that afternoon. The three of us would pick up Eleanor's date and go out to dinner that evening at a nice restaurant.

I was totally unprepared for the reception I got at O'Hare airport. As I came down the escalator to the baggage claims area I spotted these two stunningly beautiful black women at the foot of the escalator, one holding a bottle of champagne and the other with three chilled crystal champagne glasses. They were there to welcome Rufus McKinney to Chicago in a style I had never experienced before. Other arriving passengers looked at me with amazement, obviously wondering who is this short black man who is being greeted in this fashion. I certainly did not look like a celebrity or some kind of entertainer. I was simply dressed—a sports coat, shirt and tie and coordinating tan slacks. No fancy green suit, flashy jewelry or other marks of wealth or celebrity. I am not sure whether it was Donie or Eleanor's idea to stage the champagne reception at the airport. No matter who was responsible it sure gave a big boost to my ego and served as an indication that Donie cared a lot about me and wanted everybody to know about it.

Later that summer Donie came to Washington again, but this time to visit with me. I introduced her to several of my closest friends and to my Washington office staff. One of those friends and Donie seemed to get along particularly well. Her name was Jeri Reddick, a very good-looking young woman who was seeing a lot of my buddy Eddie Williams. Jeri took Donie under her wing, showing her around Washington and taking her to lunch during the day. Eddie, like me, was living the bachelor life in Washington and was having some trouble meeting all the demands on his time by several female friends. But Jeri clearly had the inside track in that competition. Jeri had a high level job at the D.C. Department of Recreation. She lived very near my house. I don't know what I would have done without Jeri since there were few if any women platonic friends of mine in Washington whom I knew outside of my relationship with Dorothy. Jeri was probably the only woman friend I had in the city I could trust to be a pal for Donie while she was here.

The time for Paula to enroll at Spelman College came up while Donie was visiting me in late August 1979. She kindly agreed to accompany Paula and me on the automobile trip to Atlanta to get Paula started in school. This worked out just perfectly. The ten-hour drive down to Atlanta gave Paula and Donie a chance to get acquainted. It also enabled me to assess Paula's reaction to this new woman in my life. The two of them got along surprisingly well. Paula opened up to Donie more than I expected. Donie talked candidly with her about the dangers and pitfalls a young lady is bound to face her first time living away from her parents. She behaved toward Paula just as any concerned mother would toward a seventeen-year-old daughter going away to college.

We arrived in Atlanta the evening before Paula had access to the dormitory where she would be staying on campus. We took a large single room at a nearby hotel and all three of us spent the night in that room together, just like family. The next day we all went over to Spelman, got Paula registered and all set up in her dormitory room. That afternoon the three of us spent time shopping for personal things Paula would need. Donie was of immense help in getting me through this task, which only a mother would love. When we returned to the dorm one of Paula's roommates had arrived and we got a chance to meet her. She was from a small town in South Carolina. We said our good-byes to Paula that evening because Donie and I planned to leave very early the next day for the return trip to Washington. We wanted to get back to the capitol as early as possible because we planned to leave the following day for a short vacation together in Nassau.

It was during the Nassau vacation that we began discussing seriously the possibility of our getting married. We did not set any date at that time; we just agreed after much soul searching that we belonged together. The detailed planning would come later. What we both were most interested in at that time was making the solemn commitment to each other. While Donie was still a young woman, neither of us were novices at this game called life. I had just turned 49 years of age. I was ready to settle down in a mutually satisfying adult relationship. I had never really liked being single in the four years since my marriage broke up. I had been married nearly all of my life, having first taken that step at the tender age of 21. I had had no real bachelorhood before and therefore was not good at juggling relationships with more than one woman at a time, as I understood single men often do. So the prospect of getting married again relieved a tension I had been living with for several years.

Because I planned to spend all my time with Donie on this vacation I did not take my golf clubs with me. Not taking the clubs was a hard decision to make, as I had become an avid golfer by 1979 and tried to play every chance I got. I was told that our hotel on Paradise Island was near a very nice public course. If I had brought my golf clubs no doubt I would have been tempted to get out for at least one round of golf during our stay. Instead, we just enjoyed each other's company, lying on the beach and meeting new people during the day and at night having a quiet dinner somewhere nearby. The casinos were all around and I liked to gamble. But I preferred poker with friends, not the fast, impersonal games played at the casino. Only once did I try my hand at the blackjack table. I left a few dollars there.

We left Nassau just ahead of a storm that was expected to hit the island the next day. Donie returned to Los Angeles and I returned to work the day after Labor Day. My secretary, Lea Tinsley, and everyone else on my office staff sensed that something serious was developing between me and Donie, although I had not disclosed any plans about marriage to anyone. I could tell because they all began treating her calls with all the deference and respect normally accorded a very special friend or the boss's wife.

I set up lunch with Bettye Treadwell soon after I got back. We went to Jean Pierre's Restaurant on K Street. While we were having cocktails I told her that I had found someone I wanted to marry and that our relationship had come to an end. This was a painful thing for me to do, but it came as no surprise to Bettye. For the last several months we had been seeing less and less of each other. I think she knew why. We parted amicably and agreed to remain friends.

I think Bettye decided to test our continued friendship a few weeks later. She called to say that Alan Beals, the executive director of the National League of Cities, asked her to inquire whether Southern California Gas Company would sponsor a reception for League officials attending their annual conference which was to be held in November in Las Vegas. I agreed to do so, not just as a favor to Bettye but because the League was one of the national organizations I had a duty to cover as part of my job as vice president for national public affairs for the company. Sponsoring such a reception was a normal thing for me to do. Bettye was in charge of planning the reception so we had occasion to be in contact with each other as the date for the League conference approached. I did not want Donie to misunderstand and that is why I invited her to join me when I came to Las Vegas for the League conference. That was when she delivered to me personally the warm sweet potato pie when I met her at the Las Vegas Airport. She knew how fond I was of sweet potato pie because I often bragged of the pies Momma baked while I was growing up. She could not have chosen a better way signaling how much she cared for me.

Things moved quite rapidly after November toward the day Donie and I would marry. The two of us visited her parents in Indianapolis in December and told them about our plans to marry. In fact, I went through the formality of asking her father for her hand in marriage. Mr. Smith was a very plain spoken man. He told me that Donie was a grown woman who not only had been living independently of him for many years, but had been married before. While he had no objection to our getting married, he wanted me to know that our getting married was solely up to the two of us. He said emphatically that he had no approval authority whatever in the matter. He and Mrs. Lillian Smith thought it quaint that I would ask permission. While we were in Indianapolis we began looking for wedding bands to exchange with each other and decided on the wedding date Friday, June 27, 1980 in Washington, D. C.

I did not want a big elaborate wedding and neither did Donie. But we did want to get married in a church. I had been attending a small Presbyterian Church in northeast Washington right off Rhode Island Avenue called Church of the Redeemer Presbyterian. This was a church whose founding pastor, Reverend Jefferson P. Rodgers, was a Washington activist during the height of the civil rights movement. I began attending that church from time to time after leaving Northeastern Presbyterian, the church where Dorothy and I had been members. Redeemer Church's pastor was a dynamic young minister named Cameron Wells Byrd, a rather urbane man who enjoyed playing tennis with my good friend Robert Bates. Although I was not yet a member of Redeemer I asked Rev. Byrd if he would perform the wedding ceremony. He said yes but with one condition: Donie and I would have to come to his office at the church beforehand for an extensive counseling session. Byrd said he realized Donie and I were experienced people, but he made it a firm policy of counseling every couple whose wedding ceremony he performed. We had no problem with meeting this condition.

The vows we agreed upon were the traditional ones. However, the ceremony itself would not be conventional. While Donie's par-

301

ents would be present, we decided that the bride and groom would enter the sanctuary together, meeting the minister, the best man and maid of honor at the altar. My brother, Dr. A. Lorenzo McKinney, was best man, and her sister, Phyllis Carr, was maid of honor. Apart from her family and mine, only a dozen or so close personal friends were invited to the wedding itself, which took place at four o'clock in the afternoon. A much larger group of friends and business associates were invited to the reception that evening at the Hyatt Regency Hotel near Capitol Hill.

Fortunately, the weather was just perfect our wedding day. I was very pleased that my children came to the wedding and related festivities. I expected that they would come, but I know they had mixed feelings about the whole thing. I think they all wanted me to be happy. However, the wedding meant that whatever hope they may have held out before that their mother and I might get back together was now lost forever. Paula had just completed her first year at Spelman College. Anne had graduated from the University of Maryland a month before and was trying to figure out what she would do next. Fred was about to complete the requirements for his doctorate in economics from Yale. Rudy was completing his final year of law school at Howard University. So their moods all were very upbeat because each of the children was moving forward toward some life goal. I was proud that the breakup of their parents' marriage did not appear to cause permanent damage to the psyche of any of them.

Eleanor Temple from Chicago was among Donie's friends who came for the wedding. One thing I learned early on was that all of Donie's friends seemed to be stunningly beautiful women. Eleanor was at the very top of that list. Being a school principal, she was articulate as well as smart; she was only a few credits short of acquiring her doctorate. The minister, Rev. Byrd, was smitten by her the moment he saw her at the wedding. He insisted on being introduced to Eleanor as soon as he showed up at the reception, and spent the entire evening trying to convince her that she should visit Washington more often. Rev. Byrd, who was a little younger than I, had been divorced for several years but was seeing a woman in the congregation at the church. The attention he paid to Eleanor that evening disclosed an aspect of his personality I had not seen before. As far as I know he and Eleanor never got together thereafter, but to this day Donie and I tease him occasionally about how hard he fell for Eleanor at our wedding. The teasing became even more intense after we learned some years later that Eleanor's first grandson was given the name "Cameron."

19
Energy on the Black Agenda—
Creating AABE

One of the more interesting people I have ever met was Clarke Watson, a black man from Denver, Colorado. I first met Clarke in early summer 1977 while he was in Washington for a meeting with one of his clients at the time, Standard Oil Company of California. Earlier I had seen a piece he wrote for the "my turn" feature in *Newsweek* magazine. That article excoriated elements of President Carter's energy proposals shortly after they were announced in April of that year. While here in Washington Watson called Bob Bates, Tom Hart, and me as well as several other blacks who were associated with energy companies. He told me that we needed to get together to talk about developing a coherent strategy for reacting to the new administration's energy initiatives. He was particularly concerned that Carter's energy policy proposals appeared to have been developed without any significant input from persons representing the black community. Watson told us that as far as he could ascertain the Carter energy task force was made up primarily of "elitist" environmentalists, no growth advocates and people with no real experience in energy matters.

Watson had some credentials in the civil rights community. He knew the NAACP board chairman at the time, Margaret Bush Wilson, and had discussed some of his ideas with her. Mrs. Wilson clearly had a somewhat different vision than her recent predecessors for the NAACP. She did not bring to the position an anti-business bias and wanted to broaden the base of support for the organization beyond elements of organized labor and certain parts of what might be called the eastern seaboard intellectuals and liberal thinkers.

Watson knew several black local politicians in Maryland and

in Colorado, including Larry Young, a member of the Maryland House of Delegates, and George Brown, lieutenant governor of the state of Colorado. Watson headed his own energy development and consulting firm and had been a community activist in the Denver area for a number of years. He was an excellent writer and was full of bright ideas. Although he did not tell me this I got the impression that Mrs. Wilson may have encouraged Clarke Watson to approach other blacks who were known to be associated with energy organizations in Washington. Mrs. Wilson herself had been mentored by a member of the NAACP national board, Jimmy Stewart, an ex-marine and veteran civil rights fighter from Oklahoma. Stewart had risen to a high level management position at Oklahoma Natural Gas Company. However, convening a meeting of black energy professionals was clearly Clarke Watson's idea and he deserves all the credit for taking this initiative.

Watson called a meeting for July 25, 1977, at the Watergate Hotel. Present at the meeting along with Watson and me were Jake Simmons of Amerada Hess Oil Company, Robert Bates of Mobil Oil, Thomas Hart and Linda Taliaferro of Westinghouse, Will Carter of Chevron, T. J. White of Phillips Petroleum, Wayne Smith of Colorado Public Service Company, John Tucker of the American Gas Association, Larry Young of the Maryland General Assembly, Mark Hyman, an independent public relations consultant from Philadelphia, Dr. Lenneal Henderson from Howard University, and John Lewis, editor and publisher of *Black Affairs* a Washington bi-weekly newsletter.

I already knew four people in this group—Simmons, Bates, Hart and Tucker; the others were entirely new to me. The common link was Clarke Watson. As convener Watson chaired the meeting and laid out an agenda that essentially called for creating some mechanism whereby blacks could credibly challenge some aspects of President Carter's energy policy proposals. He also spoke about the apparent absence of any black involvement in developing these proposals and about the need to impress upon the new administration the need to appoint blacks to high level, non-traditional roles in the new government.

Much of the discussion in the first hour of the meeting centered on the need to create a new organization and whether the immediate objective could just as well be achieved through other established groups. Naturally opinions varied on this question. However, nearly everyone agreed that at this point in time the energy issue had not been high on the list of priorities for the NAACP or the National Urban League, the two most influential organizations that primarily concern themselves with issues affecting the black community. While it probably would be a safe bet that every one at the meeting was a member of the NAACP or the Urban League, none had a significant involvement in either group's policy making apparatus. So the potential for anyone of us being able to direct or even influence either organization's decisions on a policy issue like taking on a Democratic administration's energy policy initiative was highly problematic.

Besides, it was clear that the government and Congress were under great pressure to act fairly quickly on some kind of energy legislation. If we were going to have an impact on policy in a timely manner we had to create the mechanism for doing so ourselves right away. Therefore a consensus was reached fairly quickly to form a new organization and that it would be called the American Association of Blacks in Energy, with the acronym AABE. By acclamation Watson was chosen as chairman, Larry Young as first vice-chairman and I as second vice chairman.

During the remaining hour or so of the initial meeting we discussed extensively the question of what kind of organization AABE should be, who would be targeted for membership, and where our principal base of operation should be located. Given our reason for coming together in the first place, the nearly unanimous view was that AABE should exist for a limited purpose of trying to affect energy policy, primarily on the national level. It would do so with the objectives of insuring that the interests of the black community were taken into account in energy policy decision making and that black officials would participate in the policy making process.

I believed that the credibility of the organization, initially at least, depended on the degree to which its leadership and members were men and women of professional and managerial quality. They had to have knowledge and experience in energy matters and be capable of articulating a point of view on energy issues to important national audiences. I saw in AABE a professional association created to fill a void that existed in our arsenal of weapons to combat a form of economic discrimination against the black community. I did not envision AABE as ever becoming a mass membership organization, or one that competed with other black social service, fraternal, business, or civil rights organizations. Instead, through its members who are qualified by their status as professionals in energy companies or associations in related fields of endeavor, AABE would become a resource for such organizations, helping them to more effectively address the energy issues on behalf of their constituencies.

The men and women who initially came together to form AABE were from differing backgrounds and had a wide range of skills. They included people from several sectors of the energy industry. Some were associated with major oil and gas producers; others were with organizations identified with the electric industry; the natural gas industry in all its elements were represented; academia and the government sectors were represented as well. Some people present at the meeting held policy level positions in their own organizations. Jake Simmons, an officer of Amerada-Hess, a major oil refiner, had been a high-level official at the Department of Interior office of oil and gas in the Kennedy/Johnson administration. John Tucker was the first black officer of the American Gas Association. Linda Taliaferro held a law degree from Boston College and was a lawyer for Westinghouse in Pittsburgh. Finally, I had been elected vice president of Southern California Gas Company in 1975, after becoming head of the Washington office of a Fortune 500 company in 1972. Having people of such stature gave AABE a degree of credibility that few other organizations seeking to influence energy policy could match.

The initial meeting concluded with a decision to incorporate AABE in Colorado. We agreed to hold our next meeting on September 23, 1977 to coincide with the annual Congressional Black Caucus weekend, the largest annual gathering of black political leaders in Washington. At that meeting we would settle most of the other organizational issues and develop plans for moving forward to implement our ideas.

Two of the more interesting questions that surfaced during the follow-up meeting in September were whether to admit white persons as members and whether to accept corporate memberships. A subsidiary issue in the first of these questions had to do with the

307

name we had previously agreed upon. Some organizers felt we could run into public relations problems because the name implied an organization of, by and for blacks only. Including the word "blacks" as part of the formal name was a very sensitive issue with some colleagues who felt it might be offensive to some of our non-black friends. But I argued that it was important to clearly identify ourselves and not attempt to soften or disguise the organization's purpose to promote black interests in energy matters. At the same time, we all agreed some persons had genuine concerns in this area who were not black. The issue was not the ethnicity of one who would become a member; rather it was whether the person subscribed to AABE's purposes and goals. Individuals of any race or ethnicity could meet that test and that alone should be the standard of eligibility in this regard. This is the position we finally agreed upon and from our earliest days as an organization we were fortunate to have the active membership and participation of persons of other racial and ethnic backgrounds.

Opinion was sharply divided on the question of corporate memberships. Given AABE's pro-energy development attitude, some argued that many energy companies would want to join and provide a solid financial base for AABE's activities. Others held the view that AABE should do nothing that might compromise its ability to assert an independent voice on energy matters on behalf of black people. Mine was one of the voices expressing concern that accepting corporations as members would make the organization vulnerable to control by large corporate contributors who might want to use it to promote their own corporate interests. Even more importantly, I knew that many of the energy issues AABE might wish to address were highly controversial within the energy industry itself, to say nothing of the American public at large. Accepting corporate memberships would greatly increase the risk of AABE becoming just another trade association with little capacity to act effectively on highly controversial energy matters.

Eventually we reached consensus that membership in AABE would be personal and held on an individual basis only. Persons desiring to join were individually responsible for their dues and participation. In all of our deliberations members were expected to represent their own personal views and not merely reflect positions that may be held by their employer.

AABE took advantage of its first opportunity to become a resource for an established black civil rights organization when NAACP board chairman Margaret Bush Wilson invited AABE's organizers to attend a conference being planned for November 18-19, 1977. The NAACP called this conference in Washington, D. C. for the stated purpose of examining the energy crisis and its implications for black Americans. Mrs. Wilson had invited James Schlesinger, the man President Carter had appointed to be the first secretary of the newly created Department of Energy, as keynote speaker at the conference. Schlesinger, of course, was to be the person in charge of shepherding through Congress the Carter energy policy proposals that had been announced earlier in the year.

The Carter energy plan had three major objectives: (1) reduction of U.S. dependence on oil imports and our vulnerability to supply interruptions; (2) development of renewable sources of energy for sustained economic growth in the future; (3) encouraging a shift from principal reliance on oil and natural gas to coal to meet the nation's energy needs. To accomplish these objectives the President proposed a complicated system of new energy taxes and other disincentives designed to curtail oil and gas use. The plan would maintain wellhead price controls on natural gas and extend them to sales for intrastate use as well. It called for new mandatory energy conservation measures.

Secretary Schlesinger strongly defended the administration's energy policy proposals in his speech to the NAACP conference. He confirmed my suspicion that the Carter team believed we actually were experiencing a shortage of oil and gas resources and wanted to preserve the remaining resources for higher priority uses. The government, of course, would be heavily involved in deciding what those higher priority uses were and in allocating the supply as well. Mrs. Wilson and her closest energy policy advisor, Jimmy Stewart, were uncomfortable with the message they heard from Secretary Schlesinger.

Following the session Mrs. Wilson invited several AABE members along with certain NAACP board members and staff to her suite to discuss a strategy for responding to what we had heard from Secretary Schlesinger. After much discussion the group came to the conclusion that the NAACP itself should develop and issue a formal statement about national energy policy. The statement should call attention particularly to the concerns we had about the apparent absence of black input to development of the administration's energy policy proposals, and to the potential harm implementing some of those plans would have on black Americans.

Mrs. Wilson asked me and Tom Hart to prepare a draft statement reflecting the points that had been covered in our discussions. I accepted the challenge of preparing the initial document myself because I felt very strongly that elements of the Carter plan if enacted into law would be extremely harmful to black citizens. In my view the plan reflected a no growth economic philosophy that would stifle opportunities for blacks to move up into the economic mainstream of the society. Economic growth could not take place under conditions where there were serious constraints on the availability of primary fuels for American industries. By mid-December Hart and I had completed a draft statement. I sent it immediately to Mrs. Wilson's office in St. Louis, Missouri, for her review and approval. With only minor changes she approved the draft statement. However, before submitting it to the full board which was scheduled to meet early in January 1978, she told me the statement needed to be reviewed and approved also by NAACP executive director Benjamin Hooks in New York.

Upon seeing the document the executive director initially expressed skepticism as to the connection between energy policy and the traditional mission of the NAACP. At Mrs. Wilson's request I called Mr. Hooks and we discussed at length the importance of energy supply development to the overall health of the American economy and how that relates to creating new jobs. Eventually, the executive director also approved the statement. The NAACP board of directors finally adopted the energy policy statement at its annual meeting on January 9, 1978.

The NAACP statement was relatively brief, covering only some four or five pages. The core paragraph of the text was the following:

We have examined the administration's national energy plan in the light of the agenda for economic growth and development for America's black people. What we see in the plan is an over-emphasis on conservation, and a reduction in the growth of

310

total energy demand and consumption. The plan basically takes a pessimistic attitude toward energy supplies for the future. It seems to make the basic assumptions that (1) we will run out of all primary fuels, except coal, relatively soon and (2) essentially nothing can be done to substantially increase or even to maintain existing production rates for oil and natural gas. This emphasis cannot satisfy the fundamental requirements of a society of expanding economic opportunities.

We think there must be a more vigorous approach to supply expansion and to the development of new supply technologies so that energy itself will not become a long-term constraint, but instead can continue to expedite economic growth and development in the future. . . .

Issuance of the NAACP statement drew extensive coverage in all national news media. Clearly, many people were shocked by it, including several prominent black commentators and politicians. They could not believe the NAACP would try to inject itself into the national debate on energy policy, a subject the organization was presumed to be completely ignorant of or have no legitimate interest in. One prominent newspaper columnist had the temerity to pose the question: "Does civil rights include energy?" Because the statement was critical of the Carter energy plan and advocated a more vigorous approach to production of conventional energy resources, the NAACP was attacked by various environmental and anti-nuclear groups. No doubt these attacks from sources that more often than not had been aligned philosophically with the organization were discomforting to many in the NAACP leadership. But to its credit, the organization did not back down, and reaffirmed the statement at the next meeting of the board of directors on April 17, 1978.

*   *   *

My involvement in the creation of AABE and that organization's subsequent role in placing energy policy on the agenda of the NAACP, the National Urban League and other black social service organizations I consider to be among the more significant accomplishments of my life. The period during which these activities took place was one in which my professional employment interests were almost totally aligned with my personal interests in opening new avenues of opportunity and advancing the cause of civil rights for people of color in America.

I was extremely fortunate to work for a company and occupy a position there that allowed this to happen. This convergence of personal and professional interests probably was rare during that era for a black man in corporate America. I traveled the length and breath of the nation speaking to a variety of organizations both reporting on developments in Washington concerning energy matters and being an advocate for policies I believed very strongly were beneficial to the interests of our less fortunate citizens. The ten to twelve years from the mid-1970s to the late 1980s were among the most personally satisfying years of my life. In 1978 alone my speaking engagements took me to a variety of audiences from San Diego to Newport Beach; from Keystone, Colorado, to Seattle; from Rancho Bernardo to Portland; and from Los Angeles to Pittsburgh.

The national exposure and the causes I advocated led to both praise and scorn. Praise from conservatives who interpreted what I was doing as a challenge to liberal dogma about public policies that are beneficial to black people. Scorn and derision from some on the left of the political spectrum who interpreted my position to be nothing more than a stalking horse for the new conservative political agenda.

The ideological conflict over the best path to black advancement during this period in the late 1970s and early 1980s was similar to that between Booker T. Washington and W.E.B. Dubois in the early part of the 20th century. Then the debate was over whether the focus should be on the pursuit of the common life vocations by the masses or the development of a talented black leadership class to demonstrate intellectual capabilities of the race. In the late 1970s the question was whether blacks were better off allying themselves with business interests to promote economic growth and development or continuing their reliance on the government sector to protect and advance their economic interests.

I believed, however, the liberal and conservative interpretations presented a false dichotomy. The notion that blacks should take advantage of new employment and career opportunities being offered in the private sector in the 1970s was an affirmation of the civil rights struggle of the previous decade, not a repudiation of it. Entry of young black professionals into positions in the business world that previously had been denied to them was evidence of success for advocates for civil rights. And advocacy of an energy policy that favored economic growth and development of jobs in the private sector carried neither a liberal or conservative label. Instead, it was an acknowledgment of the prevailing new economic realities. For the foreseeable future the overwhelming majority of new jobs would be generated in the private sector.

The central message I wanted to get across to black political leaders and others was that it was time to take a fresh look at who our real friends and enemies are. In the American system, every individual and group must try to define what its own fundamental interests are and how best to advance those interests. In the quarter century following the end of World War II the federal government, particularly the courts, more than any other institution in our society played a central role in black progress. (Except of course for the role played by blacks themselves through organizations like the NAACP.) The energy crisis presented a challenge that was new and different for traditional civil rights groups. The solution to the problem that seemed most consistent with the long-term interest of black people happened to be more in line with what the business community wanted than with the Carter administration approach. Advocating a more robust energy resource development policy unfortunately offended some of our traditional allies. But it showed that some black groups were capable of making an independent assessment of what was best for them.

I also felt very strongly that the so-called soft path, "small is beautiful" solutions to the nation's energy problems, a view held by many political liberals, did not offer significant benefits to working men and women. I had seen with my own eyes what having cheap and abundant energy could do to raise living standards for less well-off populations. That is what the big public hydro-electric power generating authorities had done in Appalachia and parts of the West. The American automobile industry could not have developed the way it did, creating vast new employment opportunities for poor blacks, nor would it have been feasible to undertake building the interstate highway system, if automotive

313

fuels were not abundantly available to the masses at prices they could afford.

I saw in the soft path advocates' arguments a certain nostalgia for the "good old days" of sweatshops, backbreaking labor and virtually no upward mobility for the underclass. There appeared to be a longing for the pre-industrial past where the options of the lower classes were extremely limited. Besides, the people most closely identified with that movement appeared to me to be highly educated academic types, or sons and daughters of very wealthy families who probably knew little or nothing about the struggle to make a living, or what it means to be laid off from a job because a plant closes down or moves away.

What I tried to do during the energy crisis period of the late 1970s and early 1980s was develop in the black community a more complete understanding of the linkage between energy policy and other social and economic policies. I believed this was an essential step in developing appropriate responses to the energy crisis. Certainly blacks should be concerned about higher energy prices and the adverse effects of higher prices on people with limited incomes. So it was in their interest to support measures to bring about more efficient use of energy. They too had an interest in preventing regulatory agencies from imposing unfair burdens on poor people or allowing the well-off to reap unfair advantages. These were things blacks needed to do in their roles as consumers of energy. But I wanted blacks to understand that their interest in energy issues went far beyond those they have as consumers. Artificial constraints on the availability of energy in an economy like ours could create serious economic dislocations and unemployment. Those elements in the society still striving to achieve the "good life" can only hope to do so if the economy continues to expand, thus creating new opportunities for upward social and economic mobility. It was critical therefore to insist that national energy policy recognize the need for new energy supply development as well as measures to reduce excessive energy demand.

In the first two or three years of AABE's existence its leaders all shared a similar vision about the organization. Enthusiasm remained very high and the membership grew quite rapidly the first few years as word spread around the nation that a dynamic new black organization had emerged and was having some impact in shaping national energy policy. AABE rightly claimed much of the credit for adding provisions to the Department of Energy Organization Act for the creation of an Office of Minority Economic Impact. We worked hard to see that that office was adequately funded and staffed to carry out the function of ameliorating some of the burdens higher energy prices would impose on minority communities.

The organization had a hand in sensitizing the new administration to the need to appoint minorities to policy level positions in those agencies with significant responsibilities in the energy area. These efforts yielded modest success as a black man for the first time served on the Federal Energy Regulatory Commission, the successor to the Federal Power Commission; and for the first time another black man held the number two job at the Department of the Interior. We began to see more and more state and local governments appoint black men and women to public service commissions where important decisions are made about the terms and conditions of utility rates and services. By 1984 blacks served on the regulatory commissions of at least a dozen states, many of them in the South.

In the first year of its operations AABE began publishing a quarterly newsletter, *Energy Scene,* out of Clarke Watson's Denver office with Watson as the editor. That publication served as a vehicle for getting out to various publics the AABE message in favor of aggressive development of domestic energy resources and of attracting young black men and women to careers in energy related occupations.

But by the third year of AABE's existence some differences among AABE's leaders began to surface. I felt that the chairmanship of the organization should rotate among members associated with the principal elements of the energy industry. That is, a chairman from the producer segment should be followed in office by someone from another segment of the energy industry. However, we could never reach agreement to incorporate such a policy into our bylaws. I also wanted to limit chairmen to one two-year term and provide for a chairman-elect to serve as an understudy to succeed the chairman after two years. Such a system would provide some stability in leadership and help avoid the annual meetings becoming more about elections than about dealing with important energy issues. I also felt that rotation of the leadership would reduce the chances of any one industry segment becoming too dominant a force in the organization. I thought it was important to maintain diversity in AABE's membership and rotating the chairmanship among persons from the various elements would probably help insure that. Here again, I was not able to persuade enough of my colleagues to go along with these ideas.

Also, there was an element in AABE that tended to think that greatly expanding membership ranks would enhance the organization's capacity to influence energy policy. In one sense bringing more people into AABE could help in that regard. I believed, however, that the capacity to influence policy was more a function of the power of our ideas than of our numbers: whether what we had to say about an issue clearly advanced the interests of AABE's constituency. To me it was more important to have people with knowledge and experience that enabled them to address the issues intelligently and to help guide AABE toward effective policies and strategies in the larger public policy development arena.

Energy issues often were complex and controversial. I understood that few if any of AABE's members truly were independent agents, free to advocate publicly positions that might be considered harmful to fundamental interests of the companies or organizations they worked for. But I envisioned members having sufficient status to enable them, in AABE's deliberations, to engage in reasoned discourse with others who may have a different perspective. Expanding the membership beyond the managerial and professional level might make it more difficult to maintain the organization's focus on energy policy issues.

I also envisioned AABE being around for a long time. The energy crisis that led to its creation eventually would be alleviated if the government adopted the right policies and with some changes in public behavior regarding energy use. But the need for an organization like AABE would continue as long as energy remained such a critical commodity in our economy.

Unfortunately, some of the early members began to look upon the organization primarily as a fund-raising vehicle or as a means of attracting new clients to private consulting businesses. This provided further justification, in my mind, for frequent changes in AABE's leadership so that it would not become too closely identified with one person or particular organization. For that reason I stood for election as chairman at the end of Clarke Watson's first full term and was successful.

I believed two years was a long enough time for the leader to move the organization forward. And I thought such a period of time was about as long as anyone with full-time employment elsewhere could afford to be released periodically from his or her duties there to conduct business on a voluntary basis for AABE. From the outset I announced I would serve only one term as chairman, hoping that precedent would be followed by each of my successors. To my regret, this did not turn out to be the case. But the organization still survives and has prospered as I write these memoirs some 26 years after the date of AABE's founding.

20

Leading a Diverse Staff—Creating a Positive Company Image

By 1980 I had assembled the finest Washington office staff of any utility company in the nation. In the fall of 1977 I hired Gay Friedmann for the congressional liaison job. Gay, a young woman from Minnesota, had come to Washington several years earlier to work for Senator Eugene McCarthy. After she left Senator McCarthy's staff she worked as a lobbyist in the Washington office for Enserch Corporation, a Texas-based energy firm. Her experience on Capitol Hill and with companies in the energy industry well suited her for the position in our office. She knew the lobbying business very well and quickly became familiar with southern California Gas Company and the issues we were concerned about in Congress.

I presumed Gay was a Democrat but one could not readily tell that from her demeanor. She was very comfortable working with people from both parties, which was in line with my own philosophy of not becoming obviously identifiable politically. To help her learn more about the utility business in general we sent her to a two-week training program at the Stone and Webster facility on Long Island, after she had spent a week at Socal headquarters in Los Angeles getting to know our people.

When Gay left the company about twelve years later to establish a Washington office for Northern States Power Company she had built the well-deserved reputation for being one of the finest, if not the very top lobbyists in Washington. She was a true professional, well-respected not only by her peers but also by scores of members of the House and Senate and their staffs. We had an excellent working relationship throughout the entire period of our association. I have long maintained that working with congressional people, as opposed to executive branch officials, is much more pleasant than any other aspect of the lobbyist's job. Recognizing this, others on my staff occasionally tried to encroach on Gay's Capitol Hill turf. I took great pleasure in our staff meetings watching Gay assert control over her congressional assignments whenever others made any move in that direction.

Gay too was a golfer. In fact she had the distinction of being the first female to acquire membership in her own right at Congressional Country Club. She achieved this distinction about two years before I became the first African American admitted to membership in that club in 1980. Through the mid-'80s Gay, myself and two others on my staff, Ed Irwin and John Hemphill, had an annual golf outing at Congressional where we would compete for the office golf trophy using our established handicaps. Gay won that first year and took on the task of buying the first trophy. The winner would get to keep the trophy in his or her office until the next year's outing, when it would again be presented to the winner at an office luncheon. When the trophy was unveiled we were all surprised to find this female figure atop the trophy dressed in a detachable skirt. Gay was either prescient or extremely confident of her superior golfing skills because she wound up the tournament winner almost every year.

Except for Ed Irwin, who spent his entire career with the company, and Gay Friedman, the other managers who worked for me tended to remain in the Washington office for shorter periods of time. Richard Landers, a brilliant analyst with a State Department background, joined the staff as a replacement for Jim Rooney in December 1979. Landers left after about four years and started his own consulting firm in California. Richard was succeeded by Robert Long, an ambitious young man who had previous Capitol Hill experience, who really wanted Gay's job. But I hired Long to work the executive agency beat, a position he was never really comfortable with. He left after about three years. John Hemphill, who transferred from headquarters into the job, replaced him shortly thereafter. When Gay Friedman resigned in February 1989, it took several months to settle on one of the many applicants for that job. We finally hired David Freer and he came on board later that summer. When we hired him David was working for Clem Whitaker, a California-based consultant/lobbyist, whose clients included

Socal's marketing department as well as Pacific Gas and Electric Company.

David had come to Washington several years earlier from Alaska and had represented the Western Oil and Gas Association. David was a very resourceful lobbyist and had good connections with members and staff on those committees having jurisdiction over energy and environmental matters. Eventually, David became head of the Washington office several years after my retirement. Ed Irwin decided to retire from his position as our liaison with the Federal Energy Regulatory Commission in 1990. Ed was a most loyal and dedicated employee whose contributions to the Washington office and to the company would be sorely missed. To replace him I hired one of his former staff contacts at the FERC, Bob Beauregard, who had since gone to work for the interstate pipeline trade association.

Throughout my career as a manager I made it a practice to try to find the smartest and most competent people to work for me. I believed the boss should give his people the widest possible latitude to do their jobs. I never worried about being upstaged by my subordinates. My philosophy was that a subordinate who performed in an outstanding manner should be recognized and appropriately rewarded. I thought high performance by a subordinate reflected well on the boss's judgment in selecting that person and demonstrated a high degree of confidence the boss had in his own abilities. I have always been wary of any boss who is jealous because he thinks a subordinate may know more than he does, or believes his position is threatened when someone who reports to him does his job extremely well. This approach worked for me through most of my tenure with Southern California Gas Company. With very few exceptions I worked for confident men who knew the natural gas business extremely well. That made my job much easier. In turn, I derived much satisfaction from working with highly competent people like Gay Friedmann, Ed Irwin, and Richard Landers. They were consummate professionals.

Frequently, however, one of my managers and I together would call on a government official. Usually the appointment would be made through the appointments secretary. When we showed up for the appointment, often the official or his staff on

320

seeing two people one white and one black would react in such a way as to clearly indicate their assumption that I was the subordinate member of the team. I always found it amusing to observe this phenomenon. As the meeting moved beyond the initial pleasantries to the matters we were there to discuss it was interesting to see the subtle change in demeanor as the official realized which one of the company's representatives was the senior member of the team. This tended to happen much more frequently in calls on executive branch officials than meetings on Capitol Hill where more people knew who I was. But I think Gay Friedmann enjoyed introducing me as her "boss" to some of her Hill contacts when we called on them together.

*   *   *

Fairly early in my tenure as Washington representative for Southern California Gas Company it became apparent to me that many congressional people (members and staff) and others in Washington were confused about the company's identity. We ourselves were partly responsible for this confusion. It was not easy to keep track of the multiplicity of subsidiaries under the Pacific Lighting Corporation umbrella. The similarity of our company name and those of other larger or more well-known California companies also could be confusing. The major oil producer, Standard Oil of California, was popularly known also as Socal. Southern California Edison Company, the electric utility based also in Los Angeles, was often referred to as Socal Edison. And Pacific Lighting Corporation was often mistaken for Pacific Gas and Electric Company, the much larger combination utility based in San Francisco.

The name Pacific Lighting suggested to many that the company was an electric utility. While my company was well known in Southern California, we had little if any national identity. As a wholly owned subsidiary our stock was not publicly traded on any of the national exchanges. Only the stock of Pacific Lighting Corporation was publicly traded under a symbol not readily identified with the gas company. In meetings with government officials it was not unusual, therefore, for me and my people first to spend time distinguishing ourselves from other companies the official

321

had assumed we were there to represent. This confusion about our identity was a really big problem that needed to be addressed.

I first approached my boss John Abram about our identity problem in 1977 after we moved our office from the Watergate 600 building to 1150 Connecticut Avenue. I told him one thing we might do is have Socal host a fancy dinner in Washington every year. He thought that idea had some merit but felt an annual dinner might be too much of an expense and hard to justify at the California Public Utilities Commission. Abram pointed out the Commission already was skeptical about the expense of a Washington office being covered in our rates to California consumers. In addition, Abram was sensitive to the fact that confusion about our identity as a company was really a public relations problem. That problem appropriately might be viewed as within the purview of our vice president for public relations at headquarters.

In any event, Abram was not ready to act on the dinner idea the first time I broached the subject. We discussed the matter occasionally thereafter but it was not until the spring of 1978 that it occurred to me to link the dinner with the convening of each new congress after the biennial elections. That would provide the political tie-in that I needed to overcome any problem with the vice president for public relations. Also, there is always the possibility of new members being elected who will need to have some orientation about our company and what we were trying to accomplish in Washington. To deal with Abram's concern about costs, why not bill the dinner as in honor of the California congressional delegation and make that delegation alone our principal focus. Abram and others in Socal's senior management liked the modified proposal about the dinner and approved it for implementation when the new Congress convened following the 1978 elections.

The first decision we made was that the dinner would be a first class, black tie affair for members of the entire California congressional delegation and their spouses at the Madison Hotel in February 1979. We also decided that the principal host would be Chairman of the Board of the holding company, Paul Miller. And the co-hosts would be selected other senior officers of Pacific Lighting and Socal, including the top officials in charge of each of our major gas supply projects, along with me and my managers here in Washington. The spouses of all of our people would attend as well.

The involvement of our most senior level officers insured that I would have all the support I needed from headquarters in planning for the dinner. Every year the Socal executive group held at least one "off premises" planning conference at a nice resort somewhere in Southern California, as did several other departments and affiliated companies in the Pacific Lighting group. We maintained a small staff of people to help arrange and plan for such company events. A member of that staff, Bob Mack, was assigned to help with arrangements for our first congressional dinner. Having an expert event planner like Bob Mack available freed me and my staff from a lot of the logistical work in planning an event like this. We could concentrate our efforts on the difficult task of promoting the attendance of as many of the members of the California delegation as possible, responding to whatever needs they may have and identifying any ranking executive department officials from California who might also be asked to attend.

The first congressional dinner finally was scheduled to take place on February 24, 1979. We arranged for most of our headquarters executives to arrive in town a few days before the event so that my staff and I could schedule appointments for them with key government officials while they were here. The idea was to maximize the exposure of the company and its people to official Washington. By this means I hoped to lessen the confusion about our identity as a company. I realized it would take time, perhaps several such dinners over a number of years, to accomplish our objective.

By Washington standards the first dinner was very successful. The ranking members from both parties on the House side were in attendance, along with just over half of the total forty-three member delegation. Unfortunately, neither Senator Cranston nor Senator Hayakawa showed up, although both earlier had responded favorably to our formal invitation. I had a hard time explaining to Paul Miller that such behavior by important Washington congressional figures was not at all unusual. Ellen Proxmire, the local party planner I had retained to help us with Washington protocol rules for such an event, had warned me that a favorable response to formal invitations by members of the House and Senate is no guarantee that the person will show up. The no shows did require us to make a number of changes in planned table seating arrangements. But these were handled without undue difficulty by our highly efficient event planning people and the Madison Hotel Staff, who had extensive experience in these matters.

There were no speeches, except a very brief welcome to our guests offered by Paul Miller. The elegantly done printed program simply listed the names and positions held by each company person present, the names of both California Senators and an alphabetical listing of House members and their congressional districts, the dinner menu and finally a brief description of Pacific Lighting Corporation and Southern California Gas Company. The final paragraph of that description concluded with these words: "Southern California Gas Company is one of four large shareholder-owned utilities in the state. These companies are not related. The others are Pacific Gas and Electric Company, which serves northern and central California and is a partner with Pacific Lighting in efforts to acquire new gas supplies; Southern California Edison Company, which supplies electricity to roughly the same area served by Southern California Gas Company; and San Diego Gas and Electric Company."

We continued sponsoring the congressional dinners every two years throughout the 1980s. The format for each was similar to the first. However, in 1981 Californians who had been named to the new Reagan administration's cabinet were also invited to the dinner. The Attorney General, William French Smith, and Casper Weinberger, the Secretary of Defense attended that year. The presence of such high-ranking government officials made the dinner extra special and exciting, even for some members of Congress. The first three dinners all were held at the Madison Hotel. In 1985 I decided to change the venue to the recently opened Regent Hotel on M Street near Georgetown. Two years later we carried the event to the newly renovated Willard Hotel, perhaps the finest historic hotel property in Washington. For each event my staff and I spent a great deal of time trying to select a unique token gift for each female guest who attended and deciding on some type of entertainment for the evening. We always tried to make the dinner a memorable event. The spouses especially seemed to look forward to dressing up for the Socal congressional dinners and found them

324

to be a welcomed contrast to the usual, business-oriented Washington receptions.

We continued to enjoy immense success until Paul Miller retired. His successor, a man without much background in the utility business, or knowledge about hosting social events in Washington, decided to take charge of all decision making concerning the dinner himself. I knew it was nearly time for me to bow out of the picture when the chairman decided congressional turnout could be improved by hiring a retired NBA basketball player as a celebrity attraction. The dinners were discontinued soon after that disaster.

21

Moving toward Market Solutions to Energy Problems

The takeover of Washington by the Reagan administration in 1981 represented a fundamental change in the approach and philosophy of leaders in the executive branch about the role of government in the economy and the lives of individuals. For the most part they were opposed to command and control type solutions to the problems the country faced, especially the energy problem. They firmly believed that if the government would only get out of the way, the "free market," private sector institutions and individuals acting in their own self-interest would in time solve the energy problem. "Deregulation" became the administration's central theme. They were highly skeptical about the value of the Department of Energy and gave serious thought to asking Congress to dismantle it entirely. They put people in charge of regulatory agencies like the FERC with a policy mandate to find ways to allow market forces to operate more freely, even in those areas where the law appeared to require regulation to protect consumers.

On some issues Socal clearly stood to gain support as a result of the prevailing deregulatory climate in Washington. But on a number of other issues the new administration would be opposed to what we were trying to do. For example, we expected the new administration to be in line with our view that legal restrictions on the use of natural gas under boilers should be removed. The administration's posture in favor of accelerated development of domestic energy resources also was consistent with our views. However, they were strongly opposed to the idea of government subsidies for synthetic fuels projects, such as loan guarantees for our Wesco coal gasification proposal. Socal had supported the creation of an Energy Mobilization Board to streamline and expedite the decision-making process on critical energy development projects. The Reagan solution to the problem of administrative delay was whenever possible to eliminate what they perceived to be excessive regulatory requirements that the decision-maker had to comply with, e.g., laborious environmental impact reviews. The new administration's call for total removal of wellhead price controls on natural gas went beyond what we thought was necessary to stimulate exploration and development activities. But we could live with that policy if it were phased in properly.

Before the end of Reagan's first term it was becoming clear that the energy problem had shifted somewhat from the one the nation faced a few years earlier. The energy supply picture had improved and oil prices were moving moderately lower. These trends continued throughout the late 1980s as oil prices fell to their lowest level in more than a decade. The improved energy picture can be attributed to several factors. But one of those factors had to be the market-oriented policies instituted by Reagan and his people. The Democrats, of course, argued that the improvements were the results of policies adopted by Congress, such as enactment of the National Energy Act of 1978 and the imposition of measures for conservation and more efficient energy use.

In any event, the improved outlook for conventional oil and gas supplies led many to question the need to continue costly gas supply projects Socal had been pursuing. We knew that LNG imported from Indonesia could never be price competitive with gas from domestic sources. No matter how hard we tried, the cost of producing synthetic gas from coal could not match the costs of producing gas conventionally. And some economists had been right all along when they said allowing the wellhead price on natural gas to move freely with market conditions would accelerate exploration and development and eliminate supply problems.

These developments, while solving much of the gas supply problem, created others for the company. Until 1980 hardly anyone questioned the historic structure of the natural gas industry. Oil companies produced natural gas and sold it to pipeline companies who in turn sold that gas under long-term contracts to distribution companies like Socal. Distributors then marketed the gas to all kinds of end users, some of them very large industrial customers. For many years most people seemed pleased with this cozy little arrangement. Pipelines who moved the gas from producing fields to population centers owned the gas they transported and sold it to their customers. They were not common carriers, such as the railroads or trucking companies providing mere transportation services to others who wanted their goods moved from one place to another. Pretty soon large volume end users began to ask why couldn't we acquire our own gas directly from producers or brokers and pay pipelines and distributors a fee for their service of providing transportation only? And so the problem of bypass was born.

Many in Congress thought it was a good idea to make pipelines contract, if not common carriers, and allow end users greater direct access to buy gas in the field for their own account. Gas distributors like Socal felt threatened by this idea and we began to organize efforts in Washington to oppose it. Socal felt threatened because a dozen or so of our 4.5 million customers accounted for nearly half of the volume of gas we sold. And many years ago one of those customers had tried to get federal approval to build a pipeline from producing areas in Texas to California just to supply fuel for its steam generating plants.

But our main concern was a public policy one. Rates to all our customers were set by the California Public Utilities Commission. Under public utility ratemaking concepts we were able to keep rates low to residential and other small volume customers by balancing some of the high costs of serving them against the much lower cost of supplying huge volumes to a few very large customers. Removing those very large customers from the ratemaking equation would inevitably result in much higher rates for the little guys. The big customers claimed they were subsidizing the great majority of our customers. We answered that that is the nature of utility ratemaking where the rates charged to any one customer in a class never exactly matches the costs of providing the service to him particularly. As long as the rates large industrial users paid were competitive with the price of oil, their other fuel alternative, everybody on the system was better off.

The Socal Washington office took the lead in forming a coalition of distributors to fight bypass, and various legislative proposals to make pipelines contract carriers. After much effort, in 1988 we were able to convince several House members to sponsor a bill we drafted to place severe restrictions on the ability of large industrial customers to abandon utility service in favor of independently acquiring their own gas supplies in the field. We succeeded in obtaining one hearing on the subject of bypass in a subcommittee of the House Energy and Commerce Committee. But there was widespread skepticism about our idea to limit bypass. We never could gain any momentum largely because what we were trying to do was widely perceived as anti-competitive and directly counter to the prevailing winds of deregulation.

I sensed, it turned out correctly, that we were fighting a losing battle. The two more powerful elements of the natural gas industry, producers and pipeline companies opposed our initiative, as did the large industrial user groups. Small and residential customers had no lobby that could match the forces arrayed against us. Over the next few years the business I had represented in Washington underwent dramatic, fundamental changes. It took some time for us to make the transition from the business of selling gas to that of selling gas transportation and storage services.

The transition from a highly regulated business to one marked by considerably less economic regulation was not easy. In the previous era Socal's relations with its pipeline suppliers generally were very cordial and conducted in a manner befitting dealings between gentlemen who respected each other. There were of course disputes at FERC about matters such as rate design and how costs should be allocated. But supply contract negotiations in Houston and Los Angeles usually were quite civil and business-like in tone.

The three investor-owned gas utilities in California rarely had serious disputes about encroachments on each others franchised territory or stealing customers from one another. In the new deregulation era, this all began to change. Our principal interstate pipeline supplier became a competitor, seeking to directly hook-up with our largest industrial customers. It became possible for customers themselves to begin shopping around for better rates and service from non-utility marketers as well as from utilities that previously served other markets. Suddenly, the gas distribution business became more like car dealerships and other unregulated retail businesses.

Socal continued to face other serious challenges. Contracts

that had been entered into under the assumption that the historic pattern of regulation would continue no longer fit the realities of the natural gas business. Parties did everything possible to avoid giving up voluntarily any advantage such contracts may have conferred. The Natural Gas Policy Act passed in 1978 put in place a pricing regime for different categories of gas that, when coupled with contract provisions for minimum bills, take or pay and indefinite price escalator clauses, led to near chaos in the markets. However these contract-related problems did not lend themselves to legislative or political-type solutions since they really boiled down to disputes over money between private contracting parties.

By the end of the 1980s the urgency the company felt earlier for maintaining a high profile presence in Washington had greatly diminished. I did undertake some new initiatives in an effort to put Socal and natural gas distributors generally in a better position to meet the challenges presented by pipelines and various producer interests. For years pipelines had been a dominant force in the American Gas Association. Though they too were members of A.G.A. most local gas distributors tended to be very small companies and could not match the political clout of pipeline members. Very few distributors were anywhere near the size of Socal. Only three or four of them maintained any Washington presence at all.

On the other hand, every interstate pipeline and nearly all oil and gas producers maintained Washington offices or otherwise had a strong Washington presence. Most gas distribution companies relied on the A.G.A. to represent their interests in Washington. I felt the conflicts distributors were beginning to have with their pipeline suppliers made it more and more difficult for A.G.A. to continue serving effectively as trade association for both interests. Moreover, pipelines had their own trade group, INGAA, to look after their interests exclusively. The situation demanded that some changes be made.

First, I convinced A.G.A. leaders to help me set up an informal group for distributors only whose representatives would meet monthly with an important member of Congress to discuss issues that primarily concerned natural gas distributors. And so the Gas Distributors Exchange was formed. The membership of the Gas Distributors Exchange grew quite rapidly to more than twenty companies, many of them smaller companies along the East Coast.

They would send a representative usually from their headquarters to meetings and often were the best source of help in securing congressional guest speakers from their own local districts. The idea was to use the exchange to foster understanding of the vulnerability of gas distribution companies in the inexorable march toward greater competition in the industry and the risks to which residential and other small natural gas users were being exposed.

Not long thereafter, in 1989, I took the initiative in organizing a national conference for natural gas distribution companies in Washington. The conference, called Gas Distributors Dialogue, convened in Washington September 21, 22, 1989 under the joint sponsorship of Socal, A.G.A., American Public Gas Association and two regional gas distributor groups, Associated Gas Distributors and United Distribution Companies. This conference brought together for the first time senior executives of gas distribution companies from many parts of the country for discussions about such subjects as bypass and competition in a regulated service environment from the unique perspective of gas distributors.

These companies were at the end of the natural gas marketing chain and had the least political clout among all the players in the natural gas industry. Despite the march toward deregulation at the national level, the rates, terms and conditions of service to consumers provided by gas distributors remained subject to almost complete regulation by state and local public service commissions. I envisioned the distributor's conference as a means to bring this dilemma to the attention of policy makers at the national level. We were able to attract as conference keynote speakers Senate Majority Leader George Mitchell and W. Henson Moore, the deputy secretary of the Department of Energy. Also participating as speakers were representatives of the National Association of Regulatory Utility Commissioners, as well as several individuals serving on state public service commissions.

The presence of such high profile public officials, together with the participation of well-known industry leaders such as Richard Farman, chairman and CEO of Southern California Gas Company, William T. McCormick, chairman and CEO of Consumers Power Company, David R. Jones, president and CEO of Atlanta Gas Light, and Donald J. Heim, chairman and CEO of Washington Gas Light Company, helped to make the conference a public relations success. The LDC conference and the creation of the Gas Distributors Exchange were events that helped to identify distributors as a distinct element of the natural gas business. I think they did advance our cause in Washington at a time when so many national policy makers were "aflame with the passion of deregulation." I still am very proud of the role I had in these events.

22

Approaching the End of the Line

My last two or three years as Washington representative of Southern California Gas Company, ending with my retirement on May 1, 1992, were not nearly as enjoyable as the first eighteen years I spent in that role. The later years were not as much fun partly because the excitement of being involved in the number one domestic policy issue on the nation's agenda faded as oil and gas supplies improved and prices moderated after the mid-1980s. Another reason had to do with the changes that took place in company management in the last few years before my retirement.

By 1987 the Pacific Lighting Companies had undergone a major transformation. The holding company changed its name and tried to reshape its image as well. Pacific Lighting became Pacific Enterprises. The holding company greatly accelerated its program of diversification with the stated objective of reducing reliance on the utility business for most of its earnings. Top management at Pacific Enterprises and at Southern California Gas Company also changed. The men in top management when I joined the company in 1969—Mort Jacobs, Harvey Proctor, Joe Rensch, Paul Miller, John Abram, Robert McIntyre, Ray Todd, John Ormasa, Dick Edsall, and Harry Letton—were all retired by 1989. Harvey Proctor, the Socal chairman during the critical gas supply shortage years retired in 1981. He was succeeded by my former boss John Abram, who served as chairman until he retired in 1985. Robert McIntyre succeeded Abram, another man I had reported to earlier, who served as chairman until he retired at the end of 1989.

The man who succeeded McIntyre, Richard Farman, was relatively new to the company. He was brought into the holding company initially during the mid-1980s from one of the California banks to help run one of our non-utility subsidiaries. The only senior officers I had been close to during the early years who remained in 1990 were Jonel Hill and Bill Wood.

Bill Wood, a brilliant engineer who was somewhat younger than I, became my boss in 1978. He was a principal manager in charge of our Pacific Indonesia LNG project during that period of time. Many in the company had expected Bill Wood eventually to become chairman of Socal. He had been elevated rapidly, first to senior vice president in 1981 and later to executive vice president of Socal. But Paul Miller and perhaps others had even bigger things in mind for Wood. He was moved up to the holding company as senior vice president in 1984. This move was a big disappointment to me personally because Bill Wood and I had worked well together and understood and trusted each other. I considered him and Bob McIntyre to be my biggest champions in the Socal senior management at that time. Had Wood succeeded to the chairmanship of Socal (he did eventually become chairman of Pacific Enterprises) I think my career with the company might have ended on a different note.

The new generation of company leaders were either junior to me in terms of service as an officer, were people brought in at a high level from other companies or were my contemporaries, and thus had been rivals for advancement to the more senior ranks in the company. Up until about 1987 I had the good fortune of reporting to men with great experience both in the company and the natural gas utility business. They all knew the business we were in. I had utmost respect for their knowledge, judgment and ability. Furthermore, they all recognized the value of the Washington office and what it was doing to advance our interests. As head of that office I was an integral part of the senior management team. They looked to me for leadership and insight on national political and public affairs matters.

The bosses I had from about 1987 forward also were good men but I felt their knowledge and understanding of the natural gas business was considerably less than what I believed was desirable for the level of position they held in the company. Therefore, the confidence I had before in our top management just was not there. I was disturbed by the increased use and reliance on management consulting firms to guide decisions about running the business. I had trouble understanding how some consultant just out of an Ivy

League business school who had never spent a day working at a real job could know more about the gas business than our own experienced people.

I also believe some headquarters managers thought the Washington office had had too much autonomy under previous chairmen. Some were no doubt envious of the free access to top executives we had enjoyed over the years. They were determined to reign me in and felt confident enough to begin doing that after my good friend and mentor Bob McIntyre retired as chairman of Socal. While Bill Wood was still there, he had been moved up to a most demanding job in the parent company and was busy trying to correct or recover from some bad business decisions recently made by previous top management there. He had no time to intervene in my behalf with the new Socal leaders.

In all candor, however, I must acknowledge that the fortunes of the company after about 1987 were no longer significantly dependent on policies and decisions made in Washington. We had either abandoned or scaled back many of the supplemental gas supply projects we had undertaken earlier; plenty of gas from conventional sources was now available to meet our foreseeable needs. The company needed to refocus on California and decisions to be made at the CPUC, and other state and local governmental levels.

Rather than approaching me directly about their plans for a reduced role for the Washington office they chose other ways to signal a change in my status in the organization. While they avoided changing my formal title, pay or perks it soon became evident I had suffered a reduction in rank and status. I did not appreciate having to report to someone widely perceived to be below my own level in the company. In retrospect, in light of the improved energy picture it appears that senior management probably felt there no longer was a need to have a person with officer rank in the Washington office. They really wanted to downgrade the position to manager level and have it report to a single headquarters vice president for national, state and local public affairs functions. Had such a headquarters job been offered I would have been pleased to return to Los Angeles to accept it.

I came to realize that I had reached the end of the line of my advancement to higher level office in the company during a casual conversation I had with Bob McIntyre not long after he became chairman. McIntyre and I were friends. During one of my frequent trips to headquarters about 1986 I went to McIntyre's office just to chat about Washington and things in general. We had had these kinds of informal talks many times before. He was now chairman and I no longer reported directly to him, but our relationship was such that I felt comfortable dropping by to see him whenever I was in Los Angeles.

Throughout his tenure as chairman McIntyre remained very interested in national politics and the national scene. In fact, it was he who usually would accompany Paul Miller whenever he decided to come to Washington to participate in presidential inaugural festivities during the Reagan/Bush era. While we were talking in a very relaxed manner I asked him, "What kind of future do you see for Rufus McKinney in the gas company?" Clearly, I was probing to find out whether he believed a promotion beyond vice president might be possible for me. He thought for a moment about my question, but did not ask what I might have had in mind. I think he knew full well what I was trying to find out. His answer was very deliberate. He said, "Rufus, I think you've done quite well in this company." I listened, thinking he might say more about what I had asked, but he did not and turned the conversation to another subject. I had my answer and we never discussed the possibility of my promotion again.

I interpreted McIntyre's response to mean a position beyond the level of vice president probably was not in the cards for me; that as a black man I should be grateful for the status I had achieved, being one of the highest paid vice presidents as well. (Everyone knew or could find out what all officers were paid simply by getting a copy of a report the company was required to file annually at the California Public Utilities Commission.) As of that time I had reached the so-called glass ceiling. Until then I actually believed I might be the one to break that barrier in the company. I never thought so thereafter.

Indeed, I was fortunate to have become an officer of the company. I had already surpassed the level any other person of color had attained there before. I believed, and others had said so as well, that I had been quite successful in the position I held. I also believed I had the knowledge, skill and ability to handle a higher level of responsibility if that were offered. A year or two earlier other vice presidents had been elevated to senior vice president and higher and I thought I had at least as much to offer as they did. But I did not campaign for a higher level position at headquarters during the early 1980s.

I liked the job I had immensely and was willing to move back to headquarters only if it meant a breakthrough promotion. All the senior officers knew I was not anxious to leave Washington because I thought mine was one of the best jobs in the company for me. I suppose I could have found out whether McIntyre or any of the other senior level officers had pegged me for promotion in any of their replacement planning exercises. All managers annually had to develop comprehensive plans, identifying persons in the organization they thought of as possible replacements for themselves. The thought of looking at those plans to see if I was in any of them never really occurred to me during that period.

As I look back now on my career ten years after retiring and think about some of the experiences I had at Socal, I question whether I took full advantage of the opportunities I did have. Did it make sense for me to avoid seeking out and aggressively pursuing possible promotion opportunities. Not only did I not campaign for higher level jobs at headquarters, frequently I told my boss that I preferred Washington to jobs at headquarters. In one sense this was a rather selfish posture for me to take, because it meant the company's highest ranking black employee would not be highly visible on a day-to-day basis with rank and file employees. Thus, the ability to be a role model for other black employees was somewhat diminished.

I was reminded of this by one of our black supervisors in 1980 who said he was saddened that I chose to remain in Washington and pass up an opportunity to have "a presence on the scene" at headquarters. I now realize also that sometimes it may be necessary to take a lateral career move in order to put oneself in better position to move up later on. The strategy I adopted of remaining in Washington foreclosed that avenue for advancement and I have only myself to blame for that.

I never asked for a salary increase in all my time at the company. Instead I gratefully accepted the compensation that was offered, believing that I was being fairly treated. However, my

337

attitude about compensation changed later when I saw the gap in compensation for senior officers and those at my level widen dramatically in the 1980s. During my early years the Socal chairman's pay was roughly double that of the typical vice president. By the time I retired the ratio was more like five to one. I began to wonder whether the value added by the most senior officers was that much greater than the contribution people at my level were making to overall success of the enterprise. I began to suspect that the difference had more to do with a desire to keep pace with escalating pay levels of top executives of other big companies in the area. An even more disturbing possibility was it simply came down to a matter of who was in control of passing out rewards and how much they could get away with without causing undue alarm.

I did indeed have unusual exposure to the highest level executives both in Socal and in Pacific Enterprises throughout the time I had the Washington office assignment. Beyond the biennial congressional dinners I referred to earlier I had numerous other chances to demonstrate my abilities to higher executives. Frequently various headquarters departments invited me to speak at their planning meetings, often at very nice California resort locations, about national politics and the work being done by our office in Washington. There always seemed to be a great deal of interest in such matters by many of our people in Los Angeles. I was always happy to oblige a request to come to Palm Springs, Santa Barbara, or Rancho Santa Fe in the middle of a Washington winter to make a twenty-minute talk and spend time with people doing other kinds of work.

But the most significant exposure I had was the three or four occasions I was asked to brief the Pacific Enterprises board of directors. This assignment usually came up in presidential election years. I would give an analysis of the House and Senate races around the country, discuss how I viewed the chances of the various presidential candidates and talk about the key contemporary issues affecting the natural gas industry. While the chairman and others on the board complimented my briefings as being well planned and effectively delivered, this exposure did not lead to promotions or higher levels of responsibility in the company. My rank remained the same from 1975 until my retirement seventeen years later.

An organization in Washington called the Public Affairs Council conducted periodic surveys of compensation paid to Washington representatives and their professional staffs. I subscribed to that service and made it a point to send a copy to my boss so that he would have some idea of how my pay and that of my staff compared with that being paid by other companies. Socal was not the leader of the pack but we were not at the bottom of the list either. As long as my pay was comparable to that of my counterparts at P.G.&E. and Southern California Edison, I felt I had no reason to complain.

My passivity about promotions probably was because deep down I understood how precarious a black man's position was in the white man's world. I could not escape the segregated past I grew up in and the reality of my whole experience in America. No matter how well-educated you are, what position you hold, or wherever you may be, as a black man the status you think you have achieved can be destroyed in an instant by the power of a white man's word. As much as I wanted to believe that my status in the company was no different than any other vice president, my life experiences told me that that was not really true. Wherever I looked I saw that I enjoyed a rather unique position for a black person at that time.

There was no one who looked like me at the executive group meetings at headquarters. When I came to Washington, again I was the speck in the milk at nearly all the functions I attended representing the company. We were members of the Business Roundtable, an organization for chief executives only. It was their practice, after meeting in New York, to have the BRT chairman come down to Washington the next morning to brief member company Washington representatives on their discussions and decisions. I attended those meetings and until the late 1980s was the only black presence there. I never felt I did not belong, I just always felt alone and vulnerable. Being the lone black sometimes made me feel special and stirred a sense of pride in knowing I was doing something few if any other black person had done.